The Humanity of Therapists

The Humanity of Therapists

Pursuing Authenticity and Clinical Competence

Francis A. Martin

BLOOMSBURY ACADEMIC
NEW YORK • LONDON • OXFORD • NEW DELHI • SYDNEY

BLOOMSBURY ACADEMIC
Bloomsbury Publishing Inc, 1359 Broadway, New York, NY 10018, USA
Bloomsbury Publishing Plc, 50 Bedford Square, London, WC1B 3DP, UK
Bloomsbury Publishing Ireland, 29 Earlsfort Terrace, Dublin 2, D02 AY28, Ireland

BLOOMSBURY, BLOOMSBURY ACADEMIC and the Diana logo are trademarks of Bloomsbury Publishing Plc

First published in the United States of America 2025

Cover design: Dustin Watson
Cover image © istock/tomozina

A catalog record for this book is available from the Library of Congress.

ISBN: HB: 979-8-216-27049-2
PB: 979-8-216-27046-1
ePDF: 979-8-216-27047-8
eBook: 979-8-216-27048-5

Typeset by Deanta Global Publishing Services, Chennai, India
Printed and bound in the United States of America

For product safety related questions contact productsafety@bloomsbury.com.

To find out more about our authors and books visit www.bloomsbury.com and sign up for our newsletters

With immense gratitude, this book is dedicated to
my friend, James.

Long before James T. Baker, PhD, became
Distinguished Professor of History at Western Kentucky
University,
he became my friend
and has been my friend for many years now.
His friendship has added importance to my life in
countless ways.

Contents

Acknowledgments

Colleagues and friends have influenced the composition of this book. While they request and expect nothing from their influence, except friendship and collegiality, they should be acknowledged as important to me and to the process of creating this book. With heartfelt appreciation, I wish to acknowledge Janet Turner, Richard Harmon, Janet Newsham, Brock Searcy, Nancy McWilliams, Bradley Bull, Lydia McDonald, and Roela Redd.

Introduction

We who are therapists define our professional lives by the stories that emerge from our interactions with clients. Our shared experience of these stories and interactions brings us closer to one another, as professional brothers and sisters bonded by our common pursuits and experiences. Similar to the brilliant openness of a new day, we recognize the almost limitless possibilities that our experiences give us and the bonds with one another that sustain the privileged knowledge of our shared opportunities, sometimes awed by such a recognition. This is who we are. This book is a call to honor who we are.

> They stood there, neither of them knowing what to say. As sad and lovely as it was, the moment held them in the familiar pull between wanting the moment to last forever and knowing that it should end. With smiles on their faces and tears in their eyes, the client spoke first. "I can never thank you enough. I remember when I showed up here—scared to death. I lived in a dark hole from which I knew I could never escape. I ate so much I made myself sick. Now, I'm out of the hole. My life is full of light and love now. There is just no way to say how much you mean to me. I am so grateful. I will always love what you have done for me." And with a tightness in her voice, her therapist responded, "I'm pretty choked up, too. I have come to see how very much you mean to me, too. I will remember you and

> your bravery—how you dared to change what seemed back then to be impossible. But you did it. I remember no matter how rough it got for you, you stuck with it. And, here you are. Saying good-bye. How very wonderful it is. The end of therapy is just the beginning of a lot of good things for you. This is fantastic. Thank you for letting me be a part of everything you have done for yourself."

The magnitude of such moments has become somewhat familiar to experienced therapists. They almost never take these moments casually, as if they were merely doing their job. Instead, seeing important changes toward health in their clients and hearing their clients try to express their profound gratitude for the personal and professional talent that enabled them to gain more than they could have imagined, they, too, are prone to get choked up. These moments confirm the importance of what they do. At least, in such moments, often preceded by understandable and felt anguish at times about the extreme suffering they receive from their clients, they see their own humanity. Beyond any appropriate clinical calculations and difficult clinical decisions, they see the immense potential for enabling the discovery of health that they wish for and pursue for themselves. Just as they see incalculable potential in their clients, they see it, too, in themselves.

In personal terms, as a long-experienced therapist, I aspire to join my colleagues who are concerned about the current and ominous condition of our profession and to work with them to do all that we can to improve our profession. Joining with them, this book is a heartfelt affirmation of our profession and, I hope, a source of encouragement for my colleagues. Among other compelling issues, the need for it arises from the common observation that therapists struggle with their humanity. At times, it draws from evidence that reveals the need for a book like this. Because there is so much of it, reporting this evidence may suggest that the aim of the book is to expose the weaknesses of therapists. It isn't. Reporting the evidence confirms what is true, but it also invites others to join those who work to improve counseling and therapy. It is this invitation that defines this book.

The Starting Line

This book is about therapists, not about the academic programs that prepare them. Nevertheless, appropriately credentialed and practicing therapists begin their professional development in and come from preparation programs. Therefore, analogous to the beginning of a marathon race, a comment about "the starting line," preparation programs, may be a good place to begin the longer discussion of the humanity of therapists.

Every college, university, seminary, institute, or other similar institutions that prepare graduate students for careers in counseling and therapy should have a course on "The Humanity of Therapists." Regardless of the title given to it, the reason for such a course is as simple as it is obvious: Due to the well-known and documented vulnerabilities of being human, therapists as humans take all of their vulnerabilities, along with their assets, to their provision of therapy and too often fail to provide effective clinical service due to their misappropriation of their humanity, an observation for which this book provides evidentiary support. Preparation for clinical service should equip prospective therapists to (1) protect clients from therapists' vulnerabilities and (2) deliver competent mental health care. Necessarily, therapists' vulnerabilities and their level of competence, which manifests itself through their vulnerabilities, play a significant role in therapy. Does a preparation program assist prospective therapists with their professional obligation to manage their vulnerabilities?

An immense body of information is needed in the curricula of clinical preparation programs. Evidence indicates that completers of preparation programs achieve appropriate mastery of information. After all, they usually pass licensing and other exams. However, another body of evidence raises concerns about whether completers of such programs acquire sufficient awareness of their humanity and its potential influence on their clinical performance. Generally, preparation programs advance the causes of achievement, status, markers of professional development, and other indications of personal significance, rather than preparing individuals to become effective therapists. For example, from their exhaustive examination of "the experience-accuracy effect," Spengler and Pilipis (2015) conclude that "there are real problems with training and clinical growth in mental health professionals" (p. 372) based on "little improvement in decision-making accuracy by mental health professionals" (p. 371). Compatible with others' analyses, Spengler and Pilipis (2015, p. 372) also conclude, "The results from the present meta-analysis establish that experience leads to some, but not much, improvement in clinical decision making—at least as currently and historically trained, practiced, and researched." And, somewhat ominously, they add (p. 372), "With the glaring challenge these results pose to graduate training programs and practicing clinicians, they also raise important questions about how learning about clinical decision making occurs." With their apparent proclivity for intellectualizing, academic programs understandably endorse academic prowess. They should. However, the necessary and challenging question is whether academic programs adequately prepare individuals to deliver effective therapy.

Lilienfeld (2014) asserts, "There's plenty of legitimate debate in clinical psychology and allied fields, such as psychiatry, social work, and counseling, but at least one proposition should not be particularly controversial: The state of mental health care is in shambles." With regard to preparing minimally effective therapists, are the preparation programs in shambles, too? The literature that provides assessments of licensing preparation programs appears to say that such programs may be largely ineffective, if not in shambles. A mere sampling of such literature seems to confirm this view. For example, the blunt assessment of psychology training programs by O'Donohue et al. (2008) is that training programs have failed to prepare mental health care providers with clinical competencies. O'Donnell (2011, p. 258) calls for "radical reform in educating and training" psychologists, with a needed emphasis on clinical competence. Regarding social work education, Lane (2023, p. 27) observed, "The research highlighted a gap between academic input and the realities and challenges of current social work practice, particularly in terms of depth and complexity of the knowledge and skills needed for frontline practice." Mental health counseling preparation programs also receive similar ratings. Following their examination of teaching group counseling skills in accredited mental health counseling programs, Vannatta and Steen (2019, p. 146) acknowledge that "it is difficult to understand why there is not more of a balance between attending to the development of knowledge and the development of skills." A common conclusion among those who examine preparation programs is that most programs are characterized by a disconnection between academic proficiency and clinical readiness.

Regardless of the specific strengths or weaknesses of a particular preparation program, each one and all of them together must reckon with their duty to prepare minimally effective mental health care providers. Evidence supporting the general failure to do this is consistent, readily available, and long-standing; however, substantial recommendations for improvement are also available. For example, drawing from a considerable body of relevant literature, Martin and Turner (2024, pp. 188–220) propose many specific ways to improve graduate preparation for clinical practice. In the context of this brief discussion, only four of their recommendations are listed here. They are: (1) emphasize clinical preparation; (2) move beyond teaching theories as primary sources of case formulation; (3) build on evidence that clarifies what highly effective therapists do; and (4) build an evidence-based curriculum.

Evidence in Clinical Practice

The resources are available, but the evidence that practicing therapists utilize evidence-based therapy is severely lacking. Instead, most of them deny evidence. Denying evidence reveals the humanity of therapists, not ill will or another nefarious impulse. As Knapp and his colleagues (2024, p. 212) state, "Of all the biases and heuristics, the most problematic for psychotherapists is the overestimation effect, a form of professional narcissism." Martin (2024, pp. 32–49) explains this phenomenon as "exaggerated individualism." McWilliams refers to this as "narcissistic entitlement" (2005, p. 139). Whether it is professional narcissism, exaggerated individualism, or narcissistic entitlement, the phenomenon of assigning priority to individual interests, instead of clinical evidence, as a basis for therapy, is common. Regardless of the term selected to describe it, the unfortunate denial of evidence in the delivery of therapy raises the potential for harming clients.

Denial of evidence is human. The history of the practice of medicine illustrates this phenomenon. As critically important as maintaining health is, the idea that the practice of medicine may have contradicted this belief is itself hard to believe. Nevertheless, as Gurowitz (2011) observed, "Surgery in the 1800s wasn't sterile. Surgeons operated in their street clothes—back then, a typical surgeon's operating room attire was a black frock coat that was rarely, if ever, washed." Further, she adds, "Surgeons didn't wash their hands or their surgical equipment." Worse, "Operating rooms weren't sterile either, and surgical dressings were scraps from the floors of cotton mills. Many surgeons used ordinary sewing needles and thread to close wounds and incisions, and they stuck the needles in the lapels of their coats to use on the next patient."

By the time Louis Pasteur and Joseph Lister came along, various forms of anesthesia had been adopted. They made surgery far more common, but due to poor hygiene, it was much more lethal. The deadly problem of infections is the one that Pasteur and Lister sought to solve. Despite the successful demonstration of effective infection control and publication of evidence, surgeons ignored the evidence for decades, causing numerous unnecessary deaths. (Refer to Isaac, 2017; Michaleas et al., 2022; and Encyclopedia Britannica, 2024).

The story of germs and surgery holds importance for psychotherapy. At this time, regardless of the evidence to the contrary, tens of thousands of therapists arbitrarily select and offer their respective therapies, as if they are truly therapeutic, regardless of evidence to support them. Among others who report similar data, Martin (2024) reports that he located 3,908 (p. 28) specifically "Christian" approaches to therapy, 278 (p. 20) Buddhist approaches to therapy, and approximately 6,000 religion-related approaches. However, from an accrued total of more than 38,000 presumed "clinical" approaches advertised by duly credentialed therapists, virtually countless nonreligious, aberrant approaches could be named, including the following:

- Harp Therapy
- Lady Warriors Therapy
- Past Life Soul Retrieval
- Kuro Nitraguro Therapy
- Labyrinth Therapy
- Spiritual Herbalism
- Purpose-filled Living Counseling
- Synastry
- Celestial Empowerment
- Rohun Purification Process
- Smileology
- Alchemical Hypnotherapy
- Somatic Astro Cartography
- Ancient Indigenous Healing Practices
- Brain Entrainment
- Star Astronumerology
- Swedish Massage
- Barbells-Kettlebells Therapy
- Gemstone Therapy
- Time Traveling

Along with thousands of other aberrant approaches, they are widely and openly advertised and practiced. More than expressing professionalism, these approaches express ordinary humanity. Such approaches are individualistic, narcissistic expressions of therapists. Allowing for protestations to the contrary, practicing mental health care providers do not feel ambivalent about evidence for clinical work that is research-based; they generally oppose it, just as surgeons tacitly opposed life-saving evidence for their profession. At least, the history of surgeons who resisted life-saving evidence confirms the importance of change and the necessity of adapting to evolving circumstances. Indeed, given the ordinary and very real demands of being human, therapists face the increasing necessity of adapting to the added and compelling demand for competency based on good evidence for their clinical service.

A large number—possibly a majority—of therapists fail to consider and pursue ways to acquire clinical effectiveness and maximize such effectiveness in treating their clients, according to Goldberg et al. (2016) and other researchers. Instead of pursuing clinical effectiveness based on good evidence for what they do, therapists tacitly and often overtly oppose evidence-based approaches, a phenomenon discussed by Martin (2020, 2024). Many seek to implement highly individualized approaches to therapy (Martin, 2024, pp. 32–49), while others aim to maximize their ideology-driven, usually non-clinical approaches (e.g., Choma et al., 2013; Holden & Barker, 2018; Lilienfeld, 2014; Lilienfeld et al., 2014; Michaels & Datta, 2016). As Knapp et al. (2024), Martin (2024), and Walfish et al. (2012), among others, have demonstrated, therapists commonly exaggerate their clinical prowess and presumed effectiveness.

Just as surgeons caused harm to their patients when they denied life-saving evidence, many therapists persistently practice therapy in ways that pose identifiable and potential harm to their clients. Just as surgeons have failed to implement readily available evidence, psychotherapists have demonstrated a similar failure. In contrast to Alchemical Hypnotherapy, Spiritual Herbalism, Celestial Empowerment, and Gemstone Therapy, evidence-supported therapies are available. Evidence for the effective delivery of therapy holds the potential for observable and measurable healing when appropriately utilized. The implementation of such evidence confirms that its healing potential is real, durable, and accessible. Moreover, it affirms the best aspirations of practicing therapists and, significantly, their profession and humanity.

As contributors to the ongoing and formidable problems, if not decline, in the effectiveness of mental health care, preparation programs carry a huge burden, but it is not theirs alone to bear. They cannot singularly redirect the multiple constituencies within and around mental health care. Such redirection will necessarily involve practicing therapists, professional associations, state legislatures, licensing boards, relevant corporations, social service agencies, and others. As preparation programs are critically important, a broader view of the world of clinical practice is needed.

A larger view acknowledges that therapists need to protect the rightful prerogatives of their clinical obligations while also acknowledging that therapists' services to their clients may be compromised by influences that shape their clinical work and their humanity, including those that often hold appeal for therapists. For example, the normative interests of therapists may lead them to join profit-making corporations that exist primarily for the benefit of investors, not therapists or clients. Their appeal to therapists is that they promise secure incomes while shaping clinical services in ways that may not best serve the needs of either therapists or clients. Specifically, businesses have established large for-profit and non-profit businesses that manage therapy services, including telehealth companies such as Telemynd, Talkspace, Faithful Counseling, Calmerry, Alma, Hurdle, ReGain, Teencounseling, Brightside, Talkiatry, BetterHelp, Pride Counseling, Psychology Today, Cerebral, Core, and WellVia.

The image of practicing therapy in a solo practice, where a therapist enjoys as much freedom to direct clinical services as the therapist wishes, continues to fade. Indeed, a therapist's ability to manage a practice continues to weaken, as profit-driven corporations have not only moved into the consulting room, they have determined whether there is a consulting room, which therapists will occupy the room, and how much they can earn (e.g., Yenney, 1994; Pingitore, 1999). Rudden (2022) concludes that the ongoing expansion of corporate control of mental health care poses negative outcomes for many providers who deliver their professional services in and through corporations. Professional autonomy has been and continues to be supplanted by corporate regulations (Casalino, 2004). The odd mixture of expanding necessary mental health care and the weakening of therapists' influence on such expansion has also been shaped by telehealth, artificial intelligence, evolving political initiatives, neuroscience, and rising and falling levels of access to health care. Therapists may understandably be paradoxically encouraged and confused about their roles and apprehensive about their future. The view here is that these issues pose formidable challenges, but that therapists individually and collectively can and will meet these challenges and preserve their personal and professional dignity, integrity, and clinical prerogatives.

A Brief Guide to the Book

Below, the short descriptions of the chapters are intended to provide an orientation to the contents of this book. Each chapter focuses on a dimension of therapists' humanity.

> Chapter 1, Therapy: The Embodiment of Humanity, represents humanity as may be expressed through the values and actions of therapists. For example, the chapter says, "Therapy raises potential for sharing common assets and vulnerabilities of being human, whatever these assets and liabilities may be." This chapter discusses the implications of each of the representations of humanity, describing the ways in which therapists embody humanity.
>
> Chapter 2, Given by Life: The Humanity of Surviving and Adapting, confirms common human realities—the need to survive, the necessity of adapting, and the reality of death—as significant features of humanity. More than merely confirming what virtually everyone knows, this chapter also seeks to establish the relevance of several social and clinical constructs, including grieving, language, parenting, emotions, disabilities, and therapy itself, that express the real-world implications of humanity.

Chapter 3, The Period Goes On: The Humanity of Faith, aims to take readers inside the pursuit of personal meaning without depending on sacred texts, doctrinaire statements, or common creeds. As such, it is a report about the inner world of the personal need for faith, a personal quest for meaning—possibly defined as faith—as an expression of humanity. It is experiential and confessional, not ideological.

Chapter 4, "S" Is for "Seed Digging Dynamic Therapy:" The Humanity of Clinical Adventurism, aims to analyze treatment approaches that begin with the letter "S." It makes the case for the necessity of not only understanding how out of control therapy is but also communicating this condition to others. It confirms that the gathered evidence indicates that at least 4,285 treatment approaches begin with the letter "S." Moreover, the chapter analyzes the vulnerability of the humanity of therapists.

Chapter 5, I Am Therapist: The Humanity of Encounter, presents an allegorical conversation between a therapist and a representative of the "curious public." The allegory is a dialogue between these two individuals, with the aim of clarifying what therapy is, not only as answers to important questions about counseling and therapy but also as a way to express the humanity of therapists.

Chapter 6, Cold Feet and Masculinity: The Humanity of Discovering Self, opens the lives of therapists' growth toward health, mostly through their encounters with their clients. As such, it represents the necessary process of growth that often characterizes the development of therapists.

Chapter 7, Healthy Helping: The Humanity of Being a Therapist, discusses the essential characteristics of effective therapists and the necessary relational assets that effective therapists manifest in their delivery of mental health care, when they are effective. Taken together, the characteristics of effective therapists and healthy individuals define healthy helping.

Several items in this book need to be contextualized and described for what they are and are not. Following protocols that protect clients, all illustrations of cases or situations that involve clients do not include real names or other characteristics that would enable readers to identify clients. Another clarification is that the language of "therapist" and "therapy" is more inclusive than these terms may imply. Several titles for mental health care providers, along with multiple titles for state-issued licenses and multiple specializations, are presumed to be included here and may be used when the context calls for them. Otherwise, to avoid undue and likely confusion, usually, the terms "therapist" and "therapy" are used.

The Hope of Truth

This book focuses on practicing therapists, their humanity, and the critical importance of claiming or reclaiming their humanity. As such, it comes with the hope and expectation that the importance of affirming the humanity of therapists will, in itself, benefit not only our profession but also each individual who seeks to move toward a healthy affirmation of their humanity. Whether the experience of therapists in the moment-to-moment of being with a client is daunting, ecstatic, disturbing, joyful, confusing, welcoming, heart-breaking, guilt-suffused, self-satisfied, or many other feelings, it is inescapably human, a reality that enjoins them in the life-giving obligation and potential of making therapy as clinically effective as possible.

Therapists know that truth—honest candor about reality—poses problems. Whether the truth reveals the accidental death of a sibling, a compromised fetus, the loss of a desperately needed job, or many other difficult revelations, it almost always evokes anxiety and worry. Yet, therapists hold the rock-hard belief that life for their clients can get better than immediate circumstances allow, even when they also feel doubtful about a client's potential for healing and recovery. Such doubt may be a necessity of helping because it assures that therapists will be alert to the risks of not helping clients as well as they deserve and to therapists' obligation to provide the best possible care for their clients. Understanding this, the indispensable lesson for therapists is that acknowledging difficult truths about themselves opens doors to positive change. This is the power of honest doubt and an important source of hope. Honest doubt stimulates self-examination and growth for both clients and therapists.

To state the obvious, life cannot be a flawless, pain-free, problem-free experience. Individuals who receive therapy are usually aware of this. And therapists know this, too. Yet, allowing for the truth of what is known about life—and death—clients and therapists seek to make life better, with fewer flaws, less pain, and solved problems. With this pursuit, clients and their therapists also believe in possibilities, expecting that they can and will live in harmony in their relationships, reconcile with others with whom they have had difficult-to-resolve differences, feel a lyrical quality in living, openly and freely express their most sensitive needs, exhibit the benefits of a tranquil inner world, and make reality-based adjustments to their consciousness of life being fulfilled, like a flower from a bud or a baby from a womb. Living with the expectation of living well is hope. In every meeting with every client, this is the promise of therapy. Hope. No doubt, when we are therapists who pursue authenticity, emerging like the naturalness of dawn, we move closer to the likelihood of fulfilling this promise.

References

Casalino, L. P. (2004). Physicians and corporations: A corporate transformation of American medicine? *Journal of Health Politics, Policy, and Law, 29*(4–5), 869–883.

Choma, B. L., Hanoch, Y., Gummerum, M., & Hodson, G. (2013). Relations between risk perceptions and socio-political ideology are domain- and ideology-dependent. *Personality and Individual Differences, 54*, 29–34.

Encyclopedia Britannica. (2024). *Germ theory*. https://www.britannica.com/science/germ-theory

Goldberg, S. B., Miller, S. D., Nielsen, S. L., Rousmaniere, T.,Whipple, J., Hoyt, W. T., & Wampold, B. E. (2016). Do Psychotherapists improve with time and experience? A longitudinal analysis of outcomes in a clinical setting. *Journal of Counseling Psychology, 63*(11), 1–11.

Gurowitz, M. (2011). *Pasteur to Lister to Johnson*. https://www.kilmerhouse.com/2011/03/pasteur-to-lister-to-johnson

Holden, G., & Barker, K. (2018). Should social workers be engaged in these practices? *Journal of Evidence-Informed Social Work, 15*(1), 1–13. https://doi.org/10.1080/23761407.2017.1422075

Isaac, S. (2017). *Lord Joseph Lister of Lyme Regis (1827–1912): The father of modern surgery*. https://www.rcseng.ac.uk/library-and-publications/library/blog/lord-lister-of-lyme-regis/

Knapp, S. J., Gottlieb, M. C., & Handelsman, M. M. (2024). Avoiding failures when applying principle-based ethics to difficult ethical situations in psychotherapy. *Practice Innovations, 9*(3), 205–214.

Lane, D. (2023). Social work education and practice learning at a crossroads: Challenges. *Practice: Social Work in Action, 35*(1), 27–45.

Lilienfeld, S. (2014). *Evidence-based practice: The misunderstandings continue*. https://www.psychologytoday.com/us/blog/the-skeptical-psychologist/201401/evidence-based-practice-the-misunderstandings-continue

Lilienfeld, S. O., Ritschel, L. A., Lynn, S. J., Cautin, R. L., & Latzman, R. D. (2014). Why ineffective psychotherapies appear to work: A taxonomy of causes of spurious therapeutic effectiveness. *Perspectives on Psychological Science, 9*, 355–387.

Martin, F. A. (2020). *Therapy thieves: How to save mental health care from its providers*. Oxford University Press.

Martin, F. (2024). *The challenges of integrating religion and spirituality into psychotherapy: Integrity, competence and cultural pluralism in clinical practice*. Routledge Publishing.

McWilliams, N. (2005). Preserving Our Humanity as Therapists. *Psychotherapy: Theory, Research, Practice, Training, 42*(2), 139–151. https://doi.org/10.1037/00334-3204.42.2.139

Martin, F., & Turner, J. (2024). How to improve graduate preparation for clinical practice. In F. Martin (Ed.), *The challenges of integrating religion and spirituality into psychotherapy: Integrity, competence and cultural pluralism in clinical practice*. Routledge Publishing.

Michaels, T. M., & Datta, V. (2016). Evidence, not ideology, should guide the use of psychotherapy. *The British Journal of Psychiatry: The Journal of Mental Science, 209*(2), 171.

Michaleas, S. N., Laios, K., Charalabopoulos, A., Samonis, G., & Karamanou, M. (2022). Joseph Lister (1827–1912): A pioneer of antiseptic surgery. *Cureus, 14*(12), online.

O'Donnell, R. R. (2011). Reforms in professional education. In N. A. Cummings & W. T. O'Donohue (Eds.), *Understanding the behavioral healthcare crisis: The promise of integrated care and diagnostic reform* (pp. 257–278). Routledge.

O'Donohue, W. T., Cummings, N. A., & Cummings, J. L. (2008). The unmet educational agenda in integrated care. *Journal of Clinical Psychology in Medical Settings, 16*, 94–100.

Pingitore, D. (1999). The corporatization of psychotherapy: A study in professional transformation. In K. Weisgerber (Ed.), *The traumatic bond between the psychotherapist and managed care* (pp. 217–235). Jason Aronson.

Rudden, M. G. (2022). "A weird culture of coercion": The impact of health care corporatization on clinicians. *International Journal of Applied Psychoanalytic Studies, 19*(3), 270–290.

Spengler, P. M., & Pilipis, L. A. (2015). A comprehensive meta-reanalysis of the robustness of the experience-accuracy effect in clinical judgment. *Journal of Counseling Psychology, 62*(3), 360–378. http://dx.doi.org/10.1037/cou0000065

Vannatta, R., & Steen, S. (2019). Pedagogical practices in CACREP accredited group counseling courses: A content analysis. *The Journal for Specialists in Group Work, 44*(2), 138–150. https://doi.org/10.1080/01933922.2019.1599477

Walfish, S., McAllister, B., O'Donnell, P., & Lambert, M. J. (2012). An investigation of self-assessment bias in mental health providers. *Psychological Reports, 110*(2), 639–644.

Yenney, S. L. (1994). Trends in mental health care delivery: The corporatization of a caring profession. In S. L. Yenney (Ed.), *Business strategies for a caring profession: A practitioner's guidebook* (pp. 17–22). American Psychological Association. https://doi.org/10.1037/10506-003

Chapter 1
Therapy
The Embodiment of Humanity

Therapists bring their personal histories into the practice of therapy. Therapists know this—or should know it. Quite literally, they embody all that they have been, bringing this into the practice of therapy. Acknowledging this embodiment and working to elevate their awareness of it almost inevitably leads to their increasing ability to experience themselves and their clients in such ways that their clients likely gain significant movement toward improved mental health. They can more precisely identify with their clients, maintain appropriate differentiation between their personal needs and their clients' needs, facilitate clinically relevant change, and at least avoid harming their clients. The livingness of these ideas may be seen in the experience of a therapist who talked with his friends about his history as a therapist, saying,

> If I tell you about my experience as a therapist, you may think I'm crazy, but I have to talk about our marriage, first. It says more about my history of being a therapist than almost anything else. Amy and I met when we were undergraduate students. She was a psychology major and I was studying social work. The weird thing that happened is that after we graduated, I went into a psychology program, and she went into a social work program. After we finished all of our schooling, both of us got a license and started

> to practice. We did pretty well as therapists. Along the way, we had a child, a daughter. This is around the time some heavy duty tensions began to grow up between us. Any time I was around Amy, I felt the tension in my gut. Now, keep in mind that we're talking about therapists here. The sad thing is that neither of us recognized how lonely we were coming into our relationship and how desperate we were for someone to give a damn about us. We masked it pretty well, until our daughter was born. I feel sick when I say this, but both of us were jealous of how much the other one expressed so much love and affection toward our daughter. After a while and some hard conversations, we began to let the sun shine in. And, as we saw each other for the first time as honest—I mean, truly honest—partners, we talked about how much we needed from each other. It really was like a new day. I remember reading about Aaron Beck and how he was well into his career when he realized that his interest in depression came from his childhood when he felt like he had to rescue his mother from her depression. That's sort of like what we did. We had to live with how we masked what we needed and how we denied what each other needed. I guess it's better late than never. Life is much better for us now. And, I think that our relationship closely parallels our growth as therapists. If we talk about work at all, we no longer talk about our clients; we talk about our experience of being with our clients. It's a new day—a better day.

Practicing therapy comes with a demand for the personal growth of therapists. Practice introduces massive ambiguities and other formidable challenges. Few, if any other professions are as messy, complicated, and demanding as psychotherapy. In the moment of meeting a client, craving certainty and predictability almost inevitably arise. At such moments, confidence in one's abilities often wanes. Feeling inadequate seems to frequently come with clinical practice. Competent counselors and therapists know this. They also know that their best understanding of therapy is translated into competent and effective clinical practice with a serious and perpetual lack of predictability and clarity about what, in the moment, they should do. They know that the temptation to escape from their felt uncertainty is palpable, especially during the early years of their practice. Nevertheless, as ambiguous and frustrating as clinical practice may be, competent therapists persist in welcoming the challenge of testing their own humanity and improving the lives of their clients.

At least on two occasions, I witnessed sessions that were public demonstrations of "excellent" therapy by widely recognized experts, popular among therapists, and often published scholars. Instead of witnessing superb therapy, I saw failure. While the demonstrators managed their profound awkwardness with grace and openness, they did more than this. They insightfully taught larger lessons. These were lessons that experienced, growing, and effective therapists immediately recognize. Several lessons from these therapists included their affirmation of the therapist's accountability for providing good therapy, even when immediate and positive responses from clients do not come. In short, these are lessons that require therapists to recognize the realities of being human, as therapists. These realities transcend mere coping with them. They require careful and prolonged self-examination if therapists expect to become skilled and effective therapists. Among many, many courses of exploration of the self, they hold the expectation that therapists will embody their humanity but also self-consciously embrace their humanity. Such therapists have and will wrestle with important questions. These questions are somewhat unique to each therapist and much too variable and numerous to include here. The following are some examples of possible questions.

> What makes me cry? What judgments do I make of myself when I cry?
> In what specific ways do I influence others to like me—or dislike me?
> When faced with difficulties, whom do I reasonably expect to help me? Why those?
> How do I manage loss?
> How do I manage or mismanage my sexuality?
> Who, if anyone, inspires me? Whom do I inspire?
>
> What is my perspective on parenting from the view of a great-grandmother who has become the primary caregiver for her only great-grandchild, a two-year-old boy? Or, how do I see parenting for a married fourteen-year-old female who is pregnant with her second child and whose parents enthusiastically support and encourage her?
>
> As I contemplate the importance or lack of importance of my life so far, what am I most curious about?

Self-awareness and self-knowledge are limited by one's self-awareness and self-knowledge. "I don't know what I don't know about myself." Many experienced therapists understand this. And the personally and professionally accountable ones among them see their clients' potential for change toward health as limited or expansive based on clients' self-awareness and self-knowledge. They frequently recognize that the cognitions and emotions that rumble and bubble beneath the level of awareness direct thoughts and actions, whereas clients often lack awareness of the source(s) of such thoughts and actions. Such thinking about self-awareness and self-knowledge likely arouses memories of clients for most therapists. The story of one such client is simple, but the complicated details are voluminous. A small but poignant example of complications may be seen in the following case.

A young man is told by his father that he will receive therapy. When the son introduces his need for therapy, he describes one of the precipitating events that caused his father to direct him to seek help. This is the therapist's account.

> A young man is arrested for reckless and drunk driving. In his cell at the county jail, he vigorously protests. After all, following his arrest, he is kept in jail for a long, long time, from his point of view. As a child and young man who easily and readily claimed advantages that almost all of his peers lacked, he expected to be treated as an advantaged individual. His father was well-known. His father was extraordinarily wealthy. His father held huge influence in the community. And, because of these considerable assets, this young man expected to escape from the negative consequences of his "enjoyable" behaviors or, at least, receive pleasant accommodations.
>
> On the fourth day of the young man's incarceration, he received a visit from his father. As his father approached the cell, the young man expressed his frustration with his situation, "It's about damn time you came to get me out of this shit hole." His father asked a simple question, "How many tiles are on the floor?" Reckoning with his father in the moment, the young man vented his frustration, "I don't goddamn know! Okay!" as if to suggest that his father was openly foolish for asking. Before he turned away from the cell and left the jail with his son remaining in it, his father said, "Well, you ain't been here long enough."

The story may invite analysis from several points of view. What is the meaning of "You ain't been here long enough?" What are the implications, if any, of this story for this son's and father's understanding of masculinity? What may the story say about the father's parenting skills or lack of them? Does the story reveal anything about how status and wealth may be misused? More broadly, what may this story reveal about the nature of being human? Those who read the story may speculate about many possible revelations about the nature of being human. These speculations, though, contain their respective understandings of humanity, no matter what this understanding may be. At least, events and moments like the son-and-father interaction above reveal humanity, as well as challenge any understanding of it.

Every individual human story and the much larger story of the human species evoke the question of what humanity may be. In response to this question, there is no short and convincing answer. Commonly, humanity is distinguished from other animals by referring to tool usage and symbolic language. Samuel (2020) characterizes humanity with several features, including belonging, community, creativity, curiosity, family, love, memory, storytelling, and voice. The following discussion describes the character of humanity that therapists may embody.

Therapy as the Embodiment of Humanity

How can therapists characterize or embody humanity? The importance of the question is that it calls for therapists to be clear about their views of themselves and their clients as humans. Asked another way, as a source of revelation and important meaning, does the practice of therapy define humanity, including that of humanity of therapists? If so, what is the definition? If therapy, as therapists understand it, defines humanity, what is the definition of humanity that emerges from such a consideration? Possibly, along with other components of a definition that others in the clinical community may contribute, therapy defines humanity in several ways, such as those discussed below. Analogous to the basic values upon which major codes of ethics stand, these characteristics of humanity are presumed to be truths that therapists hold to be self-evident.

Therapy raises the potential for sharing common **assets and vulnerabilities** of being human, whatever these assets and liabilities may be. Where else can anyone go to speak about the most intimate features of their inner world, particularly those that evoke humiliation and shame merely in their contemplation? At its best and most normative, humanity is sharing. This is the humanity that therapists promote and facilitate while being quite cognizant of their personal humanity. As an expression of this cognizance, Adams (2014) quite effectively reveals the assets and vulnerabilities of therapists in her confessional and analytical book, *The Myth of the Untroubled Therapist: Private Life, Professional Practice*. At least, she establishes that therapists unavoidably immerse themselves in the experience of being human, just as every other human, and take their assets and vulnerabilities into their role as therapists.

An individual, couple, family, or community may feel the stress of engaging their assets and vulnerabilities, but also potentially reveal their authenticity and relevance for healthy survival through such engagement. Therapists are well acquainted with this reality. For example, the otherwise secure adult female who is a mother and wife chooses to pursue and indulge in numerous sexual liaisons. She needs meaningful attachment with another, presumably a loving adult, but initiates actions that ensure that her needs for such attachment will not be met. The stress of her insecurities prompts her to seek to meet her needs in ways that predict her failure to meet her needs. Similarly, the man who aspires to live well and feel good about his life ensures that his aspirations will not be met because he seeks to fulfill them through his compulsive overconsumption of whiskey. He, too, ensures that his needs will not be met. Whether the specific behavior is self-defeating sexual activity, brain-numbing consumption of whiskey, or another example of inappropriately enacted human vulnerability, therapists immediately recognize the universal human reality of the ever-present potential for living poorly or living well. Human assets and vulnerabilities are always somehow enacted.

Almost all human values of consequence arise in a community. If a list of personal virtues were composed, it would surely include accepting, accountable, altruistic, benevolent, brave, capable, collaborative, compassionate, communicative, honest, to name only ten, from hundreds of possibilities. Likewise, if a list of personal vices were composed, it would surely include abrasive, dishonest, greedy, intolerant, manipulative, promiscuous, sarcastic, undependable, vain, and vulgar vices. Virtues and vices confirm that therapists recognize the necessity and advantages of identifying with others and carefully promoting healthy human relationships. This is the opposite of loneliness and isolation, self-service, greed, aggression, and harm. In other words, therapy defines **humanity as a community**. This is humanity, as therapists generally understand it. Indeed, one of the almost universally acknowledged truisms of clinical work is that the therapeutic alliance is a necessary component of competent and effective therapy. "Alliance" is an expression of community, albeit one that is limited in number.

Likewise, the altruistic dentist who commits her practice to those who cannot afford dental care and the school shooter who kills children are members of the human community. This is to say that humanity is a community and that those who plan affirmatively to build it or those who execute criminal activity come almost inevitably with having a community. Some will be good for the community, while others will be bad for it. Some not only harm the community but also sometimes destroy the potential of having a community that would enable them to survive or possibly thrive. The promise of thriving is not one believed by criminals who destroy the promise by conspicuously acting against it. However, the promise evokes major and persistent temptation to act to fulfill it, when countless individuals, churches, various social organizations, and numerous businesses represent themselves as "family." Perpetuating the promise of family has been too often an effective way to sustain community, but also a short-term device for engaging others, blatantly through commercial advertising or religious evangelism, but is seldom a reason to keep them involved. Nevertheless, the need for community appears to be a common feature of being a human. Further, those who know this and want to embody community as a positive value demonstrate this value through their actions. They are generous, altruistic, and sometimes sacrificing in response to the needs of their community. Therapists demonstrate their commitment to the community as they aim to equip clients to find a coherent and durable community when this is clinically relevant.

Inherent in the community is **communication.** Surely, one of the primary features of therapy is communication, although highly conditional, based on the nature of therapy as focusing on the clinically relevant needs of clients. Effective therapeutic communication is characterized by reason, compassion, honesty, acceptance, individualization, and an outcome orientation. With immediacy, therapeutic communication is also personal, discomfiting, risky, and healing, inducing clinically relevant changes when it works as it should. It is aspirational communication based on the role of therapists as those who aim to enable clients to move their lives in the direction of increased health. Such communication may not be anywhere close to being a universal kind of communication; however, it demonstrates the fundamental necessity of communication among humans.

Moreover, competent therapists understand and recognize the importance of effective communication in their personal lives. They place high importance on effective communication in such situations where the demand for it becomes manifest. They feel the burden of such communication when unresolvable conflict within their partner relationships erupts, for example. They carry anguish about the sometimes puzzling demands of nurturing their children during puberty. After all, living intimately with a partner or pubescent child usually brings about inevitable conflict, along with inevitable pleasure and satisfying relational security. Far from being a pleasant abstraction, effective communication is akin to the air they breathe; this is a necessity.

Clinically competent therapists exhibit high levels of self-awareness. In addition, they actively promote healthy self-awareness among their clients. Typically, they understand that a relatively high level of **self-awareness is also necessary for effective social functioning**. Likewise, they understand that low self-awareness often accompanies poor mental status. Whether the specific status involves excessive anxiety, dysfunctional spousal relationships, oppressive parenting, or many others, low self-awareness is usually an important factor. The question is never one of whether individuals possess self-awareness, but always one of whether it is high or low, or relatively accurate or inaccurate. From infancy forward, individuals steadily expand their self-awareness, accommodating their genetic heritage, family dynamics, specific influencing events, and the social world. As Rochat (2015, p. 142) states, self-consciousness may be construed as an experiential process of "fleeting attention [that] is essentially dynamic, constantly fluctuating and in essence multi-layered." The ideas of Rochat (2015, pp. 128–129) not only include the specific dynamics of evolving self-awareness beginning with differentiation but also include situation [i.e., environment], identification, permanence, and self-consciousness. Adapting his concept of differentiation, Rochat says,

> Differentiation: The evolving ability to see one's self as an individualized person. Parents and others observe this phenomenon in infants as they literally see themselves in a mirror and recognize that they are seeing themselves. Similarly, parents and others usually observe the developing self-awareness in their pubescent children as they gain important changes toward seeing themselves as exigent and somewhat rapidly emerging romantic and sexual partners.

The relevance of these dynamics is that they find their expression in specific human behaviors. Thus, whether therapists actively study self-awareness, they usually understand its importance in healthy individuals. They recognize many manifestations of distortions or lack of clarity in the self-awareness of their clients, including body image and body language, expression of feelings, relational skills, tolerance for differences and ambiguity, a wide range of decision making, and many more. Likewise, they understand that the level and accuracy of individuals' self-awareness have major implications for their role in the community(ies) in which they are members. With specific reference to the self-awareness of practicing therapists, discussions on this matter arise many times throughout this book. For now, suffice it to say that therapists who provide competent and effective therapy show high accuracy in their self-awareness and their estimation of their abilities as therapists.

Therapy actively supports the life-sustaining importance of an almost limitless variety of human experiences and expressions. Accepting as real and necessary, humanity has **multiple forms of differences.** This is the humanity that therapists embrace. Tacitly, at least, the differences are far too many for therapists or anyone else to list. Suspending the temptation to compose such a list, almost all adults immediately recognize differences, if only a few categories of differences are mentioned, such as age, race, and religion. However, numerous additional differences among humans may also be easily recognized, such as preferences for musical genres and styles. Similarly, types of food and tastes appear in extreme varieties, depending on many other differences, such as cultural heritage, geography, and personal preferences. Social norms and habits, including styles of clothing, family structures, occupations, manner of aging, language, and habitats, often cause one group of humans to see another group of humans as different to a degree that the other group is not one of which minimal sense can be made. Whatever personal, political, or other constructions are made of differences, they are obvious and sometimes seem eternal.

Some differences among Americans seem to be sources of hostility and, sadly, actions that seek to harm those who are "different." Differences in the availability of guns, race, law enforcement, gender, sexual identity, political affiliation, and reproductive behaviors too often turn in the direction of aggressive and assaultive actions. Adding to the confounding nature of many of these issues, many harmful actions are enacted on behalf of specifically religious ideologies. Among numerous examples that can be readily found, an Oklahoma state senator recently referred to LGBTQ+ individuals as "filth." According to a reporter for KOSU, "[Senator. Tom Woods] . . . called LGBTQ+ people 'filth' when asked about the death of Nex Benedict. Benedict was a nonbinary 16-year-old Owasso High School student who died on Feb. 8 [2024] after a fight in the school bathroom the day prior. While police say early autopsy results show Nex didn't die from head injuries, Nex's mother Sue Benedict said they were frequently bullied" (Bryan, 2024). When asked about his comments about LGBTQ+ youth, Senator Woods said, "We are a religious state. We are going to fight to keep that filth out of the state of Oklahoma, because we're a Christian state" (Bryan, 2024). Does "a Christian state" mandate that nonbinary children should be kept out of the state? Should they be sent elsewhere? Or, executed? Or, permanently kept in home detention? Obviously, welcoming differences becomes difficult, if not impossible, for many individuals and groups.

Humanity is **possessed by needs.** Therapists see that some of their clients who receive clinical services often develop refined skills in meeting their needs and that other clients seem to be committed to failure to meet their own needs. Nevertheless, whether the need for sleep, community, sex, food, shelter, or other basic needs, the reality of such needs defines humanity as organismic. After all, everyone has a body. The layer of needs that may be easily recognized includes food, safety, and sleep. If these needs are not met, social and relational needs may be nonrelevant. Typically, therapists do not attempt to meet their basic physical needs. Instead, they utilize their professional presence and skills to address needs such as over-anxiety, loneliness, marital conflict, recovery from addictions, depression, and many others.

The scene is a familiar one. A couple sits at their dining table and reviews their budget. Among other things, they determine how much money they will spend when they go to the grocery store to secure food for their two children and for themselves. As common and familiar as this scene may be, it provides one of the many possible illustrations of the importance of seeking to meet basic needs. Whether the need involves maintaining an adequate supply of food, getting sufficient sleep in a safe place and on a regular schedule, or many other need-meeting activities, the fact that humans possess these needs is clear and universally recognized. Further, beyond basic survival needs, many other needs can be driving forces at any given moment. They include the need for affection, social standing and support, belonging, safe and reliable transportation, or achievement. Further, every day presents another period of time during which basic needs must be met and when social and relational needs usually press humans into action.

Concomitant with being possessed by needs, the rising and falling **urgency of maintaining life** characterizes human thoughts and actions. No one, including therapists, can be excused from this urgency. Each day brings the grit and grind of staying alive, and the delights and universally welcomed enjoyments that often come with being alive. The grind may be an incorrigible child or a depressed spouse, whereas the ineffable delight may be a problem-free, ecstatic, romantic evening with one's lover. Humanity is tentative but also potentially immensely fulfilling within the boundaries of tentativeness.

Every day, everyone pays attention to survival. Each human needs to live. With some exceptions, each one feels no need to justify life, although living comes with annoying uncertainty, at times. Mostly, at any given time, life needs only to meet its needs. The urgency of maintaining life rises and falls with the degree to which the necessary resources are available. If food is readily and predictably available, the urgency of maintaining life is relatively low. If food is scarce and unpredictable, the urgency is high. No one can evade the necessity of paying attention to survival. However, more than merely surviving, the question that inheres in the delivery of psychotherapy is "How may clients live well—with meaning, hope, contentment, and relational fulfillment?" In some clinical cases, such as those involving a catastrophic accident that takes the life of a beloved person, sexual victimization, or any number of other overwhelming events, the question of the meaning of survival cannot be avoided. Still, psychotherapy holds the potential to enable clients to utilize the urgency of maintaining life to create lives that they truly want to live.

When delivering their services well, therapists assist their clients in discovering and inventing ways to enhance their well-being. Their attention is rightly focused on individuals who, due to increased personal mental health that comes from needed changes, adapt toward health. A larger picture of the human experience confirms that being human has been expressed in countless inventions that also exhibit the human capacity for channeling the urgency to maintain life, whether the specific adaptations actually maintain life. In the long history of human development, these inventions include the potter's wheel, beer and other beverages, steam engines, railroads, clocks, printing, telescopes and microscopes, plastics, numerous cordless devices, nuclear power, personal computers, many sporting games (e.g., baseball, soccer, and basketball), and the Internet. Thus, by limiting this list to only those inventions that may be readily remembered, human adaptation may enhance life or destroy it. And, confining such an understanding to individual clients, the phenomenon of misdirecting the urgency to maintain life can also be seen as harming or destroying life, or fortunately, its opposite.

For good or ill, therapy confirms the **reality of change and the necessity of adaptability**. Clearly, therapy endorses positive change, although it acknowledges the profoundly enigmatic reality of the self-defeating thoughts and actions of many of those who receive their services. The humanity that therapy confirms includes a readiness to adapt to life-affirming thoughts and actions. While some individuals wish to maintain a static, somewhat fixed way of life, they change, too, albeit uncomfortably. This is the nature of humanity.

Long before the reality of perpetual change can be discussed, individuals experience and integrate it into their ordinary functioning. A newborn suckles a breast or bottle, but soon she outgrows the need for it. One day, she rolls from her back to her side. Later, she rises from her supine position to support herself with her hands and feet and begins to crawl. Following this development, she then pulls herself to a standing position and, usually with the delight of her parents, begins to walk. And, somewhere in normative development, the individual speaks about "remembering when," tacitly acknowledging that life has involved perpetual change. Such a child may have a great-grandfather who can tell stories about several wars that were fought during his lifetime, assassinations that altered the history of his country, using telephones when they first became widely available, happy times, the loss of friends, and so on. As most humans experience it, change is relentless and sometimes crushing of personal dreams or, alternately, the fulfillment of such dreams. In the context of psychotherapy, change is programmatically intentional, specifically clinical, and usually desirable. This is a way of integrating the inevitability of change with positivity.

No one disputes the fact that basic needs must be met and that they are accompanied by the urgency to maintain life, including the need for food and physical safety, if an individual intends to survive. Similarly, but not quite as strongly, few dispute the fact that human individuals need **a reason to want to live**.

> "I live for my kids. They're what keeps me going."
>
> "I love being an engineer. It's what I was born to do. If I couldn't be an engineer, I don't know what I would do."
>
> "God put me here for a reason. I'm just trying to figure out what it is. For now, it's just being here, taking care of these patients." [A statement from a nurse.]
>
> "What gets me up in the morning? I guess it's the thought that I may be able to do something good for somebody. What else is there?"

A useful and positive reason to live cannot be based on mere avoidance of bad things, including death. Instead, while the avoidance of bad things is in itself an appropriate self-protective approach to living, it is hardly sufficient. The absence of bad things happening does not translate into a purposeful, enjoyable, fulfilled, and minimally satisfying way of life. As the statements above suggest, a reason to want to live energizes individuals to act for themselves and others and enables them to define their roles and find fulfillment within the boundaries of their roles.

The absence of a life-affirming reason to live exposes heightened and, all too frequently, fatal outcomes. Few individuals can survive long-term meaninglessness and futility. In contrast, and in response to such a view of life, the history of psychotherapy has seen several valuable expressions of the belief that a reason to live is a necessary feature of mental health. A few well-known expressions of this belief serve to illustrate its influence. Surely, Viktor Frankl's *Man's Search for Meaning* almost always stands as a major example of the belief in the human potential for overcoming the most extreme adversities. As a survivor of the Nazi holocaust, Frankl taught others to understand that having a reason to live can enable individuals to survive extreme adversity. Or as Frankl wrote, citing Nietzsche, "He who has a 'why' to live for can bear with almost any 'how'" (1962, p. 84). With thought that challenges and inspires numerous therapists, Frankl added that this dictum "could be the guiding motto for all psychotherapeutic . . . efforts . . ." (1962, p. 84).

Another affirmation of the belief in the necessity of having a reason to live is Carl Rogers's *A Way of Being*. Rogers wrote, "The central hypothesis of [the person-centered approach] can be briefly stated. Individuals have within them vast resources for self-understanding and for altering their self-concepts, basic attitudes, and self-directed behavior; these resources can be tapped if a definable climate of facilitative psychological attitudes can be provided" (1980, p. 115). However, much more than a clinical orientation, Rogers confirms the truth that countless individuals have known quite apart from experiencing psychotherapy, either as a client or as a therapist. He asserted, "When I truly hear a person and the meanings that are important to him at that moment, hearing not simply his words, but him, and when I let him know that I have heard his own private personal meanings, many things happen" (p. 10). Indeed, as many know, something wonderful and magic seems to happen when an individual sees that another person has entered "my" internal world, communicates understanding and acceptance of what is there, and endorses "my" positive potential of what has been received and managed well. For Rogers, the profound and universal need for honest and open connection with others is a reason to live or, more carefully focused, to live well. Neither Frankl nor Rogers expresses all that may be said about the reason to live, but they represent the need for such a reason among the larger body of psychotherapists.

As therapists generally acknowledge, recognizing humanity in one another necessitates **ethics and law.** Typically, therapists advocate for positive and healthy attachment instead of violence, aggression, and war. They embody kindness instead of cruelty. They demonstrate welcoming beliefs, attitudes, and actions instead of bigotry and rejection. Possibly, the collective and individual potential for doing bad things requires the establishment of generally accepted constraints on this potential, including ethics and law, along with social norms. Among other expressions of this necessity, professionally accountable therapists advocate for and comply with professional ethics.

More than codified standards that are expressed in law or ethics, the more basic human ethic is embodied in individuals who possess an ethical attitude and a belief that all members of a community share an interest in living well and inherently deserve such living. These individuals wish to live with inner peace, but also to live at peace with their neighbors. They aspire to live in a such way that their need for optimism and personal well-being, including personal and family safety, can be shared with others. In short, they seek to be life-affirming. It is this contradiction that evokes disappointment, anger, and fear, which also results in laws. Well-behaved individuals do not need laws, except for agreed-upon understandings of how they may positively relate with one another. In contrast and regrettably, those who would violate others must be constrained by laws. Generally, the well-behaved constitute the majority of every population. They need little to regulate them, but others must be regulated as a means of protecting the well-behaved majority. This is the difference between predation and harm on one end of humanity's polarities and decency and honor on the other end.

Each aspect of humanity, as associated with or emerging from therapy, could easily be expanded into large discussions. Indeed, this has been done, although the aspects presented here may not have been gathered elsewhere. At the heart of these aspects of humanity—as it may be defined by psychotherapy—is the need to avoid suffering and death, on one end of the spectrum of human experiencing, and the joyful fulfillment of life-affirming relationships, including healthy partnering and parenting, on the other end. Often, this tension-saturated reality may be observed in almost all specific activities. Whether the activity is a children's baseball game, cardiac surgery, tending a garden, masturbation, composing a poem, or almost every other activity, the fact that the activity soon passes—remembered or not—and its history becomes a necessary feature of living. Each passing, whether it is marked by a birthday celebration, the death of a grandparent, or any one of the numerous others, every adult is at some level aware of the tentativeness of life.

Professional Accountability

Encompassing the specific characteristics of humanity, along with the tentativeness of life, mental healthcare providers seek to fulfill their professional accountability. Arguably, each clinical encounter between a client and therapist may be regarded as an affirmation of and test of humanity in an experiential laboratory. As experiential and uniquely personal as such an encounter is, it is also the outcome of more than a century of growth in the understanding and efficacy of psychotherapy. It is especially personal, as it should be, but it is also representative of and an expression of the profession of psychotherapy. Framed this way, professional accountability necessarily becomes the boundary within which psychotherapy occurs. Not only an experiential and uniquely personal activity, but it is also a professional activity that should be highly conditioned by professional standards. Among these standards, the delivery of psychotherapy should depend on the best available evidence for providing clinically relevant responses to the needs of clients.

If the professional mental health community believes in evidence and evidence-based clinical practices, it should be expected to investigate its experience of manifest humanity. However, as Ling et al. (2020, p. 1728) observe, "There has been little empirical research on CH [common humanity]" among therapists." Their study suggests "that the perception of CH [common humanity] is central to the arising of compassion" (p. 1737). They conclude, "This study revealed that exposure to CH scenarios appears to boost compassion and that CH seems to be a specific perspective that is required in order to arrive at unbiased compassion" (p. 1739). Clearly, the potential for effective psychotherapy becomes stronger when therapists identify with their own humanity and that of their clients. May (1983, p. 93) succinctly articulates this reality in writing about therapeutic encounters, saying, "The encounter with the being of another person has the power to shake one profoundly and may potentially be very anxiety-arousing. It may also be joy-creating. In either case, it has the power to grasp and move one deeply." Very likely, most therapists would agree with May while also acknowledging that the evidence supporting their agreement is more experiential than empirical.

In contrast with eons, during which humanity developed, formalized psychotherapy as a means of helping one another has emerged very recently. No doubt, the positive potential for effecting significant personal change toward mental health has been widely confirmed and accepted. Surely, one of the better sources of information about the effectiveness of psychotherapy is the report from the American Psychological Association (2012), *Recognition of Psychotherapy Effectiveness.* However, while a considerable body of research confirms that psychotherapy works as it should, another large body of research clearly establishes the conclusion that most practicing therapists are not effective. Martin (2020, pp. 30–47) offers substantial documentation that supports this observation. Many others, including Goldberg et al. (2016) and Spengler and Pilipis (2015) confirm this observation. Thus, while therapy works, many therapists fail to deliver it competently, negating its immense positive potential of therapy.

A significant contributor to the ongoing decline in competence in the clinical practice of psychotherapy is the exaggerated individualism of therapists. In other words, therapy has largely become an activity that manifestly denies the humanity of therapists and instead makes therapy about themselves, as if the needs and interests of therapists transcend the importance of the needs and interests of clients. Among many considerations, this appears to be one of the triggering factors in McWilliams' article "Preserving the Humanity of Therapists." She begins her discussion with these words (2005, p. 139):

> Psychotherapists have traditionally embraced core values and beliefs that differ significantly from many values and beliefs that pervade contemporary, commercially oriented Western cultures. With their clients, therapists often question or challenge the culture's materialism, consumerism, appeals to vanity and greed, disdain of dependency and vulnerability, and abetment of narcissistic entitlement.

As such, in several statements, McWilliams avows not only that psychotherapy is "subversive" (e.g., pp. 139 & 140) but also that it is becoming much less so and losing its clinical relevance. However, more than a lament about the prospect of therapists' evaporating humanity as therapists, McWilliams recommends needed actions or, as she says, "[T]his essay contains ideas about how clinicians can act on behalf of our profession and the values that have traditionally infused it" (p. 146). Citing a considerable body of evidence from psychotherapy's history (p. 139), McWilliams refers to many of the values that confirm the humanity of therapists, including several important values and luminaries who developed them, such as "self-understanding (e.g., Blum, 1981), authenticity (Bugental, 1989; Meissner, 1983), empathy and compassion (e.g., Kohut, 1977; Rogers, 1951), egalitarianism (Sullivan, 1947), adaptation to unchangeable realities (Freud, 1971; Stark, 1994; Yalom, 1980), growth in agency and personal responsibility (May, 1958; Schafer, 1976)."

The basic values about which McWilliams writes may correctly be regarded as an excellent beginning for an inclusive discussion about what psychotherapy truly is. And, when the values are translated into clinical practice, they could also become standards by which the profession evaluates itself, along with other specific measures. However, whether discussed or not, translated into standards or not, ignored, expanded, or reduced, they exist in some form in the real world of clinical practice. The current real world of clinical practice raises the likelihood that these values and others that could and should be appropriately integrated into clinical practice will continue to slip into non-relevant oblivion if the humanity of therapists lacks emphasis in training and clinical practice.

More broadly, the apparent and ongoing decline in mental health care has been overwhelmingly confirmed by research, a phenomenon for which evidence has been cited many times in this book. Among other implications of this decline, therapists and others who want them to provide competent clinical services must invest their efforts in examining and improving therapists' experience of their humanity and clinically appropriate expressions of it. Beyond the foreseeable future, doubts about the viable future of psychotherapy will likely compel its members to consider their respective individual roles and the necessary and sufficient characteristics of their profession.

However, establishing committees of academically talented intellectuals to create another dust-attracting volume of "humanity standards" will not suffice. Instead, in quite specific ways designed to actualize the humanity of therapists, active and ongoing consideration must involve long-term, individualized, self-examination, and other examination of each counselor and therapist. The details of these examinations lie beyond this discussion. For now, suffice it to say that actualizing the humanity of therapists may be pursued through intensive, compassionate, thorough, long-term self-discipline and commitment to becoming an effective mental health care provider. Martin and Turner (2024, pp. 188–245) dedicated two chapters to proposals for strengthening and advancing the viability of therapy. Possibly, a place to begin is to reframe the aspects of humanity that are discussed above and individualize them for therapists. This is the goal of the following discussion.

Actualized Humanity for Therapists

If counselors and therapists take the view that the values that inhere in their profession should be embodied and actualized, what can they do to integrate these values into clinical practice? This discussion offers ideas on how this may be done. Generally, when ideas about actualizing humanity in the process of therapy are actively pursued, they are expressed by individuals in real, personal, and ongoing ways. Thus, the following discussion can be a source of guidance because it considers how individual therapists may apply this idea to themselves.

What are **my assets and vulnerabilities** that may increase or impair my clinical effectiveness? Extending this question, added questions inevitably become quite specific with regard to individual assets and liabilities. For example, an individual may need to wrestle with personal dilemmas that involve loss. Or, she may need to confront her challenges with the ways she mismanages her anger? Or, he may need to move toward healthy ways to ease his grip on his compulsive and excessive control of others. Or, she may need to accept the beneficial impact of her personal disclosures on her identification with her clients' struggles. Or, he may need to explore his surges of guilt around having sex with his dad's sister when he was fifteen years of age and she was thirty-one years of age. Or, she may need to pay attention to her reactions to her over-identification with a client whose presenting concerns revolve around body image.

An important corollary to these questions is "Who can competently help me to manage my assets and vulnerabilities in such ways that my clinical services are increasingly effective?" In contrast to the illusory belief that anyone can manage their growth alone, especially when they practice therapy in relative isolation, therapists who gain careful and caring awareness of their assets and vulnerabilities understand that they need help with such management. The consensus among researchers on the self-awareness of therapists includes at least two necessary emphases. One, serious self-reflection usually results in professional growth and increased clinical effectiveness. Two, healthy self-awareness usually develops in relation to and with the assistance of others. Chow et al (2024, p. 11) conclude that "First, self-reflection is necessary, but insufficient" and that feedback from others is necessary for developing self-awareness and clinical effectiveness. (For added evidence, refer to Knapp et al., 2017; Pereira et al., 2024; Mojta et al., 2014; Prasko et al., 2023; Tufekcioglu & Muran, 2015). Also, self-awareness receives added emphasis later.

As noted above, therapy recognizes the virtue and advantage of identifying with others. This is the opposite of loneliness and isolation. Humanity is **a community**. This feature of common humanity poses the requisite that every therapist should be clear about what the emotional and social place of personal relationships is in their lives. The importance of this, too, may be framed as questions that need answering. What is your place among others? How do you influence others, and how do they influence you? With whom do you feel inferior or superior? How do you promote the welfare of others in the groups to which you belong, or impair the welfare of these groups? How do you elevate or seek to manage conflict among members of your community? Can you describe your management of rejection from others? How do you and your community manage differences among members? What specific values and their enactment do you take to your community? What specific characteristics do you need to see in a prospective friend?

More broadly and significantly than individual self-examination, and no matter what their roles or personal ideologies may be, community means that therapists belong to a professional community. As such, their professional accountability transcends much of their preferred individualism, regardless of how strongly they wish to be unique as persons or how much they wish to claim that their professional services are unique. Belonging to the profession mandates loyalty to the highest standards that inhere in the community.

Inherent in the community is **communication.** Again, questions can help individual counselors and therapists assess the quality and impact of their communications. Can you describe your communication style? With whom in your community would you prefer not to communicate? What do you conclude about the quality of your ability to communicate sensitive or negative but necessary information? When is your communication style primarily a passive one, and why? Describe the communication you have frequently observed between your family members, excluding yourself, and what you have gained, if anything, from your observations. Describe a moment when you assertively communicated your sensitive and important needs to someone and your level of confidence in yourself in this moment. How do you utilize your emotions in your communications with others, including your partner, your parents, your children, your colleagues, and your clients? With whom do you prefer to disclose your inner world, including your thoughts and urges, with which neither you nor the other person may be comfortable? Apart from the one you now occupy, list five social roles that appeal to you, such as housekeeper at a hotel, church leader, parent, or police officer, and another five that do not appeal to you, and answer the question of what this reveals to you about you and how you think about relating with others.

A common refrain among clients is "I don't know who I am anymore," particularly among those who have been traumatized. Including therapists, everyone is vulnerable to losing **appropriate self-awareness.** Therapists can lose self-awareness, too, but usually more subtly than those suffering from traumatic events. When therapists isolate themselves and fail to review their work with their peers, they frequently exhibit inappropriate self-awareness. Those who become inappropriately involved with their clients exhibit poor self-awareness, for example. Similarly, in their social functioning, they recognize that their personal histories, current relationships, personal values, and other important characteristics influence and sometimes determine the quality of their self-awareness. Thus, effective therapists monitor themselves, as their clinical experience informs them about the necessity of being attuned to the terrain of their internal world. Without this, they would lack attunement to their clients.

Moreover, self-awareness changes, sometimes dramatically. No doubt, therapists see a dramatic change in their clients who, for example, have been traumatized. They also see a change when their clients confront their trauma and demonstrate extraordinary courage in looking at severe stressors that they surely could wish to avoid. Correctly, therapists who encounter such clients conclude that denial of trauma-caused internal storms may not only be protective but also life-denying. With empathic awareness and readiness to help clients, they understand the impulse to deny and avoid trauma-related thoughts and feelings. When clients dare to confront their trauma and overcome it, therapists easily admire the courage that their clients exhibit. Without trauma and the need to muster the courage to overcome it, therapists potentially harm themselves and their clients if they avoid the active pursuit of accurate self-awareness. Their vulnerability is that they decide to remain oblivious to some of their most important personal and professional assets in their misguided interest in avoiding themselves. Just as therapists witness profound courage in their clients, they should see that their courage can become a powerful antidote for such oblivion.

An undeniable truism of life in general and of the practice of psychotherapy is that humanity can be characterized by **multiple forms of differences.** There are numerous implications of this truism for clinical practice. Probably, many of the differences between therapists and their clients result in a few serious complications. However, some differences can and do betray the clinical needs of clients. For example, when an ideology, such as strong convictions about what therapy ought to be, including excessive commitment to CBT, Solution-Focused, or another approach to therapy, is out of sync with the clinically relevant needs of clients, clients may be poorly served (Noble & Rizq, 2019). Or, for example, when a specific religious ideology dominates the clinical thinking of therapists, the needs of clients are likely to be poorly served. With regard to religious ideologies, Martin (2024), including the sources cited in his book, provides considerable evidence that indicates the pervasiveness of such therapists and their deleterious impact on clinical judgment and service. These ideologies in therapy or elsewhere minimize the appropriate acknowledgment of differences.

Somewhat more narrowly, both therapists and their clients bring differences to the consulting room that mandate alertness and careful attention to the clinical needs of clients. Among many, these include political differences, attitudes and beliefs about gender or other expressions of sexuality, educational achievement, personal values, trauma history, age, and family status. Also, strong views about several emotions are also likely to be sources of differences. Therefore, in their pursuit of clinical relevance and effectiveness, therapists should ask, "What is your real reaction in the moment when a client emotes loneliness, sadness, joy, sexual desire, trust, anger, fear, guilt, shame, or gladness?" Or, "With which feelings do you feel less secure or more secure?" Conscientious therapists raise these and many other questions related to the differences between themselves and their clients.

Humanity is **possessed by needs.** Therapists engage with many individuals, families, and groups. These engagements naturally but not inevitably expose therapists to clients' pain, change, and met and unmet needs, and a lot more, that have major implications not only for the process of therapy but also for the capacity of therapists to meet their relational needs. Only at the expense of clients, therapists conclude that their relational needs have little or no influence on their delivery of clinical services. Commonly, an observation about therapists and acknowledged by therapists themselves is that they have experienced intimidation, gratitude, confusion, attraction, dread, enjoyment, acceptance, and many other feelings during their delivery of therapy. In the moment of experiencing them, these feelings and others cannot be and should not be assigned merely to thoughts about being with clients. Feeling intimidation may come from a need for status, at least, and maybe doubt about one's self-worth. Feeling confused may come from a need to understand, at least. If an exploration of only the need for status and understanding is the one that may reveal how a therapist is possessed by needs, what may a therapist do with this?

Usually, an individual needs what they also fear. A need naturally arouses some level of predictable fear. If an individual needs status, the fear is that she will have little or none among those who matter. Similarly, a need for understanding arouses the fear that they will lack understanding. The fear is normative. If a therapist or anyone else is hungry for acceptance, the normative fear is the possibility of rejection. More than normative, such fear may be healthy. It is usually and appropriately motivational. Natural fear comes to humans as an awareness of themselves and the world in which they are part and keeps them safe. The management of normative fear may not be normative, though. Therapists must adapt their normative fear, particularly in the consulting room, so that they pay appropriate attention and services to their clients. Thus, because needs and fears are relevant to their effective delivery of clinical services, they should raise questions about themselves. Who intimidates me, and why? How do I manage my intimidation in therapy sessions? When I'm confused during a therapy session, what thoughts do I have about myself? In what ways, if any, do I sometimes blame my clients for my intimidation or confusion? Do I sometimes subtly manipulate my clients so that I can avoid my uncertainty about my status or lack of understanding? Do I allow my clients to manipulate me due to my uncertainty about my status or lack of understanding? What is my reaction when a client rejects my best efforts to utilize my best skills?

More basically, therapists must engage in serious reflection on the ways they manage or mismanage their needs. For example, they know that they need sleep, just as everyone else needs sleep. They know that sleep comes, voluntarily or not, sufficiently or not, regularly or not. How do therapists manage or mismanage their sleep? Or belonging? Or sexuality? Or status? Or physical hunger? Whether these needs and others are managed in healthy ways or not, they are needs that shape and influence many of their decisions, including clinical decisions.

The rising and falling **urgency of maintaining life** characterizes human thoughts and actions. When individuals feel urgency, something is needed now. The demand for something is immediate and cannot be delayed. If one's spouse is about to give birth, planning a getaway for the upcoming weekend falls out of sight. It is no longer relevant. For most individuals and most of the time, the urgency of maintaining life is subdued because the needed resources are readily available. Nevertheless, therapists ask questions about themselves. How do I maintain appropriate focus on meeting my needs without also becoming overanxious about this? In what ways, if any, do I avoid the urgency about maintaining life that others may feel? How do I utilize my need to maintain life as a motivator to ensure that I am okay, but also to ensure that others are okay, too? Given the option of loving my life or dreading my life, how do I select thoughts and actions that will fit the real circumstances of my life, but also avoid becoming trapped in such circumstances? Who needs to know and understand my need to maintain life and help me with such maintenance? When are my needs most pressing and cause me to feel the urgency to maintain myself?

For good or ill, therapy confirms the **reality of change** as a feature of being human. On any given day, therapists are not likely to try to account for their changes, say, during the past year, or needed changes that may lie ahead. Still, if they are to maintain their clinical competence, they must pay attention to their need for change. Assuming that no individual is complete, let alone perfectly complete, change is as necessary as it is inevitable. Thus, individual therapists should ask themselves, "In what specific ways do I as a person need to change, toward improving myself and my personal relationships?" And, "In what specific ways do I need to improve my delivery of clinical services?"

Humans need **a reason to want to live**. Presumably, a therapist's reason to live encompasses being a therapist. Just like everyone else, therapists feel the need for a reason to want to live. Therefore, they may explore their answers to questions that relate to this need. They may ask, "If I were to compose a mission statement for my life, what would I say that accurately reflects what is truly important to me? As I review my mission statement, which of my personal values are expressed in it? With whom would I like to share my personal mission statement? From whom would I like to get help with my personal mission statement?" Alternately, "If I were to identify five things that I should accomplish with my life, what would they be?"

Recognizing humanity in one another necessitates **ethics and law.** Individuals live by personal ethics that may or may not be compatible with published or other socially well-known ethics. Surely, within the context of delivering clinical services, therapists often see a tension, if not warfare, between what individuals say they value and the way they act. A mother who abuses her children may also energetically state that she loves her children and would never harm them. Sometimes, therapists feel similar tensions, even if they are not quite so blatant. For example, a therapist may feel quite indifferent to the suffering of a client, maybe, due to fatigue or demands of life elsewhere, while also wanting fervently to help. Or, a therapist who is recovering from knee joint replacement surgery and returning to sessions with clients may be understandably preoccupied with his tender knee and also be somewhat less interested in his client's welfare than he usually would be. Such a therapist may feel constrained to keep clients because of a need to maintain income. Allowing for the ordinary complexities that inhere in human existence, therapists may want to ask themselves, "If I have no external ethical standards to guide my conscience, by what standards would I want to live?" Or, "What is my most important guiding ethical principle for my clinical practice?"

So, what is the most basic and vitally necessary feature of therapists' humanity? The answer to this question probably includes many answers, depending on the opinion of those who wish to answer it. However, in the context of this discussion about the humanity of therapists, a good possible answer looks like this: A therapists must, first, decontaminate their clinical judgment, insofar as possible, of any impulse, feeling, relational distortions or other potential interferences with their capacity to meet the clinically relevant needs of their clients. Martin (2020, 2024), reports a large body of evidence that confirms the importance of therapists knowing themselves and reckoning with their limitations, including carefully studying their performance as therapists for many years and demonstrating their commitment to improving their clinical competence and integrity. Usually, therapists who can acknowledge their vulnerabilities, including those that arise during their therapeutic contact with clients, recognize their discomfort, to be sure, but also gain clinically relevant awareness of their client and, therefore, elevate their effectiveness.

For all humans, life is experimental, a lived experience of immersion in a process that captures them in comforting and secure moments and the tandem necessity and inevitability of painful surprises and unmitigated pleasure. A few moments of reflection likely clarifies this for anyone who thinks about the nature of this human experience.

Mom had a stroke. We aren't sure what to expect.

When we are together, I feel like I am a part of a glorious universe.

Back then, I had nowhere to turn. Once the thought of suicide entered my brain, I was scared to death. My next stop was a therapist's office.

Prostate cancer? Well, damn, that's not good news.

We love to visit with our granddaughters. What could be better than that?

Let's go. We can't be late getting to the hospital. They're not going to wait on us to get there before they start James' surgery.

I love our house. Inside is okay, but I really love being out there, swimming in beautiful flowers. I feel like God made flowers just for me to enjoy.

War. I don't understand it. Why can't we live in peace and just take care of one another?

Allowing for obvious inconsistencies in the quality of life, including the specific settings in which people live, the human experience is universal, incorporating countless variations in its details. It enwraps everyone, including therapists. Like every other parent in a similar situation, as desperately as they may wish to do so, they cannot stop the teen angst of their son. They can have great sex. They can see the signs of physical decline, as they anticipate their seventieth birthday. They can feel the joyful excitement of attending the celebration of their spouse's significant promotion at work. They can claim the exhilaration of being independent from the irrational expectations of their aging parents. In other words, they can acknowledge and openly experience their humanity, but also welcome it.

More than being enwrapped in being human, therapists also can determine that they will welcome their humanity—all of their humanity—and manage themselves in ways that they can respect and truly enjoy. Allowing for their darkest days, they can claim and embrace gratitude and other life-affirming attitudes as their primary responses to living a human life. Still, the idea of welcoming one's humanity can be as repulsive as it is compelling. Generally, it is repulsive because it often involves acknowledgement of unwelcome revelations about one's self. In contrast, it is also compelling because claiming one's humanity and immersing in it activates excitement about living. As Peck concluded, "If someone is determined not to risk pain, then such a person must do without many things: having children, getting married, the ecstasy of sex, the hope of ambition, friendship—all that makes life alive, meaningful and significant" (Peck, 1978, p. 133).

The demands of life, with particular emphasis on providing clinical services, require acute vigilance to the possibilities that life presents. For therapists, the essential question is "How adaptive is my/our profession, in response to these demands and to the immense potential of competently delivered psychotherapy?" More ominously, "Shall I/we continue to let our profession slip into non-relevance?" Alternately, to extend Peck's thoughts, shall we risk the pain of encountering the realities of life and justly claim the immense potential of psychotherapy for our clients so that they and we, too, can feel the consequential excitement of being alive and full of positive meaning because we helped to produce significant changes, because we dared to deliver ethical, professionally accountable psychotherapy? As we seek to answer these questions, a major challenge for individual therapists and their leaders is to reckon with our/their humanity.

References

Adams, M. (2014). *The myth of the untroubled therapist: Private life, professional practice*. Routledge.

American Psychological Association. (2012). *Recognition of psychotherapy effectiveness*. https://www.apa.org/about/policy/resolution-psychotherapy

Blum, H. P. (1981). The forbidden quest and the analytic ideal: The superego and insight. *Psychoanalytic Quarterly, 50*(4), 535–556.

Bryan, M. (2024). *Oklahoma state senator calls LGBTQ+ people 'filth' when asked about death of nonbinary student*. https://www.kosu.org/local-news/2024-02-26/oklahoma-state-senator-calls-lgbtq-people-filth-when-asked-about-death-of-nonbinary-student

Bugental, J. F. T. (1989). *Search for authenticity: An existential-analytic approach to psychotherapy*. Irvington Publishers.

Chow, D., Lu, S. H. X., Kwek, T., Miller, S. D., Jones, A., Hubble, M. A., & Tan, G. C. Y. (2024). Improving responses to challenging scenarios in therapy: A randomized controlled trial of a deliberate practice training program. *Training and Education in Professional Psychology.* Advance online publication. https://dx.doi.org/10.1037/tep0000493

Frankl, Viktor E. (1962). *Man's search for meaning: An introduction to logotherapy*. Beacon Press.

Freud, S. (1971). Analysis terminable and interminable. In J. Strachey (Ed. & Trans.), *The standard edition of the complete psychological works of Sigmund Freud* (Vol. 23, pp. 209–254). Hogarth Press.

Goldberg, S. B., Miller, S. D., Nielsen, S. L., Rousmaniere, T., Whipple, J., Hoyt, W. T., & Wampold, B. E. (2016). Do psychotherapists improve with time and experience? A longitudinal analysis of outcomes in a clinical setting. *Journal of Counseling Psychology*, *63*(1), 1–11.

Knapp, S., Gottlieb, M. C., & Handelsman, M. M. (2017). Self-awareness questions for effective psychotherapists: Helping good psychotherapists become even better. *Practice Innovations, 2*(4), 163–172.

Kohut, H. (1977). *The restoration of the self.* International Universities Press.

Ling, D., Olver, J., & Petrakis, M. (2020). Investigating how viewing common humanity scenarios impacts compassion: A novel approach. *British Journal of Social Work, 50,* 1724–1742. https://doi.org/10.1093/bjsw/bcz124

Martin, F. (2020). *Therapy thieves: How to save mental health care from its providers*. Oxford University Press.

Martin, F. (2024). *The challenges of integrating religion and spirituality into psychotherapy: Integrity, competence and cultural pluralism in clinical practice.* Routledge Publishing.

May, R. (1958). *Existence: A new dimension in psychiatry and psychology*. Basic Books.

May, R. (1983). *The discovery of being: Writings in existential psychology.* W. W. Norton and Company.

McWilliams, N. (2005). Preserving our humanity as therapists. *Psychotherapy: Theory, Research, Practice, Training, 42*(2), 139–151. https://doi.org/10.1037/0033-3204.42.2.139

Meissner, W. W. (1983). Values in the psychoanalytic *situation. Psychoanalytic Inquiry, 3*(4), 577–598. https://doi.org/10.1080/07351698309533515

Mojta, C., Falconier, M. K., & Huebner, A. J. (2014). Fostering self-awareness in Novice therapists using internal family systems therapy. *The American Journal of Family Therapy, 42,* 67–78. https://doi.org/10.1080/01926187.2013.77287

Noble, A., & Rizq, R. (2019). "It's led me astray": How cognitive behavioral therapists experience personal therapy in clinical practice. *Counseling and Psychotherapy Research, 20*, 29–38.

Peck, M. S. (1978). *The road less traveled: A new psychology of love, traditional values and spiritual growth.* Simon and Schuster.
Pereira, R., Pazo Pires, A., & Neto, D. (2024). Therapist self-awareness and perception of actual performance: The effects of listening to one recorded session. *Research in Psychotherapy: Psychopathology, Process and Outcome, 27*(1). https://doi.org/10.4081/ripppo.2024.722
Prasko, J., Ociskova, M., Abeltina, M., Krone, Kantor, K., Vanek, J., Slepecky, M., Minarikova, K., Mozny, P., Piliarova, M., & Bite, I. (2023). The importance of self-experience and self-reflection in training of cognitive behavioral therapy. *Neuro Endocrinology Letters, 44*(3), 152–163.
Rochat P. (2015). Layers of awareness in development. *Developmental Review, 38,* 122–145. https://doi.org/10.1016/j.dr.2015.07.009
Rogers, C. R. (1951). *Client-centered therapy: Its current practice, implications, and theory*. Houghton Mifflin.
Rogers, C R. (1980). *A way of being*. Houghton Mifflin Company.
Samuel, L. R. (2020). *The 10 universal human traits*. https://www.psychologytoday.com/us/blog/boomers-30/202012/the-10-universal-human-traits
Schafer, R. (1976). *A new language for psychoanalysis*. Yale University Press.
Spengler, P. M., & Pilipis, L. A. (2015). A comprehensive meta-reanalysis of the robustness of the experience-accuracy effect in clinical judgment. *Journal of Counseling Psychology, 62*(3), 360–378. http://dx.doi.org/10.1037/cou0000065
Stark, M. (1994). *Working with resistance.* Jason Aronson.
Sullivan, H. S. (1947). *Conceptions of modern psychiatry*. Norton.
Tufekcioglu, S., & Muran, J. C. (2015). Case formulation and the therapeutic relationship: The role of therapist self-reflection and self-revelation. *Journal of Clinical Psychology: In Session, 71*(5), 469–477. https://doi.org/10.1002/jclp.22183
Yalom, I. (1980). *Existential psychotherapy*. Basic Books.

Chapter 2
Given by Life
The Humanity of Surviving and Adapting

Everyone who reads this has a lineage that reaches back in time to the first molecule. After a couple of billion years, those self-conscious descendants of the first molecule refer to it as "life." The first molecule was life or, maybe, pre-life, as today's humans would understand it. Regardless of its precise designation, life began with it. And, while everyone lacks awareness of such an event, they would not exist without the first molecule having happened. Obviously, in a more direct, personal, and existentially real way, everyone whose consciousness allows them to be aware of their existence knows that they came from a man and a woman who combined their respective biological contributions to life—a sperm and an egg—intentionally or not, to begin their respective lives.

From the first molecule to the birth of each human being, life found a way to perpetuate itself. Obviously, for each one of us, we had no choice in the matter of creating life or becoming an expression of life. Likewise, none of us will have a choice in the matter of our respective lives ending. Each of us will end.

As paradoxical as this may seem, life found that death was a way to perpetuate itself. Stated differently, if all living things almost never died or if all living things were alive now, the planet could not sustain them. The inevitable outcome of an indefinitely long life for everything is that all life would perish, having exhausted its potential for sustenance.

The first molecule became the first cell. Well, maybe. Quite possibly, the first molecule that could have become life, as it is currently known, did not survive. Somewhere, though, one of those molecules replicated itself. It became two molecules. Then, over the span of, maybe, a couple of billion years, life created you and me. Along with every other form of life, you and I came from a replication process that began with a molecule. The first cell became two cells. Long before any combination of evolving cells had enough consciousness to think about evolving life, the expressions of life multiplied. They included slime, bacteria, odd sea creatures, and thousands of life forms that have long been extinct. But, later, they also included flying mammals, creatures that sprayed venom, migratory insects, and termites, along with buffalos, anacondas, giraffes, and every other life form.

If nothing else, the long, persistent, inexorable, complex, and diversifying expressions of life repeatedly confirm that life finds a way to exist. It adapts. It accommodates. It adapts to bitter cold, according to human standards. It adapts to acid pools. It adapts to human-exterminating, high temperatures. It adapts to deep ocean pressures. It adapts to swamps. It adapts to deserts. Life adapts in large and complex ways, but it adapts.

No doubt, among humans, life adapts, too. Obviously, humans have adapted to all habitable locations on Earth, along with some that are not so habitable. And, the expectation is that habitable locations will be built on planets that have not yet been reached by humans. Human adaptations have also involved massive, murderous, warring conflicts. Dictatorships. Famines. Diseases, including pandemics. And, as human life consumes—or overconsumes—almost anything that the planet has available for consumption, along with climate change, our adaptive capacity may be entering another time when it is stretched to maintain the survivability of our species. All of this and more state an essential fact about life. Life adapts. And, with every adaptation, life becomes more complex, more diverse.

Life becomes more diverse? Surely, it does. Botanists see the expansive diversity of plants. The modest, ground-clinging moss shares space with the massive white oak tree. Adding to these two expressions of botanical diversity, there are another four hundred thousand (400,000) different kinds of plants (Mongabay, 2024). However, botanists generally believe that many more plants have yet to be identified.

Life becomes more diverse? A detailed account of diversity among humans would occupy more space than this book should or could allow. Whatever the specific content of diversity may be, it has served the primary purpose of survivability, primarily through replication and adaptation. From the development of the first replication of life to the present day, replication has, among other things, characterized human life. However, as inviting as simple characterizations of replication may be, such as reducing life to expressed sexual impulses, they are hardly sufficient. Instead, replication of life and the necessity of engaging in it become immediately complicated by many of the features of life that can be readily recognized and many that may not be generally recognized. Among those that are easily recognized, the replication of life and sustaining the species involve

Social status. Wealthy families who live in gated communities are not likely to arrange play dates for their children with children from families who live in government subsidized housing. Or, no matter how sincerely spokespersons may be, say, for a church congregation, their message is not likely to be taken seriously, if the message is cluttered with egregious grammatical errors and manifestly poor information.

Health. A terminally ill adult is unlikely to engage in activities associated with replicating life. Accompanying health, genetic inheritance, sometimes, determines the capacity or incapacity to engage in life-replicating activities.

Personal values. Often, this involves protecting one's family, with emphasis on enabling children to reach adulthood and to replicate the species. Protecting one's family and children cannot exist apart from protecting others, too. Thus, personal values become social values. Several personal values are listed, next.

Social values. The list of these values could likely extend into the hundreds. Suffice it to list only a small selection of commonly acknowledged social values. They include justice, dependability, orderliness, honesty, freedom, equality, and equity. The question of is not one of whether these values influence replication and adaptability, but one of how.

Age. A three-year-old child is not likely to engage in activities associated with replicating life, while a forty-two-year-old will likely work to ensure that food, shelter, and other needed resources are available for their family.

Countless contingencies. Tornadoes, childcare, floods, political changes, economic recessions, war, regulatory and other legal changes, pandemics, food supply, access to education, transportation, along with many other contingencies, often determine whether survival and replication are possible.

While being a human involves the ongoing necessity of replication, it also involves adaptability. More personally, each individual embodies adaptability or the lack thereof, always accompanied by beliefs about replication, adaptability, and various cultural factors. The most visible agent of replication and adaptability is the human body. At the core of being a human, the human body endures as the essential, universal feature of human life. Apart from this feature, none other comes close to it as an essential and universal one. Color, nationality, sexual orientation, ethnicity, environmental context, education, age, intellectual capacity, social status, family size, family resources, and cultural and personal values, among many other features, appear among humans with extraordinary diversity, but everyone has a body.

Embodiment and Culture

Lust and desire promise life. Obviously, some individuals conflate lust and desire with the possibility that their unrecognized but motivating, large deficiencies will be overcome by unwanted sexual seduction, overwhelming power, oblivion to one's self, or blind and too often culturally held expectations that approve of violating others. Indeed, lust and pleasure aim to meet the need for the species to perpetuate itself. Without this otherwise inexplicable need, the species would have faded into non-existence eons ago. Expressed in a healthy manner, lust and pleasure-seeking promise both momentary satisfaction and the expectation that life will be indefinitely sustained, despite its short-term limitations. Thus, by the time death comes, as it does for everyone, the promise of expressed lust and pleasure-seeking will have been fulfilled. It will be counted as another generation that will adapt to the new world in which it lives, with the fresh expectation that its generation will produce another generation.

Not only lust, desire, and pleasure, but also quite apart from them, this is the character of competently delivered therapy services. Authenticating lust, desire, and pleasure as essential to mental health shapes the foundation for validating the positive impact of therapy, even when sex-related matters are not the focus of treatment. With the belief that therapy can make life better than it would be without treatment, the problems addressed through therapy become solvable or resolved as therapist–client interactions affirm the basic realities of healthy relating. As such, this involves clear and necessary authentication of their reality-based and common humanity—the therapist's and the client's—as it is lived in the moment. This is to say that survivability, adaptability, and replication have been and will be common human agendas.

More of this theme is discussed later. For now, the ideas here are likely more familiar—akin to breathing or urinating—than they may appear. These ideas manifest themselves when two individuals' authentic selves meet. The reality and truth of this are close to the personal experience of therapists when they meet with clients and when they deliver competent clinical services.

Therapists did not discover empathy or related interpersonal phenomena. Instead, they found ways to validate their significance in the effective delivery of professional services. As it is generally conceived, accurate empathic awareness has not been viewed as all that is needed for the conduct of effective professional services, but viewed instead as one of several necessary characteristics of effective therapist–client relationships. Quite apart from the therapist–client relationship, the importance of empathic awareness is commonly understood. When a family member suffers a heart attack, other family members also feel the stress of the event and usually do all they can to help. When a friend moves through a relational schism and divorce, friends who meet at a coffee bar to support their divorcing friend feel the anguish associated with this momentous change. When a child gets hit with a baseball during recess at school, often other children gather around to support them and to ensure that their classmate is okay. Along with many other circumstances, the importance of empathic awareness is commonly recognized, if not carefully conceptualized. Further, it is also recognized as an affective, cognitive, and physical experience.

Many years ago, following almost two decades of careful research on the therapeutic relationship and its ancillary features, Rogers (1955, p. 274) stated, "Science exists only in people. Each scientific project has its creative inception, its process, and its tentative conclusion, in a person or persons. Knowledge—even scientific knowledge—is that which is subjectively acceptable." Whether they are formally involved in conducting research or not, many therapists likely approve of the view of science that Rogers provided way back then. Significantly, he added, "Scientific knowledge can be communicated only to those who are subjectively ready to receive its communication" (p. 274). Possible implications of this view of science for practicing counselors and therapists should be considered, but such a discussion exceeds the interests of this discussion. However, in the same article, "Person or Science? A Philosophical Question," Rogers addressed some of these implications as he discussed his personal experience of conducting therapy. As if to invite his readers to enter his internal world, he wrote,

> I launch myself into the therapeutic relationship having a hypothesis, or a faith, that my liking, my confidence, and my understanding of the other person's inner world, will lead to a significant process of becoming. I enter

> the relationship not as a scientist, not as a physician who can accurately diagnose and cure, but as a person, entering into a personal relationship. Insofar as I see him only as an object, the client will tend to become only an object.
>
> I risk myself, because if, as the relationship deepens, what develops is a failure, a regression, a repudiation of me and the relationship by the client, then I sense that I will lose myself, or a part of myself. At times this risk is very real, and is very keenly experienced.
>
> I let myself go into the immediacy of the relationship where it is my total organism which takes over and is sensitive to the relationship, not simply my consciousness. I am not consciously responding in a planful or analytic way, but simply in an unreflective way to the other individual, my reaction being based (but not consciously) on my total organismic sensitivity to this other person. I live the relationship on this basis. (pp. 267-268).

If Rogers's words are carefully read, little imagination is needed to place them in this discussion. Whereas this discussion emphasizes the importance of authentic selves coming together, with the therapist clearly shouldering the larger accountability for it, Rogers speaks in terms that have resonance with this accountability. He says, "I enter the relationship as a person, not as a scientist." Then, "At times, the risk is very real, and is very keenly experienced." And, with more relevance, "I let myself go into the immediacy of the relationship where it is my total organism which takes over and is sensitive to the relationship, not simply my consciousness."

To speak of letting one's self go into a relationship, as Rogers does, evokes an equivalent experience—albeit in a boundary-clad clinical setting—of entering a deep friendship or a romantic, procreative relationship. Somewhat more directly, May (1983, pp. 21–22) wrote, "Erotic feelings of his [the therapist's] own need to be frankly faced by the therapist, otherwise he will at least in fantasy, act out his own needs with the patient. But more importantly, unless the therapist accepts the erotic as one of the ways of communication, he will not listen for what he should hear from the patient and he will lose one of the most dynamic resources for change in therapy." Both Rogers and May call on therapists to acknowledge what is human and ordinary in the process of interacting with others, whether they are interacting in a clinical setting or elsewhere. To do otherwise is to make human relational experiences less than honest, healthy, and effective humanity. Their view of what is human and ordinary acknowledges the importance of understanding one's personal experience of the inexorable manifestations of survivability and replication. Their view also acknowledges the extremely complex and intricate cultural expressions of survivability and replication. In short, survivability and replication, along with the adaptability that they require, are always uniquely personal and individualized but paradoxically always universal.

To acknowledge what is human and ordinary within one's self, including basic bodily functions and the noblest aspirations, such as raising healthy children or composing music, is to validate and express one's capacity for successful and fulfilling adaptability, enhancing survivability, and potential for replication. Obviously, replication that sustains the species involves sexual activity. Therapy is life-sustaining, too, as it rightly expends considerable effort and talent to enable clients to live well while excluding sexual intimacy in the therapeutic relationship. To fulfill this expectation, the therapeutic relationship necessitates clinical competence and healthy outcomes for clients.

Easily and sometimes with automaticity, lust becomes obsessive thoughts, desire becomes skewed expectations, and pleasure becomes incongruous and self-defeating behaviors. While such thoughts, expectations, and behaviors may appear to be inconsistent with common humanity, at least at a glance, they are instead the image of all humans when they look into a mirror. From "A" to "Z," when viewing themselves as individuals who embody common humanity and when they see themselves as they are, they see that they are capable of being the following:

Adaptable, but also Avaricious

Benevolent, but also Bigoted

Competent, but also Complaining

Delightful, but also Defiant

Ethical, but also Envious

Fair, but also Fake

Generous, but also Gluttonous

Honest, but also Hypocritical

Insightful, but also Insecure

Judicious, but also Jealous

Knowledgeable, but also Know-It-All

Loyal, but also Lazy

Moral, but also Manipulative

Neat, but also Negligent

Open, but also Opinionated

Pious, but also Prudish

Questioning, but also Quarrelsome

Resilient, but also Resentful

Serene, but also Sarcastic

Tolerant, but also Thoughtless

Unique, but also Uncooperative

Visionary, but also Vindictive

Wise, but also Wicked

Xenophilic, but also Xenophobic

Yeomanly, but also Yapping

Zealous, but also Zonked

All these attributes and many more of them are embodied in almost all, if not all, individuals. As desirable as one side of these attributes may be, or as undesirable as the attributes on the other side may be, they are the outcomes of the human organism's need to survive and replicate. Each human embodies the potential for exhibiting any of these attributes. The particular expression of one or a combination of these attributes comes from a tacit or self-consciously known belief in outcomes that will further enhance survivability and replication. Both benevolence and bigotry may be adaptable and may contribute to survival, whether one is more pleasant in the moment than the other or not. This is neither merely animal-driven-ness nor fully self-conscious intentionality. It is embodied ambiguity, albeit noble, heinous, healthy, life-affirming, corrupting, murderous, or other conclusive characterizations of enacting ambiguity. As embodied realities, they are also common. As common as leaves are to trees, many of the qualities of being human confound those who have them, to be sure, along with others who observe them, but they are also real and human, nevertheless.

Such ambiguity may be easily seen in common behaviors. One person carefully scrutinizes every physical movement, wondering whether it helps or hurts her physical health. She asks, "Is this helping me to be healthy? Does it give me the exercise I need?" In contrast, another person seems to care little about physical movement, using large amounts of time as a somewhat mindless spectator of streaming programs or an addicted player of video games. One person assesses the health value of nearly every bite taken, while another person consistently consumes foods known to be unhealthy. Probably, the health-oriented person lusts for junk food, while the junk food consumer understands that physical health is truly desirable. This is the lived experience of ambiguity—of being human.

Embedded in ambiguity, humans aspire to minimize their real, presumed, or perceived adverse consequences. In many situations, the uncertainty that may be intensified with ambiguity understandably feels overwhelming. When a father sees his four-year-old son running toward the heavily trafficked street with fast-moving vehicles, his moment of uncertainty understandably and predictably intensifies his terror in reaction to the scene before him. In contrast, a tired husband and father arrives at his home, expecting to take a few minutes to relax following a hard day's work at his labor-intensive construction job, but encounters a surprise birthday party for him, complete with friends and family screaming, "Happy Birthday, Larry!" He, too, feels uncertain as he reacts to the loud, good wishes, but almost immediately smiles broadly and immerses in the celebration. In either situation, with its terror or enjoyment, the individual rapidly interprets the ambiguous situation, but also feels the moment in his body.

The felt experience of terror may be much too familiar for some, while the felt experience of enjoyment may not be experienced frequently enough for others. Neither terror nor enjoyment nor any other specific feeling encapsulates the full range of embodied, felt experiences. These experiences are highly individual and deeply personal, while also expressing the outcome of evolution, since the first molecule became life several billion years ago. Thus, these experiences are not only individual and personal, to be sure, but also evolutionary and, more importantly, cultural. Further, when either of these individuals is placed in the larger context of cultural development, their respective reactions—terror or enjoyment—can easily and correctly be interpreted as adaptive and as necessary for survival and replication. As Whiten et al. (2011, p. 938) observe in their analysis of evolving culture, "Culture, broadly conceived as all that individuals learn from others that endures to generate customs and traditions, shapes vast swathes of human lives." The relevance of culture and its importance for the delivery of therapy appear in the discussion below.

The Place of the Therapist

So far, this discussion has considered the biological heritage of humans, the necessity of survival as expressed in adaptation and replication, the inexorable ambiguity that inheres in human experience, and the historic and ongoing relevance of culture to understanding individuals. These emphases may appear to stray from the consideration of the humanity of therapists. The necessary consequent question is "How are these things relevant to the discussion of the humanity of therapists?" The response to this question could expand into large spaces that exceed the aspirations that guide the creation of this book. Instead of such expansion, suffice it to provide brief answers that discuss topics that hold potential for clearly affirming the humanity of therapists in the context of the issues already presented. The topics include grieving, language in therapy, parenting, disabilities in therapy, and emotions in therapy.

Grieving as a cultural phenomenon. Many different cultural patterns of behavior and interactions within a specific cultural context could easily demonstrate the pervasive reality of individual behaviors as cultural phenomena and their relevance to the practice of therapy. As a category of possible behaviors and interactions and the specific practices and traditions that come with them, this discussion briefly focuses on the universal phenomenon of grief. As Sebola (2021) stated, "Grief has specific social and cultural meanings" (p. 2). This observation may be both obvious and much too abstract. The reality of it, though, is almost never abstract. It is personal and usually deeply felt when individuals and families carry the pain of grief. To represent this reality, the following illustration reveals the sensitive, specific, and very personal presence of cultural differences in the experience of grieving. The real identities of the individuals are masked.

> Married for twenty-seven years, Lincoln, along his young-adult daughter, grieved the loss of his wife and her mother, Wilma. They expected that the large extended family would celebrate the life of Wilma, in ways that they would appreciate. They did, mostly. However, after the funeral service and internment provided comfort for them because they were surrounded by reassuring others, the family gathered at the home of Lincoln's niece. This is where their expectations met traditions with which they were not familiar and that confused them. When they anticipated being a part of the family gathering at the home of Lincoln's niece, they expected to be comforted by family member's kindly reminiscences about Wilma, sharing a quiet meal with others, hugs and other loving greetings, and a time to turn into thinking about how they may manage their lives without Wilma and with assurances of their interest and support. Instead, they walked into a raucous party that included loud music, energetic dancing, and heavy consumption of beer, whiskey, wine, vodka, and other alcoholic beverages. They heard no mention of Wilma. Almost no one hugged or greeted Lincoln or his daughter. Instead of the warmth of belonging that they expected, they felt abandoned by everyone else in the family, as they sat among them and observed the party. Generally, the clash of expectations and activities included divergent cultural heritages around grieving.

Sebola holds that grief has specific cultural meanings for individuals, families, and larger groups. Among those who study grief, this view is taken as a truism of human functioning. Silverman et al. (2021, p. 4) explain this in the following manner.

> Grief researchers have long recognized the important role of culture in framing the mourning experience, as processes of meaning reconstruction and relationship transformation are inherently situated in interpretive communities and social relationships. . . . Rather than a solely individual process, extensive research has shown that the response to loss is always intersubjective.

Such experiences as Lincoln and his daughter endured may or may not be common. More generally, the fact of individual behavior as an expression of culture is common. Neither Lincoln nor the other family members decided to exhibit grief as they did without family and cultural influences. Allowing for the near-universality of the emotional and physical pain associated with grief, they did not invent how to grieve. Or, from the view of ecological psychology, there is "the mutuality of the environment with the organism" (Read & Szokolszky, 2018, p. 191). Thus, whether the focus of concern is grief, child development, money management, leisure endeavors, or other specific features of human activity, the human individual can and should be an object of study and analysis, but will be poorly understood without commensurate attention being given to the individual's social world and larger culture of which the individual is a member. After all, therapists should remember that they are members of, contributors to, and products of culture, too.

Language in therapy. Conversations among therapists, not to mention the contents of their many publications, include references to their professional services. Such communications include terms such as PTSD, ADHD, DSM, TFCBT, and numerous other acronyms, along with another expansive volume of terms such as alloplastic defenses, narcissism, tangential thinking, and triangulation. The language of therapy is extensive. Mental healthcare providers should not assume that their clients or the larger culture understands and accepts their language. More narrowly, in providing professional services, they must bear accountability for their language as it may be heard in the process of therapy. Confirming this, for example, recent research attempted to answer questions about "language style matching," or LSM. Aafjes-van Doorn and Müller-Frommeyer (2020, p. 452) concluded that LSM "was not predictive of the working alliance [between therapists and clients], but that it "positively predicted the frequency of ruptures." Further, they concluded, "[T]he client tended to adapt to his therapist's language style, rather than the other way around" (p. 452). Another example of recent and relevant research comes from Palmer et al. (2023). In short, using quantitative text analysis techniques, they compared the language of cognitive behavioral therapists and their clients with that of focal psychodynamic therapists and their clients. Among other things, they affirm the importance of coherence between the identified method of psychotherapy and the implementation of the therapy through language associated with the identified method. The language between therapists and clients must have coherence, and, depending on the language and language style of clients, alternative approaches may be needed.

These representative references to recent research on language in therapy belie the fact that far too many therapists generally show little positive regard for the importance of language, particularly their own, in the process of therapy. This observation is easily confirmed in Chapter 4: "S" Is for "Seed Digging Dynamic Therapy:" The Humanity of Clinical Adventurism. Among other things, Chapter 4 reports a number of approaches to therapy that, in and of themselves as numbers, cause concern about the current condition of psychotherapy. As reported in Chapter 4, the total number of approaches to therapy located so far is 38,373, and the number of approaches within those that begin with the letter "S" is 4,285. Quite apart from these staggering numbers, the chapter also refers to a vast array of truly absurd approaches to therapy offered by practicing therapists. A number of these approaches could occupy a large volume of space in this discussion. Instead of including all or most of them, a short list of them will suffice. Table 2.1: So-called Approaches to Therapy that begin with the Word "Soul" includes a sampling of only twenty (20) of the two hundred forty-one approaches (241) to therapy that begin with the word, "Soul."

Presumably, these approaches to therapy come from good intentions. Including them here should not be construed to be a judgment about the character of those who advertise these approaches. In contrast with judging their character or intentions, the clinical judgment of the therapist must be questioned. In this discussion, though, while clinical judgment is an issue, the potential misuse of therapy through language is the topic of consideration. As Waldman (2021) trenchantly observes, "Perhaps the language of mental

Table 2.1: So-Called Approaches to Therapy That Begin with the Word "Soul"

Soul Biofield Tuning	Soul Circle
Soul Detective Protocols	Soul Entrainment Practice
Soul Expansion Shamanic Mentorship	Soul Journeys for Akashic Studies
Soul Reparations	Soul retrieval & past life regression
Soul Surfing	Soul Synergy and Coherence Therapy
Soul Travel	Soul Work and Biblical Affirmation
Soul Work—Christ-centered	Soul Writing
Soul-centered Psychoshamanic	Soul-focused Feng Shui
Soul-Life Integration/Crystals-Essential Oils	SoulCollage Cards Counseling
Soulshine Astrology	Souluminatio

health is burgeoning because actual mental health is declining." Waldman adds that the way individuals talk about their thoughts and feelings " . . . prefigures both what we want for ourselves and for others." If Waldman's thought is correct, the significance of the language used by tens of thousands of practicing therapists is that they want therapy to be centered on their highly individualized needs and thoughts and their nonclinical approaches to therapy and not on the needs of their clients.

Maybe, in contrast to Waldman, the language of therapy is not burgeoning because therapy is declining, but therapy is declining because language is burgeoning. Through their highly individualized, randomly chosen nonclinical approaches to therapy, individually and collectively, these therapists are enshrining the predictable, ongoing decline in counseling and therapy. Or as Nuttgens (2023, p. 29) says, "The proliferation of therapeutic models, with their untold numbers of purportedly unique interventions, serves as a source of division, confusion, and retrogression for the field of psychotherapy." The professional peers of these therapists may be constrained to conclude that their colleagues must be presumed to be competent only because all of them share the same training and credentials—a graduate degree and government-issued license. Unfortunately, this constraint also contains the terribly uncomfortable conclusion that all of them are deleteriously influenced by the deception that they have integrated into their selected "therapeutic" language, denying their humanity. Goodman asserts, "As therapists, it's important that we use language that is accessible to our clients" (2020, online).

As obviously important as it is to use language that is accessible to clients, the implications of Goodman's advice expose challenges for individual therapists along with their leaders. Minimally relevant clinical reasoning must question whether clients can access language, such as Soul Biofield Tuning, Soul Journeys for Akashic Studies, Soul-centered Psychoshamanic [Therapy], Soul-focused Feng Shui, Soulshine Astrology, or thousands of other approaches that utilize their respective vocabularies. From the view of language that professional accountability may prescribe, what is the clinical rationale for utilizing Sound Alchemy: Tuning Forks, Crystal & Tibetan Singing Bowls and their compatible vocabulary? Or, South American Toltec Shamanic Principles? Or, Splankna: EMDR TFT NET ACT RRCMT? Can clients be expected to make minimal sense of these approaches to therapy? Should clients be expected to disrupt their psychological standing in reality and dive into the exotic vortex of highly individualized approaches to therapy? Setting aside the potential confusion, if not harm, that clients likely experience, what do other therapists experience, if they see only the approaches in this paragraph, along with their own approaches to therapy? When honest with themselves, they very likely see languages for therapy that, at best, are foreign to them and alien to minimally appropriate approaches to counseling and therapy.

Parenting in psychotherapy. Within the mental health community, parenting receives widespread attention and analysis during and around treatment. Therapists can and frequently do offer their understanding of parenting styles, for example. And, in relation to matters that are more specifically clinical, they also interpret many of their problems as products of various failures of parenting. Probably, common understandings of parenting styles and the presumably parent-caused personal problems need significant changes. They need refinement, subtlety, and expansion. As Gaztambide emphasized, "Our patients [clients], after all, bring us wounds that serve as windows to our social, economic, and political world" (p. 2033). The challenge of integrating such understanding into therapy may be more formidable than most practicing therapists recognize. What is this challenge?

Toward achieving refinement, subtlety, and expansion, "There are many factors that influence how parents perceive their parenting roles, how well they think they are doing, and the level of support they get for the struggles they experience" (Kirby et al., 2019, p. 252). Neither parents nor therapists are likely to be surprised by this somewhat normative view. However, Kirby et al add, "[I]n competitive cultures, the issue of social evaluation and shame becomes a prominent theme in parenting roles" (p. 252). Kirby et al. explain the results of their research.

> [C]hildren who are growing up in more hostile environments and where parents are themselves relatively isolated, unsupported, and under high competitive pressure will be patterning their children to survive in that cultural context. Hence, what they pay attention to in their child, what they model for their child, what they reinforce in their child, and what they punish in their child will all be patterned by the competitive context. In this way, children internalize a competitive way of being in the world making them more vulnerable to shame and self-criticism and when becoming parents themselves entering this role with the burden of self-doubt, self-criticism, and the need to achieve success and prove themselves competent in their parenting roles. (p. 254)

Insofar as parenting is defined and shaped by its culture, parents absorb and adopt as their own the values, attitudes, and behaviors associated with their culture. While this generalization, no doubt, cannot be tightly and neatly applied to all parents who live in, say, the American culture, the truth of it is easily recognized, nevertheless. The report by Kirby et al concludes that American parents feel "shame as a prominent theme in their parenting roles." In this discussion, necessary questions arise with regard to therapists. How does your culture influence your view of parenting? When you consider the likelihood that parents in American culture are influenced by its competitivism, how does this shape or reshape your understanding of parenting problems? Or, as you review another statement by Kirby et al, what is your reaction to it? They state, "Parents have a challenging yet rewarding role in nurturing their children. However, competitive cultures amplify the pressures parents' experience making them vulnerable to shame, and increasing the likelihood for psychological controlling and dysfunctional parenting styles" (p. 255).

Emotions in therapy. Therapists have fairly consistently and nearly universally shared the belief that they should seek to achieve accurate empathic awareness, with particular concern about being accurately aware of the emotions of clients, during their sessions with clients. This very likely rests on added beliefs and assumptions about the emotions that clients bring to sessions. Insofar as these characterizations of therapists are correct, they reveal a common failure to recognize that "empirical research supports the perspective that emotions are co-constructed, sociocultural categories rather than triggered, universal internal states," according to Givens and Wilkinson (2022, p. 433). They say, "Recent research on the neurobiology of emotion provides strong evidence that emotions are created in the moment rather than being triggered reactions that one discovers or recognizes" (p. 433). They explain Barrett's statement, "Emotions are constructions of the world, not reactions to it" (p. 433), when they conclude,

> In accord with the classical theory of emotion, counselors perceive, intuit, recognize, reflect, articulate, and categorize feelings (Neukrug et al., 2013). It is assumed that proficient counselors disclose hidden emotions and support accurate identification of feelings. However, the theory of constructed emotion questions whether a counselor's use of specific feeling labels can inadvertently alter client emotional experiences. In effect, standard clinical practices related to accurate feeling identification can overlook how counselor-imposed emotion labels might influence, shape, truncate, or distort a client's complex affective experience in the moment. (p. 439)

At least, therapists should pay attention to their understanding of emotions, including their own their thinking about how they approach emotions during their clinical contacts with clients and their vulnerabilities associated with the potential for imposing undue influence on their clients. Without this, as Givens and Wilkinson suggest, therapists manipulate their clients' emotions, albeit with good intentions, and truncate the potential of their therapy.

Disabilities in therapy. In an explication of barriers to mental healthcare for some individuals, Avci (2023, p. 335) concludes, "Ablest thinking restricts access to mental health care for people with disabilities." The reality of these barriers, as a cultural dynamic with real clinical implications, may be illustrated with a story of a young woman who is slightly overweight—a manifest cultural issue—who also complains in therapy about how her disabling spina bifida "turns guys away." She is romantically and sexually frustrated. In American culture, almost anyone who sees this young woman is not likely to think that she may be or could possibly be interested in a romantic and sexual relationship. After all, from her view of herself and the view of many, if not most, others, she is not desirable. She fails to possess and show herself as sexually alluring. She is not trim and physically fit, proportionally packaged like the models who, after all, are models who possess images of what desirable women should look like. Therapists may easily assume that this young woman's frustration and disappointment fail to rise to a level of importance that needs clinical assistance. Insofar as this happens, therapists deny the humanity in the client, but also deny it in themselves. Ablest thinking frustrates humanity, rather than enhancing it.

Psychotherapy as a social construct. If understanding therapy as a social construct is deemed to be correct, does this minimize its importance? If so, this would be an unfortunate outcome of such an understanding. Similarly, in many specific ways, femininity and masculinity have been understood as social constructs. This does not minimize the importance of femininity and masculinity. Instead of minimizing them, this understanding increases the likelihood that seeing them as social constructs equips viewers of males and females to exercise options that may improve their self-management, particularly with the assistance of therapists. For example, instead of being resigned to the often-made observation among therapists that men do not seek to utilize their services as much as women or as needed, therapists—male or female—must review their own assumptions about masculinity and invent ways to effectively help men when they receive professional services.

Much more than understanding therapy as a social construct, those who practice therapy must augment this understanding with questions about the extent to which they may be captive to their collective and individual constructions of therapy. The need for these questions is manifestly clear. Without the questions, accompanied by serious and prolonged efforts to answer them, therapy will likely remain captive of constructions of therapy that have little or no basis in clinical reality. As Chapter 4 illustrates, therapy has much too frequently become romanticized and fantasized interpretation of what therapy is or could be. Obviously, as a consequence of ignoring the multitude of distortions of professionally accountable therapy, mental health-care providers have decreased their potential for delivering professional services that effectuate positive outcomes. In fact, exaggerated individualism as a social construct has largely neutralized mental healthcare as professional and therapeutic.

The evidence is overwhelming, indicating that therapists continue to decline in competence. The conclusion is that therapists commonly abdicate professional accountability. The citations that support this conclusion can fill many pages. For now, suffice it to say that the citations appear in various places in this book, but surely include Goldberg et al (2016), Spengler and Pilipis (2015), and Martin (2020). Many sources are identified throughout this book. In this discussion and without undue repetition from it, the evidence in Chapter 4 may suffice as a basis for concluding that therapy has been captive of the misconstrued but real humanity of therapists. Such a conclusion stems from exaggerated individualism, nonclinical thinking and actions, a failure to monitor and regulate clinical practice, a widespread decline in competence and compliance with professional ethics, and the supremacy of ideologies that belie appropriate clinical judgment, among many characteristics.

In ways that may be obvious and unambiguous, as well as mostly unrecognized, the culture in which therapists are members influences their clinical judgment. At least, it should be acknowledged that counselors and therapists live in a permissive American culture that allows them to believe that they can arbitrarily invent and practice numerous approaches to therapy that have no basis in clinical reality. Apparently, as interpreted in Chapter 4, many therapists hold the belief that "I want to do what I want to do and, because I want to do it, I am comfortably justified in doing it as therapy." As a reflection of their culture, consideration must be given to other ways that their culture may influence their clinical judgment and transform it into approaches to their clients that are sometimes conspicuously nonclinical.

Living as a Therapist

Clients present massive ambiguities to therapists. This is easily confirmed when reference to any one of several features of being human is made. The feature may be intelligence, sexual orientation, relational skills, or, as discussed above, grieving, language, emotions, parenting, or disabilities. Guidance for therapists can be easily located, with regard to these features of being human or many other topics, such as advice about how cognitive behavior therapy works or how to provide effective clinical services for children when their parents are divorcing. Without minimizing the importance of these categories of advice, the focus of this book is different. The difference may be stated in many different ways. In short, the focus is that the healthy humanity of therapists must be recovered and preserved so that competent clinical services can become far more common than they currently are. Edge and Lemetyinen (2019) capture this idea in their discussion of providing counseling in multicultural contexts. They state, "[E]ffective therapeutic engagement requires therapists who are competent and confident to work with diversity and difference, utilizing insights into their own as well as their clients' internal and external worlds" (p. 261). Lacking such insights, they further advise that the "unintended consequences can range from barriers to help-seeking; incongruence between the help seeker and the health care provider's views of the help seeker's presentation and/or treatment; prolonged family burden; and experiences of structural, public, or internalized stigma and discrimination" (p. 268). Along with this advice, they assert that "given the social distance and power imbalance inherent in therapeutic relationships, it is important to acknowledge that therapy can be harmful" (p. 268).

Whether the topic of discussion is the inherent ambiguities of living, grief, language, emotions, parenting, or the influence of culture on clinical judgment, or many others, the conclusion that large numbers of therapists deny their humanity is clear. The answers to the question of "Why?" are not so clear, although some of them seem to be apparent.

The massive contamination of therapy with incompetence and other problems is a misuse of presumed, professional freedom. Every therapist who provides clinical services must make numerous and often difficult clinical judgments. The requisite demand of having to make clinical judgments also requires individual discretion. In the immediacy of the moment-to-moment of interacting with clients, taking time to peruse relevant research literature, consult with a specialized expert, or seek advice from a colleague is not a luxury in which practicing therapists can indulge. However, the relative isolation that inheres in such immediacy and its accompanying exaggerated individualism become temptations to "do what I want to do, just because I want to do it." Succumbing to this temptation, therapists easily rationalize their individual decisions to invent and/or select foolish approaches to therapy [Refer to Chapter 4], presuming to be experts with treatments for which they have no training and experience. Rather than thinking and acting clinically, these therapists accommodate the culture in which they live. This is a misuse of personal and professional freedom. More than this, it is a denial of their humanity.

Freedom lives in ambiguity. Simple questions illustrate this. Should one vote for one candidate or another? Should one accept a job offer or not, knowing that there is much about it that cannot be predicted? Should a family buy a home or continue to rent an apartment? Should a couple pursue having another child or not? What will intimacy be like, now that his prostate cancer surgery resulted in his inability to get or sustain an erection? And so on. The list of living ambiguities is virtually endless. The terrible paradox of avoiding the angst that stems from ambiguity is that it is also an escape from freedom, personally and clinically. And, sadly, one of the outcomes of escaping from freedom necessarily involves the denial of one's humanity. To be sure, freedom lives in ambiguity. However, when the inevitable angst of ambiguity triggers the urge and actions needed to suppress this angst, freedom can be lost. In therapy, the consequences of this loss of freedom dramatically accelerate the loss of clinical competence and poor, if not harmful, service to clients.

In the context of providing clinical services, this loss of freedom, incompetence, and poor service to clients should be examined by practicing individual therapists, possibly by trying to answer questions such as the following: Do inadequate services for clients permit therapists to maintain safe distances while creating the illusion of intimacy? Do such services invite openness while therapists safely remain closed? Do aberrant approaches to therapy and the presumed expertise that accompanies them demonstrate clinical inadequacy, feigned expertise, and pretense of professional accountability? With such services within a critically important relationship, can therapists ensure empathy, while remaining indifferent to the suffering that inevitably comes during many sessions with clients, when therapists over-rely on approaches to therapy that too often represent therapists' conscription into ideologically and highly individualized approaches to therapy that do not include real or accurate empathy? Do such services blunt therapists' sensitivity to diversity? Do such services suspend the normative disciplined naïveté and spontaneity of clinical judgment? Do such services enact the therapist's preferred personal beliefs or other ideology and channel the thoughts and feelings of clients into controlled and not usual clinical processes?

The concern that professionally accountable therapists should address is not one of whether these things currently characterize their profession but whether they can and will endure. The needed changes hold expectations that are not new to the profession of therapy. As important gestures toward a useable, viable, and professionally accountable future, the profession may want to remember the qualities of healthy individuals, as several luminaries in the history of the profession have carefully and insightfully shared. Its importance cannot be exaggerated. After all, *health* is the necessary aim of therapy. A discussion of *healthy helping*, including an emphasis on *healthy helpers*, appears in Chapter 7.

With wars, imposed famines, oppressive dictatorships, economic turmoil, and other threats to personal, family, and social security, life finds a way forward. The way may be healthy or unhealthy, life-affirming or life-denying, optimistic or pessimistic, confused or neatly clear, or other understandable responses. Within an individual or family or larger social group, reactions to threats may similarly reflect the complexity of being human, with a profuse mixture of hostility and hope, mercenary impulses and merciful caring, self-protection and other-avoidance, and so on. Within the mental healthcare community, competent therapists will honor their humanity in the context of such complexity and refuse to vent their personal issues on their clients, overtly, subtly, passively, seductively, or otherwise. The temptation to vent is an ordinary human expression of reactions to the stressors referred to above. Such a temptation and others not only expose the raw nerves of being human but also pose moments of testing for therapists' humanity.

The urgency of maintaining life through sustaining it in any given moment and replicating it for the pleasure of the process and for sustaining the species translates into the commonly recognized fact that life finds a way. Evolutionary processes have brought humans to this. The replication of life—the capacity of an organism to reproduce—began without consciousness, although humans have acquired a level of consciousness that gives them options that various preceding forms of life could not have had. Primitive plants depended on photosynthesis and chemical processes, not intentions and aspirations. Reproduction occurred, whether the primitive plants wanted to reproduce or not. Replication became ever more inevitable, as the actions that sustained it involved irresistible pleasure. From Puffer Fish to Bald Eagles, along with their evolutionary predecessors, reproduction compulsions drove them to generate their descendants through some form of genetic programming. Whether the pleasure and instinctual driven-ness arose in tigers or teenage humans, it pervasively shaped their existence. But now humans have an expanding number of options and an accommodating level of consciousness that gives them the freedom to choose how they wish to sustain life—or, possibly, to end life.

The freedom to choose has been abrogated in numerous ways. Among therapists, when abrogation of freedom to choose is avoided, consciousness of this mandates action toward remediation. In general, action involves honest reckoning with the humanity of being human. Just as therapists believe that such an honest reckoning has been a core feature of significant psychological and relational improvement, they carry within themselves the potential for this honest reckoning. The experience of honest reckoning will, no doubt, take many forms. For some, it will require self-care differentiation between being a caring parent versus an overly indulgent, controlling parent. For others, it will require self-caring differentiation between healthy lust and angry lasciviousness. After all, human functioning includes love and hate, physical health and sickness, success and failure, gains and losses, life and death, as some of the many unavoidable paradoxes that inhere in human existence. Therapists have within themselves the capacity to choose to live honestly and with integrity and, in such living, to honor their real human needs, knowing that this involves integrating the wonder and joy of living, along with its inevitable, accompanying discomfort.

This discussion includes several issues relevant to the humanity of therapists. One is the biological heritage that imbues all living things, with emphasis on survivability, adaptability, and replication. It includes brief analyses of grieving, language, parenting, disability, and emotions, with emphasis on the ways that culture shapes the adaptive possibilities for all members of a culture, including therapists. The conclusion here is that many therapists express their survivability, adaptability, and potential for replication in specific ways that frustrate if not deny their humanity, but retain the potential for authenticating their humanity. Competent therapists understand that their professional services should sustain the capacities of their clients to improve their well-being. This is mental, emotional, relational, and social replication.

This chapter adds the matter of the culture in which therapists practice. At this time, many counselors and therapists practice in such ways that express their potential for denying their humanity, but, more critically, the humanity of their clients, as they indulge in and translate cultural norms into unusual clinical theories and practices. In short, therapists express the professional and social culture of which they are members. Analogously, this is similar to a physician determining that dark chocolate-covered blueberries should supplant diet and exercise for maintaining a healthy heart. After all, consuming dark chocolate-covered blueberries is much easier to recommend than a heart-healthy diet and exercise.

The proliferation of blatantly inappropriate approaches to therapy should not be construed as only an evasion of professional accountability. More significantly, it is the evasion of professional accountability that results from tens of thousands of therapists' evasion of themselves. Through such an evasion, they deny their humanity. However, along with others who share concern about the condition of therapy, the widespread denial of humanity among therapists should not be taken as a condition that cannot change. Indeed, so long as professionally accountable therapists continue to occupy a profession that remains committed to change toward mental health, the story of the profession will be open to possibilities. Or, as McWilliams (p. 149) concludes in her advocacy for preserving the humanity of therapists,

> I am hoping that the values that brought most clinicians to the difficult but rewarding work of psychotherapy can be reclaimed despite the power of substantial interests now threatening them. By taking on the hypocrisies

and conceit of our own era and culture, perhaps we can do a better job of preserving our humanity in the therapeutic role and, in the process, inoculate our clients against the worst aspects of living in this confusing and fragile world.

References

Aafjes-van Doorn, K., & Müller-Frommeyer, L. (2020). Reciprocal language style matching in psychotherapy research. *Counselling & Psychotherapy Research,* 20(3), 449–455.

Avci, O. H. (2023). It's a taboo: Women with disabilities applying for psychological counseling due to romantic relationship and sexual problems. *Sexuality and Disability, 41*(2), 335–355. https://doi.org/10.1007/s11195-023-09779-x

Barrett, L. F. (2017). The theory of constructed emotion: An active inference account of interoception and categorization. *Social Cognitive and Affec-tive Neuroscience, 12*(1), 1–23. https://doi.org/10.1093/scan/nsw154

Edge, D., & Lemetyinen, H. (2019). Psychology across cultures: Challenges and opportunities. *Psychology & Psychotherapy: Theory, Research & Practice, 92*(2), 261–276. https://doi.org/10.1111/papt.12229

Gaztambide, D. J. (2019). Reconsidering culture, attachment, and inequality in the treatment of a Puerto Rican migrant: Toward structural competence in psychotherapy. *Journal of Clinical Psychology, 75*(11), 2022–2033. https://doi.org/10.1002/jclp.22861

Givens, J., & Wilkinson, B. D. (2022). More than a feeling: Constructing emotion in theory and practice. *Journal of Counseling & Development, 100*(4), 433–441. https://doi.org/10.1002/jcad.12437

Goldberg, S. B., Miller, S. D., Nielsen, S. L., Rousmaniere, T., Whipple, J., Hoyt, W. T., & Wampold, B. E. (2016). Do psychotherapists improve with time and experience? A longitudinal analysis of outcomes in a clinical setting. *Journal of Counseling Psychology, 63*(1), 1–11.

Goodman, W. (2020). The language of therapy, explained. https://www.psychologytoday.com/us/blog/healing-together/202001/the-language-therapy-explained

Kirby, J. N, Hayley Sampson, H., Day, J., Hayes, A., & Gilbert1, P. (2019). Human evolution and culture in relationship to shame in the parenting role: Implications for psychology and psychotherapy. *Psychology and Psychotherapy: Theory, Research and Practice, 92*(2), 238–260.

Martin, F. A. (2020). *Therapy thieves: How to save mental health care from its providers*. Oxford University Press.

May, R. (1983). *The discovery of being: Writings in existential psychology.* W. W. Norton and Company.

McWilliams, N. (2005). Preserving our humanity as therapists. *Psychotherapy: Theory, Research, Practice, Training, 42*(2), 139–151. https://doi.org/10.1037/0033-3204.42.2.139

Mongabay. (2024). *How many plant species are there in the world?* https://news.mongabay.com/2016/05/many-plants-world-scientists-may-now-answer/

Neukrug, E., Bayne, H., Dean-Nganga, L., & Pusateri, C. (2013). Creative and novel approaches to empathy: A neo-Rogerian perspective. *Journal of Mental Health Counseling, 35*(1), 29–42. https://doi.org/10.17744/mehc.35.1.5q375220327000t2

Nuttgens, S. (2023). Of interventive doppelgangers and other barriers to evidence-based practice in psychotherapy. *Journal of Psychotherapy Integration, 33*(1), 20–33. https://doi.org/10.1037/int0000279

Palmer, S., Brockmeyer, T., Zipfel, S., Wild, B., Resmark, G., Teufe, M., Giel, K., de Zwaan, M., Dinkel, A., Herpertz, S., Burgmer, M., Löwe, B., Tagay, S., Rothermund, E., Zeeck, A., Herzog, W., & Friederich, H-C. (2023). Words count in psychotherapy: Differentiating language characteristics of cognitive behavioral therapy and focal psychodynamic therapy for anorexia nervosa. *Psychotherapy, 60*(4), 488–496. https://doi.org/10.1037/pst0000499

Read, C., & Szokolszky, A. (2018). An emerging developmental ecological psychology: Future directions and potentials. *Ecological Psychology, 30*(2), 174–194. https://doi.org/10.1080/10407413.2018.1439141

Rogers, C. R. (1955). Person or science? A philosophical question. *American Psychologist, 10*(7), 267–278.

Sebola, B. R. (2021). Interaction of culture and grief amongst women who terminated a pregnancy in adolescence: A narrative approach. *Curationis, 44*(1), e1–e6. https://doi.org/10.4102/curationis.v44i1.2247. PMID: 34879686; PMCID: PMC8661433.

Silverman, G. S., Baroiller, A., & Hemer, S. R. (2021). Culture and grief: Ethnographic perspectives on ritual, relationships and remembering. *Death Studies, 45*(1), 1–8. https://doi.org/10.1080/07481187.2020.1851885

Spengler, P. M., & Pilipis, L. A. (2015). A comprehensive meta-reanalysis of the robustness of the experience-accuracy effect in clinical judgment. *Journal of Counseling Psychology, 62*(3), 360–378. http://dx.doi.org/10.1037/cou0000065

Waldman, K. (2021). The rise of therapy-speak: How a language got off the couch and into the world. *The New Yorker*. March 26. https://www.newyorker.com/culture/cultural-comment/the-rise-of-therapy-speak

Whiten, A., Hinde, R. A., Laland, K. N., & Stringer, C. B. (2011). Culture evolves. *Philosophical transactions of the Royal Society of London. Series B, Biological Sciences, 366*(1567), 938–948. https://doi.org/10.1098/rstb.2010.0372. PMCID: PMC3049105.

Chapter 3
The Period Goes On
The Humanity of Faith

Précis

The idea that the sentence ends but the period goes on may seem to be a peculiar one. Possibly, the idea that the period goes on may appear to be slightly absurd, if not annoying by its apparent naiveté and, maybe, its obliviousness to serious adult thinking. After all, the period at the end of a sentence ends the sentence. And, presumably, there is nothing that follows the period. What could possibly remain following the period? In short, almost everything—almost everything of importance to living life—follows the period. It includes situations such as these:

> Having gathered a huge volume of information about breast cancer, a wife and mother of two adorable pre-school children feels anguish about what may happen to her and to her family, now that she anticipates surgery. Will she survive? Will she emerge from surgery and receive the news that medical interventions cannot save her? Will she be deformed, lacking treasured signs of her femininity? Will she see pain and rejection in her husband's eyes? She knows that there is no sentence that satisfactorily covers this.
>
> Following the observation that his daughter has not only begun to show the signs of sexually maturing, but also interest in sex-related things, dad worries about how secure or insecure she is, how many stressors have begun to arise in her inner world, or how she may be expressing her sexuality. He tries to remember every sex-related conversation with her, along with other experiences, hoping to assess his role in her healthy development and to confirm that he did almost everything right. He knows that there is no sentence that satisfactorily covers this.
>
> Along with taking almost everything associated with her childhood, the house fire also took her parents, while she was vacationing with her college friends in Freeport, Bahamas. She feels the losses so deeply and widely that she doubts her ability to recover. For now, seeing and feeling the visibility of her trauma, she believes that recovery is not possible. She knows that there is no sentence that satisfactorily covers this.
>
> The chaplain, a stranger to Jake Boyle, entered Jake's hospital room. Looking grim, the chaplain introduced himself, ensured that he was speaking to the right person, and then said, "Mr. Boyle, I'm sorry for this. Your physicians tell me that there is nothing more they can do. They asked me to visit with you." In this moment, Jake's world dropped from his mind. He heard nothing more from the chaplain. There is no sentence that satisfactorily covers this.

Taken seriously, the idea that the period goes on nicely reminds all of us of what we know to be true. Namely, no matter how thoroughly we fill in the blanks of our lives—with schooling, watching television, showering, working, sleeping, shaving, vacuuming, or any of the thousands of activities that occupy us—there comes the inevitably long, seemingly everlasting period that follows everything. It defines who we are, when nothing is there to occupy us—no solid emotional ground, no solid relational ground, and no cognitive ground on which to stand with reasonable confidence. It is the time we wait, maybe, staring into the abyss of everything that follows from the present moment. It is devoid of plans that matter, because it compels us to answer some of the basic questions of human existence, if not the most basic ones. Does it matter that I am? What truly matters to me? Am I living a fulfilled life or a meaningless one? If anything of importance, what comes next in my life?

If these and other existential questions are seldom considered, what may this apparent lack of questioning say about the individual?

Does it matter that I am? Or, more specifically, can I take good care of my sexually maturing daughter? Has breast cancer terminated my basic security and maybe my life? If I can't work any longer, what is my significance? If I have lost everything, including my parents, do I really matter any longer? If we cannot have a child, how do we redefine our long-held, heartfelt expectations? How does a man cope with the announcement of his impending death? And, how can we fill the gap—the great unknown—that waits eternally for us?

The Period Goes On is an attempt to reflect the experience of getting inside these questions and the answers that may emerge from these questions, with regard to personal meaning and faith.

Note to readers: Read *The Period Goes On*. Reflect on it. My hope is that it may bring you peace and hope. I have come to refer to *The Period Goes On* as a memorandum of hope. If it serves this purpose for you, it will have achieved my best expectations.

Introduction

The "blessing" below is reported to have been prayed over Henri Nouwen by his spiritual teacher and leader.

> May all your expectations be frustrated.
> May all your plans be thwarted.

> May all your desires be withered into nothingness.
> That you may experience the powerlessness and the poverty of a
> child and sing and dance in the love of God the Father, the Son and the Spirit.
>
> (Livestream, 2006)

Seldom will any of us select a message like this one as a guide for our lives. Nevertheless, while the words may be repugnant for many who read them, they contain truths that we may wish conveniently to ignore. Among these truths, life itself is enigmatic, sometimes disappointing, and worse, requiring us to adjust to unwanted realities.

Why life? Or why not life? More narrowly, if life has interminable goodness, pleasure, and, well, life, why would anyone want it? At our core, in those parts of our thoughts and feelings that feel the ever-present reality of termination—of death—the moment of goodness or pleasure can be so very much more treasured and reassuring. Or, as Hazo (2005) wrote so eloquently in "The Necessary Brevity of Pleasures,"

> Like lovers seeking heaven in excess,
> the hopelessly insatiable forget
> how passion sharpens appetites
> that gross indulgence numbs.

To be sure, the fulfillment of wishes can and does often lead to numbness of mind and desire, outcomes that no one aspires to achieve. The expectation that heroin or cocaine can produce unending pleasure, much too commonly, ends in misery and death instead. Maybe some individuals who die from their pursuit of pleasure through cocaine or countless sex partners self-consciously wish to die, but most don't. Similarly, those who act, think, and feel that being absorbed in religious ecstasy as a source of unending pleasure die, too, usually deluded by the certainty of the ideological cage in which they have opted to live. Much like the heroin addict, they energetically seek relief from life and profess that they have found the answers and seldom recognize or wish to recognize the behavioral-intellectual-emotional cage in which they too often have placed themselves.

It is one thing to work with great energy to make life good and another to immerse oneself in denialism as a way to avoid being authentically human. Unfortunately, these two approaches to life may look a lot alike. For example, without exception, everyone who knew "Bob" saw him as welcoming and friendly, optimistic, industrious, effective, secure, relationally attached, along with other positive and desirable characteristics. So, when he reportedly told his wife to wait inside while he warmed the car, no one suspected that he would or could have connected the exhaust from his car with the passenger compartment and killed himself. He was such a good and solid human being. What was he masking so very well that realized itself in suicide?

To live well until living well becomes impossible disturbs and disrupts one's senses. Thoughts and feelings that were dependable become squishy and strangely uncertain. Relationships become muddled and tormenting. Longstanding commitments take the quality of no longer mattering. Planning for what may come and believing that it may lead to reasonable predictions about what may happen becomes a warily nagging voice, antagonizing and erasing the best of possibilities. This is the reality of living in a period where dreams come true and nightmares abound.

The Period Goes On

The period goes on.

The sentence ends but the period goes on. And, like driving fast in a dense fog, I have lived in the likeness of faith, seeing beyond the known only far enough to keep going and hoping, aching to see further, afraid of the needs that drive me.

I need God.
But how do I find God?
What if I don't find God?
Can anyone lead me to God?
And how would I know if I found God?
Worse, what if I recognize that my search was vain and stupid?

Old Dreams

The saints saw through the fog. Their dreams brought them to see more clearly than ordinary vision someone beyond the known. Their dreams, full of passion and age, remake me into a saint of sorts, because the saints who dreamed them tell me what to think and believe, whether they want to or not. Their dreams hold the greatest power, the power to promise what I want: "If you believe as I do, you, too, can see beyond the known. God is there if you look. If you do not see God, you have not looked hard enough. You do not believe enough." Their dreams are powered by promise, sweetened with oughts and shoulds, set with certainty in stained glass, and passed on to me as mine to protect and to pass on. Their dreams are commandments to accept, to praise, to obey, and to sell to others. Their dreams—life-giving to them—are served to me with authority from the lectern and the pulpit by dreamers whose dreams died as seeds pressed into the fine carpets of well-appointed houses of worship and into the minds of desperate seekers there.

I hear what they say, desiring to believe and to take life from them. But their dreams are their history. And the religion I get from them is dust. It is dust. It is the dust that glows when the brightness of the sun exposes it.

Religion is the dust settled from their rush to the edge of the ordinary to see beyond the known. They saw and told what they saw. And I have heard their story from their messengers' messengers, told and retold in broken voices as they pant, choking on dust, in fear of not telling and not panting, and they choke, suffocate, and die. And I have said, "Yes," too, to their message and work hard to patch the holes of doubt in my "Yes" because I am afraid, too. I have said yes to their message, accepting their brightness as the sun itself, following them, and getting lost where I should have been found, because I am afraid. I have let the fear possess me. But shall I let this continue? Shall I be more and more an anchor to the past for someone else, telling their dreams over and over, acting out their tired rituals, panting after dust and dying? If I'm not an anchor for their truth, what am I?

Can their dreams survive my mind? Can their past survive my present? Their sentence ends. It ends me. It is a sentence to serve until dying in the lies of it, to pay until my soul is spent, to know until I die in life, as if life is a book that begins and ends with only the last word, leaving me to read the unknown on my own. It is a word known only to the saints. Known to countless searchers, the saints had the last word. Can their word truly be the last one? And can only they know it? What about me having the last word, for me? Can I make sense of their word on my own?

The sentence ends me, unless I raise these questions. The sentence ends, but there are questions.

What do I do with their dreams? Can I have a dream of my own? Are their dreams good for me? They are giants, after all. Some have centuries of followers. I have no followers. None. If I can't get my own dream, ought I to follow theirs? Ought I to put my questions in a locked box that has no keys to open it? What must I do or know to live by their dreams? Must I know myself?

I look in the mirror of their reflections and see myself bent and in pain, confused and wondering why I am afraid. And, of what?

My fear is that I must believe and speak the same thing all the time forever, sinking slowly into a life-long grave filled with agreed-upon but irrelevant certainties. My dread is that I shall be a dust keeper in the faith-house monuments to their dreams, valuing the truth I found, even claiming it as mine, but choking and dying. Finding and claiming my own dream or knowing myself even without a dream requires me to break the subtle code of chain link assumptions given to me as truth, as faith to be claimed and lived.

Ticking away in me, like a loud clock in an empty room, is the feeling that my life is balanced upon myself. And I either carry it or kill it. Carry it or kill it. Carry it or kill it. Carry or kill. Carry or kill. Carry or kill. I can carry it if I grow beyond their dreams. Or I can kill it if I stand for their dreams and let their dust settle on me like a shroud, weakening and dropping life into a dark hole of mindlessness where conscience strains and shouts from lungs without air and where breathing sucks in the lies of borrowed truth, and dying.

The sentence ends, but the period goes on.

Such hard thinking, like an assassin, quiet, invisible, tireless, stealthy, and deadly, sneaks through the fence of faith guarding my struggle for a dream of my own, kills their dreams, and sets me free. Their dreams—from Abraham, Moses, and Paul to Bonhoeffer, Merton, and King—are dead in their time, in their history, in their past, and I can't revive them. They belong in their graves, even if I want them out. Their truth gave them the inspired energy to defy others who would readily crush them. My truth feels vapid in this moment.

If hard thinking is the killer, time is the great dream thief: certain, constant, indifferent, eternal, teaching me and preaching at me that I am not supposed to care about things so far away as the dead dreams of dead saints.

> The message of time aims itself at my body: Do not care,
> except for what your body wants now, while lower needs go
> on and on and are met or unmet, depending on where the sun is.
> The message of time aims itself at my heart: Do not care for
> the father who abandoned you when you were a suckling babe.
> He is dead to you. Don't grieve for loss that isn't yours.
> There are other fathers. Find them. They can love you.
> The boys coat, held in place with angry hope
> That is long since dirty, heavy and tired and
> Shadowed by hunger-thinned wrists, from
> His father's clean-Jesus greed and cathedral comfort.
> The boy's coat is the one his father neglected to buy,
> One coat after another, one long winter after another,
> Until the boy could buy his own, clean and warm coat.
> The boy is never as warm as he should be, as
> He is always the man who learned to feel cold.

The message of time aims itself at my spirit, too: The voices
of the saints are dead. Only their words survive, but they,
too, are dead to me. And what was spoken about by the saints
is lost from me. That is my search, feeble, frail and fresh
as a newborn.
At least, knowing what is lost gives me something to look for.
"Your search is for a dream of your own, a dream that is felt,
known, immediate, real, and specially yours. Find it."
The sentence ends, but the period goes on.

But like the saints and their dead dreams, I am stuck in my time, in my history. Where do I get my dream here? And if I get it, can it survive my mind? Can my future survive my past? Will I kill my dream as I have killed theirs? When both theirs and mine are dead, then what?

My dream seems always to be in the future, always deferred, always anticipated, but seems always also to take me back to where I began, again and again:

From city lights and newsy nights,
from college trips and well-formed hips,
from brainy capers and daily papers,
to the old mailbox:
As we throttle around a graveled country curve,
we see a surprise.
"Look at that." "Can you believe it?"
"It's grampa's mailbox!"
We look at it, unbelieving and joy-struck.
Eight—almost nine—long decades after he posted it,
more than a half of a century after he died there,
his name—his name—peers faintly, but shouting,
through the distant darkness of time.
His name stirs in drivers-by who loved him,
yet who moved on to post mailboxes of their own,
memories of him and memories of their own lives gone.
They are memories of my own life gone.
And the past holds me there
in a tight and eternal embrace of decaying ecstasy.
That is the meaning of old mailboxes
with grandfathers' names on them.
My soul soars with discovery of filler
for gaps in my past and sinks
at recognition of its significance.

I bought the old mailbox and took it home. But the hours I've spent reminiscing measure only what is gone. Religion, borrowed from the dreams of saints, goes back, too, to its beginning, again and again, forgets its present, studies at its beginnings, reminisces, measures what is gone, and snaps its mind shut with self-proclaimed joy. Shut or open, past or present, dead or alive, my need for a dream, the need for God, maintains itself only by the will to not let the need get away.

The sentence ends, but the period goes on.

The Search

The period goes on, beyond mailboxes and religion, beyond the consumption of empty promises that their promoters do not embody, like empty calories too long consumed. And my life goes on, too, in pursuit of a dream, a driving, energizing passion—something or someone who can see my needs and... I need my dream, not theirs, nor a passing flash of passion among millions of passing flashes. Nothing of sartorial elegance or soterial promises will do, but maybe something common and simple like a bean or an acorn that contains survival and the expectation that my life will matter. For want of a dream shop to sell it to me or a savior to lead me to it, I search. My search is energy, not life. It is purpose, not discovery. It is a need, and needs not yet met.

> It's like I've got to carry water from the spring back to the house to be sure that I will have water to use when I get there and to survive, but I get so thirsty carrying it that I drink it along the way and get to the house with no water.
>
> So, I've got to carry water from the spring back to the house to be sure that I will have water to use when I get there and to survive, but I get so thirsty carrying it that I drink it along the way and get to the house with no water.
>
> So, I've got to carry water from the spring back to the house to be sure that I will have water to use when I get there and to survive, but I get so thirsty carrying it that I drink it along the way and get to the house with no water.
>
> So, I've got to carry water.
>
> I've got to keep going. I must let my needs take me to a future that I cannot yet see, let alone understand.
>
> So, I've got to carry water. . . .

I may have no water when I get where I'm going but I'm dead without making the trip. So, I search.

The sentence ends but the period goes on.

As I search, I am warmed by honest personal reality, mine and others, but the cold calculations of the clock bring such a chill that old ideas—beliefs I hold closely to my chest—freeze. I hold them close, but I can't keep them warm beyond their time to be alive. So, like all living beings, they grow old and die, falling limp in my arms. And I grieve my losses:

> Pretty. I saw the sheen of her golden hair. It seemed like a friend whom I had not met. She went for a walk in the early morning and drowned herself. But she looked so good. Mom and Dad said she was such a nice girl who "never gave us any trouble. She was a fine Christian girl."
>
> Ornamental. I saw the Christmas Star on their tree, calling me to believe, to celebrate their holy days with them. He shot his wife, his two children, and then shot himself. But he was a good father and a loyal member of his church.
>
> Cosmetic. I saw the gold-flaked blue on her eyelids when she explained that no one likes her, but that she would do anything to get herself liked. She also explained that God loves her and that that makes life wonderful. But she holds sexual seances with anyone who wishes to enter her, an innocent woman who refuses to confront her fear of being worthless, masking it with quick faux romances, painting over it to attract her pseudo-suitors.
>
> Achieving. I saw the finely lettered and framed ordination certificate on his wall as he sweat through his anguished confession of guilt about incest with his child. "How could I have been so goddamned stupid! Just plain damned stupid." He may have felt the fire of the Spirit, but he didn't seem to be able to take his torch to light his way through life with it.
>
> Competitive. I saw the faint afterglow of believable praise, the dusty and tarnished trophies his championship muscles had won. Like them, his dusty and tarnished emotions are strangers to him as he takes them out and says, "God's been good to me, but these goddamn pills are killing me. Why am I alive, anyway? I ain't worth shit. I'd be better off dead!"
>
> Theological. And I saw him, a theological pig rooting in his carefully crafted abstractions of God, who becomes so familiar to him through his relentlessly pursued and eternally stale studies that God is nicely styled to fit his most deeply felt desires that he cannot acknowledge, let alone honor as a human. God is as disposable as the stuff in which pigs root. And old beliefs devour people like these.

Pretty religion makes slaves of those who would look good at almost any price.

Ornamental religion seduces them to trade stars, coins, and crosses for honesty, realness, and vitality.

Cosmetic religion decays them from the inside out as they conceal unspeakable misery.

Achieving religion polices them and captures them in a conspiracy to be perfect in all they do, ultimately confirming their fear that they are simply and totally unworthy.

Competitive religion joins them to forces bigger than each of them to win a loss for all their souls, for it is in making god from winning that they lose.

Theological religion feeds them dust and watches them starve to death, nourished only on lovely, correctly composed ideas.

Old dreams die hard. They are my dreams gone. They are my religion of a past I cannot revive. So, I search.

And my religion is so evident to me that I hurt because I am no longer a creature but a creator, an omnipotent white knight rescuing himself from the fierce dragon of loving self-examination. The job is too lonely, though. Too lonely, yes, but everyone expects me to be certain, including me. But no one loves the creator, that self-sufficient wonder-boy whose giftedness evokes their smiles of affirmation or, in words kept unheard, "that self-sufficient son-of-a-bitch"—and lover of a good image, and often a shadow of a human being.

No one loves the creator whose creature is too much like himself. No one loves the creator when the mystery is gone. Maybe that's why God was killed when He became Jesus.

Old dreams die hard. And some of us hang on to them even after they and we are dead.

The minister and his family, along with hundreds of others, kept a two-day prayer vigil to bring back to life their drowned seventeen-year-old son. When the body began to smell, the minister called the funeral home to come get his son's body. He said that it was not God's plan to keep his son alive. He could not explain God's failure to act.

Old dreams die hard. And some of us hang on to them long after they and we are dead.

Joe turns away as I search his eyes. With unrequited joy, he says that he is doing great, that he has been sober for three months, that he is going to marry Jenny, that Reverend Potts is keeping him clean, that this time is different, that he understands what is necessary to keep himself sober, that he is not on another religious fanatic binge, that he is grateful that I am

> there for him. His shoulders slump as if he has nothing to lift him up, his eyes fix on nothing. Through a reddened blur as if he knows that his vision will not clear, his voice cracks with fear, and his soul wishes to confirm that "God is good." "God is good." Joe talks as if he needs to prove it and as if he fears that death will come before God is real to him. God. God is good, but Joe works too hard to prove it, as if he sees and fears his death. If Joe dies, he will lose his life in a cave, a labyrinth, of fear.

And where is God in this? Is he dead? To me, yes. After all, how do I know God, now that I have seen their deaths, their dreams' deaths, and mine, buried the victims, and mourned their passing? Can they find life again? Can I find life in believing or dreaming? Can I find God in believing or dreaming again?

Old dreams die hard. And some of us hang on to them long after they and we are dead.

And by hanging on, we lose. God, how we lose! Can we ever get back what we lost? Can I ever get back what I have lost?

Can we ever get back what we lost? I read about ancient sailors who sailed between almost every continent and island on the planet. They used no instruments. None, except their bodies. Over spaces many times the distance of their vision, they sailed between continents and islands. They used no instruments. None, except their bodies. They followed the swells and doldrums as if they were fixed, like streets on a city map. They followed stars as if they were common landmarks. They felt the speed and temperature of the wind on their skin and trailed it to their port as if it were a well-worn path. And they tasted the water to fix their place in a placeless mass of water, as if their tasting lighted their sightless dark. **Their story tells me about what I have lost.**

Can we buy back the souls we've lost to fancy gadgets and to fancy religion that deaden our instinctual talents to be one with our world? And what's the price of buying back the souls we lost? And, God forbid, what happens when the gadgets and our religions fail? I read about ancient sailors who sailed between almost every continent and island on the planet. They used no instruments. None, except their bodies. And I am overwhelmed by their beauty, by their simplicity, by their mystery, and by their oneness with their world.

Where did I lose my beauty, simplicity, and mystery? When did I lose the oneness with myself, my others, and my world? Can I find God without finding or, maybe, losing myself?

I see beauty. I see simplicity. I see mystery. The oneness eludes me, though, like the fragrance of last summer's honeysuckle. But when I go on what I know and see, I believe that there must be something or someone beyond what I can know and see who brings everything together. Someone beyond what I know and see.

The sentence ends, but the period goes on. In silence. Silence.

Silence

Yes, the sentence ends. I feel its death within me.

The race will end. Yes, the human race. Long after I (and you) have died, every descendant from me (and you) will have died, too. Every fragment of my (and your) existence, all bones and products, whether they were made of paper or plastic or steel, will have ended, too. But in unimaginably distant years from my (and your) end, when the Earth and Sun are dust and gases scattered through boundless space, someone will write, "The race will end. Yes, the human race. Long after I (and you) have died. . . ."

The sentence ends, but the period goes on.

And the period shines so brightly that I am blinded by it, but still get enough light through my tight-eyed squinting to make old habits look good when I turn away from it. How could I use this, I wonder? Could the period ever be popular? Is it mine to claim and to sell? Could it make me famous? I hear my questions and know that my old habits cause me to chasing rainbows in the dark, to turning life itself into profit, and making profit the goal of life. Still, even if God may be trying to get through to me, **the allure of profiting from the period claims my attention.** I hear those voices telling me to go for it. It's all about marketing:

"How do you get silence to come when you call it?"

"I just love new silence, so sweet smelling and colorful."

"Never mind, don't answer the door, that's just another one of those damned silence salesmen."

"At McSilence Fast Spirits, we have all the silence you could possibly enjoy."

"Ladies and gentlemen, presenting the King of American Silence. . . ."

"The Federal Government is negotiating silence rights in the United Nations."

"Have you seen the new silence commercial on T.V.; the one with the cute little chipmunks?"

"I took a course in silence, and it was okay, but it shouldn't be required."

"Great! The Cincinnati Silents are playing tonight at eight and I can't go."

"Do you happen to have a little silence I could borrow 'til pay day?"

"Welcome! Our show features over a thousand talented silent contestants. Let's get started!"

"Hi, I'm new in town. Can you tell me where I can find a good silence shop?"

"The Silence Action Committee has formed its new policies and procedures on silence."

"My old silence is getting a little tattered; I've got to go shopping. The new silences aren't what they used to be."

"As many of you know, a good prevention program includes silence to reduce the risks of cancer, heart disease, sexual dysfunction, and, of course, hemorrhoids."

"Okay, where did you hide the silence; it's never where I left it."

"Mr. President, can you comment on your practice of silence?"

"This public service announcement invites you to a silence rally, to protest against a noise rally."

Headline: "GUN BATTLE BETWEEN GANGS ENDS IN THE COUNTRY'S LARGEST MASSACRE IN DISPUTE OVER SILENCE."

"Hi, I'll be a little late getting home; I'm going to stop to play a little silence."

"Tell us honestly, Governor, are you going after the silence vote?"

"This is my first Silence Convention. I just love the silent greats, don't you?"

"The most effective psychotherapeutic intervention today is psycho-silence."

"I've been to a lot of padded gymnasiums like this one. The silent competition just keeps getting better and better, you know?"

"This is the best silence money can buy, in capsules, powder, or handy suppositories."

I hear these voices, and the sentence ends for me. I want to forget it, no longer to grieve its passing. The sentence is dead and gone.

The sentence ends, but the period goes on. And I feel the period, like thunder drumming its threat, its promise, its invitation, its approach to my thirsty, dust-coated soul. So, Lord, wordless and nameless thunder, don't put words between us to keep us from feeling each other.

Words to worship? No more sermons.
Words to protect? No more lectures.
Words to obey? Forget the mindlessness.
Words to follow? Forget the lesson.
Words to heal? Forget the gesture.
Words to sell? Damn the words!

Lord, if you're there and listening, forget the words. Let's take the period, the silence that follows all the words, and go with it. Let's go with the silence. Let's go with just you and me.

The silence gains weight as I immerse myself in it. It is the weight of livingness, of feeling alive in the moment, craving for more of it than any moment can give me. Worse, just as I crave more aliveness than I can get, I see them—the others who desperately crave what they need. They are lonely. They are bleeding. They are hungry. They are embattled. They are homeless. They are ailing. They are like me—needy and searching for food, shelter, companionship—and maybe truth and themselves.

"Love one another."
"Do unto others as you would have them to do unto you."
"Love your enemies as yourself."
I feel the voice that I cannot hear, telling me these things. Is it my voice? Is it... No, it can't be. Maybe it is the voice of life or possibly God?
Whose voice do I feel?

Are you the One beyond? Beyond all that I see, beyond all that I hear. Beyond all that I know through words, are you the One who brings all living things together? I want to say yes. Help me to say it. Yes? Yes to life and living. Yes? Help me to say it. Yes. Help.

Yes! Scared to say it, but yes.
Yes, to life and living.

Yes. Yes. Yes! And so I begin to dream, as I feel the silence calling me home, welcoming me to life and living. I feel the passion of a dream, my dream, being born. I am called by it and soar. I am lifted by it and soar without effort, to places where life pulses in wordless and nameless promises that it shall not stop pulsing.

In this moment, the drag of wanting to maintain my grip on my carefully groomed worth causes tension, a demand that I turn toward death or turn toward living.

> I work as easily as I breathe. I expose my mind and body to the slavery of believing that work makes me good, just as the earth exposes the grave that awaits me, ready to hold all that I have tried to accomplish.
>
> My love of work has lowered my love of myself to the point that I feel like I am dying, as if I am already in a grave.
>
> My hand on the keyboard, mower, steering wheel, and everything else that means work, grips hard and cold and stiff, holding me where I chose to be. It is a hand of deadening dread.
>
> But I'm not dead, yet.

Yes. Yes. Yes, along with the ever-present temptation to retreat into "no." Saying "no" to life is what I know how to do well. Still, in this moment, I begin to dream. I dream of saying yes to the One Beyond, but in the language that invented language, the language of the searcher—the free self who dreams life as a full and beautiful livingness, always made and, yet, always in the making—who seeks to be at one with himself, at one with the world, at one with the One Beyond. I learn a little more of this language when my spirit, time, and the One Beyond collide in silence. And, in a mind without words, I speak in words only because I am so limited in my capacity to report what I know:

> Silence, you call and I listen, feeling the vibrations of your deep voice upon my soul and seeing the rhythm of your heartbeat pulsing life and pushing life beyond itself. Your sky will be there when every skyscraper is gone. Your sun will be there when every light bulb is gone. Your green grass will be there when every dollar bill is gone. Your air and bird will be there when every aircraft is gone. And, new life, of forms greater than all those I know or could imagine, will be there, being itself, when all the known others are gone.
>
> Silence, let me know who you are. I believe we've met a thousand times, but I don't recognize you. I don't remember you very well. I understand you, yet, know almost nothing about you. You were here before I was (and before everything else, too), I know that. But more than that, you follow everything—everything:
>
> > Moonshots and whirlwinds, a gay-pride march and an egg laid. If I name it, you follow it, except, maybe, for eternity. I look and listen after everything I can, only to see and hear that I've missed you, as if you work hard to stay ahead of me. No matter what I say or do, you take over precisely then, when all is said or done. And you take over with an ease that disturbs me and tells me that I must know more.

Silence, I want to argue with you, but you have the advantage. You have argued with millions upon millions just like me. You know what I have to say. You know me but I don't know you. You fill more space and time than all that's ever been said and done by every person who has ever lived, but I know only a mere trace of what might be known by any person. You go everywhere without stirring the slightest particle of dust. You surround my daylight and dark. You watch me, silently or not at all. You don't frighten me, though. I frighten myself. Be sensitive to my need for you. Let me touch you, while you touch me, and let me feel how complete you are, and maybe, I can let myself go with you. You must know that I am no mere vagrant, poor and trapped in my frantic rush from one empty-hearted busyness to another. Nor am I fragile. You will not break me. Still, I feel at great risk with you.

Silence, primitive, you are always there, always the winner over all that I make, which is usually loud, unnatural, and deadly. Primitive silence, you call me and ask me to lie. You ask me to know, to really know, that when all is said and done, when no one can say or do another single thing, you reign supreme, divine, as the home of God, as the beginner of life and eternity. A casualty of old dreams that hurt even when they were good, I don't want to lie about believing that what I say and do is so very important. What I say and do is important to me. But you challenge every word and deed.

Decision

Sentence or period. The sentence ends, but the period goes on. Shall I choose the sentence with all its noise or the period with all its silence? Do I get loud or quiet?

The choice attacks me, assaults me with a vengeance. Certainty or uncertainty. Real or pretend. The period or the two-minute rum-filled chocolate orgasm that my fast and loud world promises?

I can have everything, my pleasures and my possessions, by being nothing. The promise screams at me from the fast voices of moneyed sellers who tell me that I can fool my passions, that I can satisfy myself ultimately, that I can crown myself King and kill whoever frustrates my passions.

The sellers know that the magic of orgasmic America is its capacity to kill for pleasure, persuading me that pleasure and grace are mortal enemies:

To win a victory in sports is to receive god-worthy praise. When the Final Four becomes the Final One, the winners presume to make God envious.

> To profit in business while others are buried in losses is to approach heaven, stirring feelings of Godliness.
>
> To body-count the church upward is to know god's providence, as if they know that God smiles on rising numbers and frowns on falling numbers.
>
> To score in a bargain for sex is to find a new fun form of acceptable human sacrifice.
>
> To heal a client in therapy stands as an endorsement of clinical righteousness.
>
> To see and love a glamorous face in the mirror makes the viewer superior to others.

No temptation is greater to me than the offer to buy the world at the price of my soul. No temptation offers so much more than can be delivered to me. I want what I can't have, nor can anyone else, except when I betray my senses. When I listen to myself and accept what I hear, I move toward others with clearer, more compassionate awareness of them. I see them as life, as a living presence that inspires me to protect life for both of us.

Never inclined toward martyrdom, I wonder why those who chose it decided to die. Why did they die? Willingly, those whose conscience and grit cost them their lives influenced others, far beyond their deaths.

> Good Friday has never made sense, to me. Jesus died on Good Friday. When King was shot and killed, his followers did not think that it was a good day. When Bonhoeffer was hanged and killed, his followers did not think that it was a good day. When Gandhi was shot and killed, his followers did not think that it was a good day.
>
> Jesus' followers felt the devastating loss of their model, their hero, their leader—a man who gave them promises of more than they could have invented as promises for themselves. As discouraged as his followers were, when Jesus died by crucifixion, they eventually changed. They came to see that Jesus taught them how to die. More than dying, though, he taught them how to live. Live for life. Live for your own life, but be ready to give it up for others.

The decision sometimes screams at me, although I have put a lot of energy into sound-proofing my ears in my internal world. The screams sometimes become mellowed, inviting, persistent, and curious: The period or pleasures and possessions? To be or to have? The question is about the territory of spiritual warfare within me. It is a question of salvation or sin, of wholeness or fragmentation, of being all that I can be—transcendent, whole, and becoming—or of having all that I can get—temporary, broken, and dead.

The Risk I Take

Someday, I may retreat into risking nothing, but for now, I risk looking into new eyes, her eyes, among them. Her laser-like look punches holes in my concentration on her dark eyes so that my interest in her crashes into those black holes of interpersonal space from where the assurance of a liking presence rarely escapes. That is the risk I take.

The period goes on.

Someday, I may retreat into risking nothing, but for now, I look into my own eyes, too. I want to give and get the look of kindness, the look of "I am with you, caring for you" that comforts those hurting and attracts those estranged. But I am afraid I cast upon the world the kindly eyes of a bargain saint who knows more about living and dying than he ever cared to know. I am afraid that my eyes tell the story of growing up old and dying before my time, losing life in its living. So, my scared, knowing eyes look upon the buy-minded patrons at the world's soul-emptying shelves who trade in bread and guns to feed and to kill with equal passion. And I see them looking at me as if I had sold myself too cheaply. That is the risk I take.

The period goes on.

Someday, I may retreat into risking nothing, but, for now, I risk looking into my own soul. The risk is that I may look too long, too deeply, and pull into the safety of my aloneness, like a turtle pulls into its shell, and have no one to hear me softly with needed love, only loudly from a distance, so that aloneness, good and needed, becomes loneliness, bitter, and angry. As if in a rodeo, though, I will ride my aloneness to tame it, break it, and use it, or I will be broken by it, looking not into my own soul but at the tail end of my own foolishness. That is the risk I take.

The period goes on.

Someday, I may retreat into risking nothing, but, for now, I risk looking into the present. The trees outside my window bend in the wind. If I knew which would break, instead of just bending, and on which day, I would cut it down now to avoid unpredictable damage. But I don't know. I take each tree as it is, not as it will be or as I think it might be. Anticipating my life too closely feels similarly futile. I may break and fall, doing unpredictable damage to myself, by looking into the present too long and feeling the wind too strong upon me, but that is the risk I take.

The period goes on.

Someday, I may retreat into risking nothing but for now, I risk looking into my own dreams. My head is full of dreams about times to dance while lovers and workers wait. My dreams say that I am at ease with all of the many selves within me. I am friends with squirrels and cardinals. I have perfect intimacy, with love birthing more love. I embrace hurting people and heal their pain. I romp on the beach, blessed with sunny freedom. I vote and speak my conscience and shape a better world. I give what I have to anyone who needs it, living simply and in peace with all those who desire peace and many of those who don't. I work with the contented joy, timeless fascination, and simple effectiveness of a three-year-old's delightful discovery of gravity. To dream is the risk I take.

Workers, warriors, and lovers are no match for the dreamer. But the dreamer is no match for himself. The risk is that my dreams will tell me how little I am. That is the risk I take.

The period goes on.

Living with and accepting risk makes me vulnerable to faith and susceptible to hope.

Expectation

The period goes on. I am in expectation.

Period. Expectation.

So here I am. I've come to look for the One Beyond. No longer planted in my own lies or theirs, I am in the expectation of experiencing God. I come to look for God, knowing now that the sentence fails me and that, as always, believing the sentence is the final treason against self. The nearer the sentence, the closer God is. The nearer the period, the further God is. Or, so it seems. But the sentence goes no further than it has gone. God is close in it, but dead. Surely, though, the sentence speaks with certainty and clarity. The period is silent. The sentence says, "God is alive. Believe this and be whole." I understand that—and maybe, if I repeat it over and over, I could come to believe it—but understanding isn't enough. The period says nothing. I don't understand its silence, but it frees me to hear the mystery, the "I am" who excites wonder, the "I am" who is the strangest of strangers who comes and stays forever, and to feel the stranger's presence. My dream is to get acquainted in silence, with the stranger whose silent presence brings my spirit into harmony, like the composer who finishes her masterpiece—one genuine masterpiece is never like any other—and to say yes to the One Beyond.

The period goes on.

In expectation of harmony and reconciliation, I sing a song without words and play the music without notes. I sing and play the morning as it brightens, but lie peacefully in the cold brown wrappings of winter when summer's warmth is far away. The toys of tan-days are stashed away for a sleepy solstice song, a song Who lullabies all life to rest and to wait under gray blankets until the morning warmly burns away the gray seals of winter, as if in sexual heat, welcoming and coaxing life from all its wombs to sing a greener song.

The period goes on.

In expectation, life is coming out now, like a flower from a bud or a baby from a womb. It is a time to be human, a time to be reborn. I have wanted to go back, though, to believing that all is well and that, if I want it to be, there is no death. But death is there. Nothing I could believe takes it away. And I could count time until death in nail-biting agony, in ulcerating indecision, and in starving loneliness, deciding whether to eat the apple of life or not. Or, I could shake the whole damn tree, bringing down its fruit until I stuff myself on it and am full of life. I choose to shake it and eat, shake it and eat, shake it and eat! And in the winter of my life, I'll stand beneath its barren, black branches, squinting into the brightness beyond, wondering which apple will fall next. This is born-again expectation.

Now is a time to be reborn. The period goes on.

In expectation of harmony and reconciliation, the sweet light of a new dawning warms me like spring's fresh breath, catching me up in a life force, and showing me the fullness of freedom in surrender to it. I am a snap of the fingers, a droplet of rain fallen—an instant come and gone. Yet, a snap and a droplet without whom the force cannot be. I am needed, ultimately and eternally, for the life force to be the life force. I am it and it is I, when I surrender to it. I—We—affirm life as life's only need. Life is to be. And my need is to be. Just be. The period goes on, welcoming me into its fullness, a grand prize of human existence that I don't have to win, but, harder, that I have only to accept, to receive without conditions—no votes to be taken, no program, no committee to approve it, no costuming, no hidden fees, and no waiting. Life is to accept and to receive. The period calls me to be. Alive and living.

For now, and maybe for always, I am in expectation of harmony and reconciliation. I dream of saying yes to the One Beyond. I have learned that, only when all is said and done, I have only begun to find how the One Beyond comes to me.

In silence—in the holy now of living—because the period goes on.

A New Sentence

When the sentence ends, something or someone happens to me, moving me to living and to awe, surprising me, terrifying me, delighting me, in my discovery that I am discovered and that the Word comes to me in silence.

Yes. The Word comes in silence.
Yes. Has God given birth, again?
And a new sentence begins. A New Sentence?

Who or what calls me to a New Sentence? Is it God? Is it Life? Is it Me, wanting to live?

Do I have to know the answer to these questions? Maybe, it could be that, for a finite and short span of time, I am the New Sentence?

I am the new Sentence. And when my Sentence ends, the Period Goes On. It is theirs to enter and to discover life in it, in the silence that follows me, and where they discover themselves as life.

I am the sentence, but the period goes on.

The period goes on.

The Clinical Significance of Faith

Competent therapists understand that their first obligation is to provide professionally accountable mental healthcare for their clients in response to their clients' clinically relevant needs. This is a necessary, duty-bound obligation. More narrowly, they also have an obligation to understand and respond to faith-related challenges brought to them by their clients. Whether therapists want to receive clients' faith-related concerns or not, clients bring them anyway. Further, as the information in this discussion has already indicated, faith is a feature of being human. God or institutional religion may not be universally endorsed by humans, but the experience of faith is universally human. Searching for meaning—something or anything to give one's life significance—beyond the obvious terrain of human existence is normative.

The nature of faith—broadly defined to include religion and spirituality—may be much more prolusory than illusory, no matter what skeptics may want to say. Honest faith may have much more in common with skeptics than the terms "faith" and "skepticism" may suggest, mainly because their obvious commonality is that they are expressed by humans. And, the nature of being human is that nothing can be known with absolute certainty. This is a human limitation. Human judgment is always tentative, just as genuine faith and genuine skepticism are always tentative. However, the conspicuous tentativeness of human experience gives added clinical relevance to the faith or non-faith of therapists. As she writes about therapist's personal history, Kegerreis (2022, p. 248) sagely observes, "[If] a therapist has a faith, she is less likely to be as closely attuned to or curious about what it means that her client believes in a similar way, while a therapist who is an atheist will think that there is a lot to understand in the meaning of the client's religious experience." Similar necessary clinical reasoning may be applied when therapists and clients come together as politically liberal, vegan, lesbian, or other emotion-evocative features of being human.

Within the context of providing therapy, the significance of faith is that it embodies the desire, hope, need, or whatever term best fits, to make sense of the immense senselessness that often confronts humans. Adults recognize a fact: "I will die." Commonly, they feel, "Yes, but this fact makes no sense to me. Why do I have to die?" The fact stands, whether it is interpreted or not. No one can change the fact any more than they can change the course of the sun as it takes its leisurely, one-million-year orbit around the center of our universe. However, despite the helplessness that attends to reckoning with existentially real challenges, individuals can decide to enjoy the brevity of life and the warmth of the sun.

In short, the clinical significance of faith is that is enables therapist to find for themselves a bridge between the stark terror of termination and the pleasant and sometime ecstatic tentativeness of living, while they live well and, in addition, attend to the problems that clients bring to therapy. And, through providing competent therapy, therapists can enable their clients to live well, too.

When clients' needs give therapists clinical problems of, say, chronic depression, unrelenting marital stress, self-abusive consumption of alcohol, an over-active and anxious third-grade student, or almost countless other problems, they respond to these needs in a professional, largely neutral, and clinical manner, as they should. Usually, competent therapists avoid easy, prescriptive ideologies as they respond to their clients. Congruent with competent professional mental health care, therapists also avoid easy religious, spiritual, or faith-related ideologies as treatments for their clients. Regardless of their level of sincerity with which their individual ideologies may be held, they are mostly non-relevant in the delivery of competent mental health care. A commonly recognized axiom of therapy is that the more ideological therapy is, the less effective it is, regardless of the ideology or the sincerity of those who embrace the ideology.

The title of Auger's article (2004) "What we don't know CAN hurt us: Mental health counselors' implicit assumptions about human nature" supports the need for caution among therapists with regard to their management of their individual beliefs. From their research, for example, Bilgrave and Deluty (2002) concluded, "Most respondents labeled themselves as politically liberal, and almost half claimed that their political ideologies influenced their practice. The humanistic therapeutic orientation was positively related to Eastern and mystical beliefs, atheistic and agnostic beliefs, and political liberalism; the cognitive-behavioral orientation was positively related to conservative Christian beliefs; and the psychodynamic orientation was negatively related to Eastern and mystical beliefs and positively related to political liberalism" (p. 245). Similarly, Silander et al. (2020) advised,

> Clinical psychologists as consumers, and co-producers, of research must consider the impact of bias on their clinical research and practice. Failing to effectively monitor the influence of ideological bias in research and practice, in the midst of an ever-polarizing political climate, may continue to threaten the legitimacy of social and psychological sciences and alienate those otherwise in need of psychological services. The most admirable qualities of clinical psychologists (e.g., self-reflection, empathy, and dedication, etc.) may very well be the qualities that allow consideration of the ideological bias problem and foster motivation to develop the knowledge, skills, and desire to approach the provision of clinical services in a nonpartisan and sociopolitically sensitive manner. (p. 10)

From the view of clients, faith in the capability of therapists to improve their lives is but another example of the reality of faith. However, faith in their helpers is not enough to improve the lives of clients. Therapists also need to be clear about how they understand faith-related issues that their clients bring to therapy. They need also to implement applicable and specific clinical skills. As the ensuing discussion indicates, Martin 2024, pp. 169–187) sought to promote a clinical orientation to clients' presentations of their faith-related problems.

For now, only a list of client's commonly presented faith-related concerns is given here. The list illustrates some of the compelling concerns that clients bring to therapy. Implicit in the list, clients seldom present religion and spirituality when these aspects of their lives serve them well and may be observed as being healthy. Instead, far more likely, clients will present complaints and problems that emerge from their faith, religion, and/or spirituality. While these complaints and problems arise and should be the focus of treatment, they are not in themselves an assessment of religion. Similarly, when a client reports sexual exploitation by, say, an attorney, a therapist need not assess the practice of law.

Among many religious and spiritual complaints and problems, clients present the ones below. The issues represented in the descriptions below are extremely abbreviated. In the crucible of clinical work, they are far more complicated than these descriptions may suggest. Mostly, the idea here is to offer a list of common presentations of religion-related issues, not to explain them. Also, while the list includes several issues that many therapists will likely recognize, it is not intended to identify all possible such issues. No doubt, there are others.

Religion as a failed source of strength and meaning. Following the loss of his wife to death as a result of breast cancer, a widower says, "I guess I figured that somehow God would come through for us. You know, something would happen that would save her."

Desperate search for positive meaning. "I just feel like I should have something in my life that I'm lacking, you know? I should be doing something with my life, but I have no idea what it is. I'm just lost, you know? I don't know what it would be like, but I somehow want to connect with God, you know?"

Hurt, embarrassed, or betrayed by one's faith community. A pubescent teen brings her friend to the church. She is met by individuals who tell her that bringing her dark-skinned friend to their Caucasian church is inappropriate.

Religion integrated into mental-emotional distortions and disorders. Generally, therapists recognize that some of their clients who suffer from mental-emotional problems and disorders express religious ideas that are commensurate with the skewed view of their world that bespeaks their problems and disorders. While religious and spiritual concerns may be integrated into a mental-emotional disturbance, their integration is usually presumed to be a manifestation of the disturbance and not a specifically religious or spiritual issues.

Moral dilemmas that stem from faith commitments. Among counselors and therapists, various affectional orientations are almost universally accepted as appropriate. However, the larger social world poses challenges for countless individuals, say, whose son or daughter has identified as gay, lesbian, bi-sexual, trans, or another orientation. "My religious orientation says that it's wrong, but I love my child."

Conflict between a client's beliefs and behaviors. Commonly, therapists hear clients speak about their inner turmoil that emerges from their violation of their values and their religion. An abbreviated form of such a disclosure may be something like this: "I'm torn. What I'm doing goes against everything I believe is right—as a Christ follower. I have partners outside my marriage. The guilt and frustration have take over my life."

Political divisions and alienation from religion. Without explanation or illustration, this reference may be sufficient, given our current political environment.

Controlling, manipulative religion. The so-called "purity culture" induces shame in children and adolescents. Typically, advocates of purity culture hold that sexual self-stimulation is bad and that only sex between a man and a woman and only within the boundaries of marriage is acceptable sex. Abstinence is the absolute standard of sexual behavior.

Disturbed parenting. Among individuals who have been traumatically damaged by "good Christian fathers," those who have been sexually victimized epitomize the reality of disturbed parenting. Numerous other parental failures by presumably devoted religious also come from disturbed parenting.

Godly or Godless Squabbles. A wife and husband struggle to make sense of their differences. She comes from a family of "conservative Baptists," while he comes from a family of "rigidly loyal Mormons." Her parents and his family raise doubts about whether they can accept their marriage or the alien member of the marriage.

Abandonment of family and religious traditions. The client says, "I can't talk to my mom or dad any more. They will want to talk about religion. I know I can't go there with them. I will have to leave, or a fight will break out."

Anxious exploration of alternative religions. The client reports, "I'm pretty comfortable with my outlook on life. I practice Buddhism. But I lived in torment for decades—not to mention conflict with my family—before I found that I could have faith that gives my life meaning. I'm still exploring how to live. That's why I'm here."

Abuse by religious persons. The evidence that defines sexual victimization by various religious leaders is prolific and consistent. Other kinds of abuse occur. Financial manipulation is one of them. Another is coercive actions toward those who disagree with prevailing attitudes, behaviors, or beliefs in a religious community.

Harmful Discrimination. The client says, "A while back, I went to work at a Christian company. They hired me knowing that I was a practicing Muslim, but they have made my work a living hell."

Compromising Transference-related Challenges. Professional accountability has often been challenged by clients who request or demand a therapist who shares their religion. Their eagerness to assign their beliefs to their therapist holds the potential for compromising the potential of clinical services.

Religious Beliefs as Accelerants of Personal Problems. For many clients, religion/spirituality adds fuel to the fire of disturbance in their lives. They carry the burden of guilt and alienation because of their experience of religion and their addiction. Such a dynamic is common among non-hetero-normative sexualities, too.

Normative Developmental Issues. Many pubescent adolescents question almost everything, including their religious views and, of course, the religious views of their parents. Their parents sometimes wonder whether their confrontational and probably annoying adolescent will ever grow beyond such thoughts and actions and become likable again.

Personal, Religion-related Quirks. A former client found "God's messages" in almost everything. He referred to the angles of the tablecloth as having religious meaning. Similarly, he referred to the color of clothing that others wore. He referred to the flames in his fireplace. He asserted that it was God's presence in fire that compelled him to become a fireman. And so on. Incidentally, in the long history of religion, many groups associated God with fire.

Therapists can and will confront many, if not all, of these religion-related challenges in their clinical practices. Meeting these challenges, along with all of the others with which they are already well acquainted, such as depression, marital conflict, career frustrations, and so on, is the reason that they do what they do. And, as caring, objective, and consummately professional as they are, therapists welcome these challenges, akin to welcoming one another when they relate well with their peers. In doing so, they embody the highest integrity and competence of which they are capable.

Guidance for Integration

The client-presented problems named above invite and compel therapists to provide professional services. Such services should be guided by the best available evidence for addressing specific problems, accrued wisdom from the profession, and a careful, thorough assessment of clients' concerns. In addition, therapists should be as reality-based and as specific as they can be when they seek to provide treatment for their clients. Toward achieving this, Martin (2024, pp. 125–150) discussed several guiding principles for providing effective mental health care in response to clients' faith-related problems, including references to several relevant research reports. The principles appear in the outline below.

Think and Act Clinically

Clinical thinking places the needs of clients at a much higher level of priority than one's own needs.

Clinical thinking intentionally and self-consciously addresses client needs.

Clinical thinking draws from the accrued wisdom and established evidence for good clinical work, regardless of the therapist's personal feelings about the client.

Clinical thinking expresses genuine interest in and curiosity about clients, instead of reacting to the client's presentation.

With the necessary recognition of the critical importance of intentional and persistent professional accountability, clinical thinking demonstrates itself in a wide array of measurable and commonly accepted clinical skills.

Clinical thinking necessarily involves the ability to appropriately examine, assess, and address clinically relevant client needs that arise in practicing counseling and therapy.

Think Critically about the evidence from clients, including the evidence inherent in their religious problems..

Seek and Rely on the Best Evidence

Endorse, Affirm, and Practice Diversity

Attempt to Make Ideologically Neutral Clinical Judgments (Selected references to research related to this principle are cited above.)

Maintain a Professional Perspective

Integrate Clients' Religion into Clinical Decision-making

Complete Relevant Training

Demonstrate Support for Religious Freedom

Adapt to the Limitations of Faith and Religion

Affirm Highly Effective Therapists. The research literature affirms several qualities that are commonly possessed by highly effective therapists. Many of the sources are discussed in Martin and Turner (2020, pp. 61–64) and in Martin (2024), pp. 147–150). Among the important qualities of highly effective therapists, the following ones are frequently identified. [Highly effective therapists are discussed in Chapter 7.]

Including devotees of various religions and those who hold hostility toward religion, along with everyone else between these polarities, faith is a human experience. In response to faith experiences, allowing for virtually countless ways to express faith, competent counselors and therapists possess the gift of therapy that enables their clients to move toward health, including religious and spiritual health.

References

Auger, R. W. (2004). What we don't know CAN hurt us: Mental health counselors' implicit assumptions about human nature. *Journal of Mental Health Counseling, 26*(1), 13–24. https://doi.org/10.17744/mehc.26.1.q2r31fh0na9efbv0

Bilgrave, D. P., & Deluty, R. H. (2002). Religious beliefs and political ideologies as predictors of psychotherapeutic orientations of clinical and counseling psychologists. *Psychotherapy: Theory, Research, Practice, Training, 39*(3), 245–260.

Hazo, S. (2005). *A flight to elsewhere*. Autumn House Press.

Kegerreis, S. (2022). The role of our own history in our therapeutic work. *Psychodynamic Practice, 28*(3), 243–253.

Livestream. (2006). *May all your expectations be frustrated.* https://www.lifestream.org/may-all-your-expectations-be-frustrated/

Martin, F. A., & Turner, J. P. (2020). *Clinical supervision in the real world: A practical guide to ethics, legal Issues, and personal development.* Routledge.

Martin, F. A. (2024). The challenges of integrating religion and spirituality into psychotherapy: Integrity, competence, and cultural pluralism in clinical practice. New York, NY: Routledge.

Silander, N. C., Geczy Jr., B., Marks, O., & Mather, R. D. (2020). Implications of ideological bias in social psychology on clinical practice. *Clinical Psychology: Science and Practice, 27*, e12312.

Chapter 4
"S" Is for "Seed Digging Dynamic Therapy"
The Humanity of Clinical Adventurism

This chapter analyzes approaches to therapy that begin with the letter "S." Such an analysis may seem strange, given that this is a book about the humanity of therapists. How could the analysis of "S" and the larger discussion of the humanity of therapists possibly relate to each other? In short, this chapter presents an analysis of treatment approaches that begin with "S" and from this analysis reveals the condition of the humanity of therapists. Thus, while the analysis of "S" reveals a great deal about the condition of therapy, it also reveals many features of the humanity of therapists. As the title of the chapter suggests, the characterization of therapists that emerges from the analysis here is that therapists likely engage in clinical adventurism. This is discussed at the end of this chapter.

To be clear, this discussion aims to accomplish three things. One, it aims to analyze treatment approaches that begin with the letter "S." This is a way to establish a foundation for conclusions about the humanity of therapists. Two, closely related to the theme of the book, it aims to provide observations about the humanity of those who advertise and presumably practice aberrant approaches to therapy. Three, it aims to describe some of the clinical implications of the issues developed from the analysis of treatment approaches. Embedded in these three aims is the expectation that professionally accountable colleagues will want to raise questions about themselves, but, more importantly, invent actions that may constrain clinical adventurism.

The Numbers within "S"

The information in this chapter includes a report on a commonly recognized phenomenon: therapists persist in advancing highly individualized approaches to therapy as if there are no professionally appropriate constraints on their clinical judgment and actions. More than reporting, though, the chapter also includes an analysis of this phenomenon and offers conclusions about it. Far from an isolated phenomenon, highly individualized approaches to therapy have become massively prolific.

The mental healthcare movement, as it is known today, likely began with psychoanalysis. As the primary approach to psychotherapy, psychoanalysis was the dominant approach for approximately seventy years, or roughly one-half of the history of psychotherapy. Clearly, during its seventy-year dominance, psychoanalysis was not the only approach, as several other major orientations to psychotherapy emerged, including various forms of behaviorism, psychoanalytic and psychodynamic approaches, and humanism. Now, with a massive proliferation of approaches to psychotherapy, only one approach to therapy, Cognitive Behavior Therapy, is offered by a majority of practicing therapists (e.g., Martin, 2020, p. 75).

As the mental health movement arose, critics arose with it. Among its severest critics, a common acknowledgment is that the movement has made numerous positive contributions to the communities in which its therapists have been members. Further, the evidence that supports the effectiveness of therapy has been consistent and affirmative for many decades. However, almost since the beginning of the mental healthcare movement, the secure foundations for aberrant approaches to psychotherapy were laid. Namely, therapists saw and still see their professional work as almost entirely contained within their highly individualized prerogative to enact almost anything that they, each individual therapist, believe to be therapy, regardless of the potentially adverse consequences for their clients. The tacit and virtually universal mantra among therapists goes something like this: "I believe what I believe and, because I believe it, I am right to believe it and to enact my belief as therapy."

The facts do not necessarily "prove" the correctness of this mantra but affirm the probability that the mantra aptly accounts for the massive proliferation of approaches to therapy. This will remain a topic for discussion. For now, a brief explanation of the source of information that supports this discussion is necessary. Ignited by encountering therapists who advertised bizarre approaches to therapy, Martin began to review the practicing, duly credentialed therapists in an attempt to understand their approaches. Over a period of years, he compiled a list of approaches to therapy. The procedures and detailed analyses are included in two earlier books (Martin, 2020, 2024). So far, with acknowledgment of his astonishment from locating so many treatment orientations, Martin reports that he has gathered 38,373 treatment orientations from practicing therapists' websites. Due to its size, he refers to the list as "The Big List." With more than 38,000 treatment orientations on the list, the number and size of the big list are truly big. This is a staggering number. As a personal aside, I readily acknowledge that I would never have imagined that anyone could locate as many approaches to therapy as I have reported. The possible skepticism of readers is readily understandable.

Long before Martin began to gather information about treatment orientations, many others had led the way toward identifying aberrant treatment orientations. Nearing thirty years ago, Singer and Lalich's book (1996), "Crazy" Therapies: What Are They? Do They Work?, may have been the beginning of a long and desperately needed conversation. Since then, several researchers have sought to identify and explain the stunning proliferation of aberrant therapies and their deleterious impact on clinical practice. Among others, they include Barlow and Brown (2020), Bilgrave and Deluty (2002), Bowes et al. (2020), Campbell and Kay (2014), Hodson (2014), Holden and Barker (2018), Lilienfeld (2014), Lilienfeld et al. (2014), Martin (2020), Martin et al. (2023), Martin (2024), Michaels and Datta (2016), Noble and Rizq (2019), Nuttgens (2023), Plante (2022), Thyer and Pignotti (2015), and Whitney (2021).

An important, closely related issue in the discussion of aberrant therapies and the humanity of therapists is that the evidence supporting the decline in competence among counselors and therapists is strong and expanding. Some of the sources that provide support for this conclusion include Goldberg et al., 2016; Spengler and Pilipis, 2015; Bowes et al., 2020; Cuijpers et al., 2010; Cummings and O'Donohue, 2011; Lilienfeld et al., 2014; Martin, 2020; Martin and Cannon, 2010; Martin and Turner, 2020; and Ronnestad and Skovholt, 2013.

The fact of more than 38,000 treatment orientations does not speak for itself. This calls for a few caveats. First, while researchers have consistently and correctly concluded that therapy is effective, aberrant approaches have usually fallen below the "research radar." Typically, researchers have not located or sought to study aberrant approaches, such as

Ceremonial Magic	Tarot Cards
Running Therapy	Armenian CBT
Biblical Solutions	Kundalini Arousal
Metaphysical Teaching and Healing	Past Life Soul Retrieval Therapy
Transpersonal Theology	Wisdom of the Mystics

Each of these approaches was advertised by a small number of therapists. As such, each on was an outlier, advertised and practiced beyond the observation or acknowledgment of most practicing therapists. However, along with numerous other aberrant approaches, collectively they represented a significant proportion of clinical orientations and are much more normative than outlying.

Second, the number, 38,373, could and will undoubtedly be larger. Surely, while additional approaches to therapy will be located, the number 38,373 compels analysis. Third, within The Big List, some treatment approaches overlap with other approaches that are very similar. For example, both Rogerian Therapy and Person-centered Therapy are included because, while they are commonly associated, their presentations by practicing therapists indicate that they are sometimes very different approaches. Similarly, both Christian Creation Therapy and the Christian Creationist Approach are included in The Big List because those who advertise them imply that they are overlapping but different approaches.

Fourth, because of overlapping approaches, a reasonable conjecture is that the total number of approaches in The Big List may be inflated. Utilizing the number without qualification must be avoided. Thus, to eliminate the potential for viewing the total number of approaches as an inflated number and any concern that may come with this, perhaps the number of treatment approaches identified by practicing therapists should be arbitrarily reduced by 20 percent or approximately 8,000. This reduces the total to approximately 30,000 approaches. The reduced number far exceeds common estimates about the number of approaches to therapy.

Fifth, numerous acronyms pose a challenge. Approximately 3,500 acronyms appear in The Big List. The meaning of many of them cannot be known. For example, EFT, ACT, and CBT are usually and correctly presumed to refer to Emotion-Focused Therapy, Acceptance and Commitment Therapy, and Cognitive Behavior Therapy. However, such a presumption may be an understandable or even predictable mistake. What is "EFT?" Is it Emotion-Focused Therapy? Or, is it "Emotional Freedom Techniques?" Or, is it "Energy Field Therapy?" Or, is it "Emotional Freedom Tapping?" Or, is it "Energy Freedom Therapy?" When an acronym cannot be associated with a known approach to therapy, it is included in The Big List.

Sixth, no doubt, numerous approaches advertised by counselors and therapists make little clinical sense. Regardless of the conclusion regarding any one of them, the fact is that there are numerous. Those who see them for the first time will likely have many quizzical head-scratching moments. And, if they could peruse The Big List, they would surely have many such moments. For now, suffice it to report that, taken together, therapists identify a zoo-like menagerie in their advertising, including

Chicken Therapy	Fishing Therapy	Fly-fishing Therapy
Dolphin-assisted Therapy	Mini-mule Therapy	Llama Therapy
Goat Yoga	Bunny Therapy	Therapy Pigs
Duck Therapy	Goat Therapy	Therapy Lamb
Turtle/Tortoise Therapy	Pigmy Goat Therapy	Geese Therapy
Mini Pig Therapy	Canine Therapy	Equine Therapy

along with many others. What else could compare with such a menagerie? Well, if almost any activity that occupies time and gives enjoyment to human beings, therapists have likely made it into a therapy. For example,

Piano Therapy	Rock Climbing Therapy	Guitar Therapy
Running Therapy	Harp Therapy	Hiking Therapy
Cinema Therapy	Farming Therapy	Culinary Arts Therapy
Sailing Therapy	Painting Therapy	Gardening Therapy
Wire-sculpting Therapy	Punching-bag Therapy	Hockey Therapy
Pet Massage Therapy	Golf Therapy	Ballet Therapy

and hundreds—yes, hundreds—of others. All of these appear on The Big List. Their relevance here is that they add energy to the necessity of examining the humanity of therapists

With added analysis later, this discussion concludes that multiple orientations to psychotherapy make a statement of clinical adventurism. The number of aberrant therapies gives substantial, detailed, and comprehensive evidence that psychotherapy lives precariously with extraordinary jeopardy, now and into the foreseeable future. This view stands with many others who share it. As one of many examples, Nuttgens (2023, p. 29) says, "The proliferation of therapeutic models, with their untold numbers of purportedly unique interventions, serves as a source of division, confusion, and retrogression for the field of psychotherapy." For now, much, if not most, of the jeopardy is likely an expression of clinical adventurism that manifests itself in tens of thousands of practicing therapists who make up stuff that they call "therapy."

Based on numbers alone, the rationale for the analysis of "S" is clear and compelling, along with being urgent. Such an analysis likely holds interest for various constituent groups, such as client legislators, licensing boards, juries, insurance companies, attorneys, and others. If based on nothing else, such interest comes from the numbers. So far, the category of "S" contains 4,285 approaches to therapy. With 38,373 treatment orientations gathered, the complete list should not be duplicated for inclusion in this book because the list alone would occupy almost a thousand pages. In lieu of the complete list, a representative sample of approaches that begin with "S" can be presented and analyzed.

Many approaches to therapy that begin with the letter "S" include familiar words. However, quite separate from their familiarity, the words are important because they hold implications for the current condition of therapy as well as its future condition. Thus, while a recitation of the facts may be interesting, they may also evoke a variety of thoughts and feelings. Regardless of reactions to them, the facts should be stated before an attempt to draw meaning and conclusions about the condition of therapy as well as on a list of approaches that begin with the letter "S."

Among the 4285 approaches to therapy that begin with the letter, "S," a list of the most common ones appear in Table 4.1: The Most Common Words among Approaches to Therapy that Begin with the Letter "S." The table also includes the number of these approaches that appear elsewhere on The Big List.

While a discussion of its meaning comes later, the "S" words that relate to "Spirit" exceed any other word by far, as the numbers clearly show. The almost inevitable question is this one: "Does the frequency of the appearance of treatment orientation related to "Spirit" have broad implications for the current condition of therapy?" As this discussion evolves, observations about this will be offered. For now, the numbers in Table 4.1 may astonish those who see such numbers for the first time. As a personal note, I continue to be astonished by these numbers, although I have been gathering treatment orientations for several years.

As noted, the item that appears most frequently among "S" therapies includes various forms of the word "Spirit." For comparison, some of the common and numerous therapies that appear elsewhere in The Big List may help to establish a larger view of the context in which the "S" approaches may be placed. Table 4.2 includes some of the Most Frequently Used Words in Advertised Treatment Orientations, including only those with more than 1,000 appearances on The Big List. The selection of only those with more than 1,000 appearances is entirely arbitrary. The selection could have included numerous others that appear many times on The Big List, including the Bible (486 times), Energy (981 times), Gestalt (203 times), Yoga (810 times), or Nature (366 times). Similar to the likely responses to Table 4.1, the responses to Table 4.2 may include shock, simple disbelief, or other understandable responses. Nevertheless, the numbers are what they are.

The analysis of "S" therapies and referencing The Big List implies the inevitable question, "Do these most frequently advertised approaches to psychotherapy constitute an operational definition of counseling and psychotherapy?" If they constitute a definition, what is it? Moreover, what does this extraordinary number of therapies say about the humanity of therapists? Responses to this question appear later in this chapter, generally characterizing these therapies as clinical adventurism.

As Table 4.1 indicates, a word may have associated words that add to the total number of related appearances on The Big List of treatment orientations. In trying to understand the current condition of psychotherapy, these associated words become significant. Some of these are briefly discussed below. Also, some of the titles for approaches to psychotherapy will not likely

Table 4.1: Most Frequently Used Words in Advertised Treatment Orientations: The Most Common Words among Approaches to Therapy That Begin with the Letter "S"

Letter "S"

Word	Number of Appearances in "S"	Number of Appearances Elsewhere on The Big List	Total
Support	97	188	285
Stress	94	171	265
Shaman	125	96	221
Structural	120	69	189
Sex	148	165	310
Social	159	211	370
Strength	163	104	267
System	221	522	743
Solution	271	435	706
Soul	260	191	451
Somatic	296	238	534
Self	306	305	611
Spirit	789	1063	1,852
Totals	3,049	3,758	6,807

Notes: Most of these words appear on the list in more than one form. For example, "Support" also appears as "Supportive." Similarly, "Spirit" also appears as "Spiritual," "Spirituality," and "Spiritually." Also, a small number of the advertised approaches to therapy include two of the words on the list above, such as "Structural and Solution-focused Model." Noteworthy, among the advertised "S" approaches to therapy located so far, 2,524, including various forms of "Shamanism," "Soul," and "Spirit," refer to religion-related approaches.

receive attention in this book or elsewhere, but cumulatively constitute a very large number of approaches. For example, selected from those that begin with the letter, "S," The Big List includes ones that seldom appear in advertising by therapists, such as Sacred Drumming Circle, Sai Shakti Healing, Salt Cave Therapy, Salvation Divine Therapy, Sanctuary Counseling,

Table 4.2: Most Frequently Use Words in Advertised Treatment Orientations

Word/Orientation	Number of Appearances
Body	1,192
Christ/Christian	1,309
Coaching	1,214
Cognitive Behavioral/CBT-related	1,488
Integrative	1,508
Life	1,089
Mindful	1,084
Relations/Relational/Relationship	1,155
Trauma	1,168
Total	

Notes: When these items alone are tallied, the number of presumed clinical approaches to therapy comes to 11,208, keeping in focus that there may be a small number of overlapping approaches.

The titles of Christian-related approaches is much larger than the numbers in this table, when they include others, such as "Biblical," "Divine," "Lord," "Sacred," "LDS," and "Scriptural." When various specifically Christian approaches are tallies, they come to a total of 3,809. If the websites of therapists were further examined, this number would surely rise.

Santosha Psychotherapy, Sat Nam Rasayan Healing, Satvic Living, Scientific Wisdom, and Secret Garden Healing. These 10 somewhat rarely advertised approaches represent a large but unknown number of therapists. If each of these approaches to therapy is practiced by, say, only 10 therapists, the cumulative number of therapists who offer them would be 100.

If any frequently used word in the psychotherapy world is attached to an approach to therapy, an extraordinary variety of approaches can be located. Some of those located will contradict or at least appear to contradict some of the others. Whether the word is person, psychoanalysis, Gestalt, Christian, or hundreds of others, it has likely been attached to an extraordinary number and variety of approaches to therapy. To illustrate this phenomenon, 20 clinical approaches that include the word "Support" were selected from those that begin with the letter "S" from a total of 97.

Soul Support Counseling
SPACE (Supportive Parenting for Anxious Childhood Emotions)
Spirit-Supported Faith-Based Counseling Marriage & Family Therapy
Spiritual Golden Angel Healing Support
Spirituality Enrichments and Support
Sport-fitness support
Support for Extraordinary Experience (SEE)
Support Living & OT Orientation
Supportive Christian Counseling
Supportive Expressive Psychotherapy
Supportive Healing Arts
Supportive Milieu Therapy
Supportive Touch Work/Massage
Supportive Touch-Yoga Therapy
Supportive Vegan Therapy
Supportive Yoga
Supportive-cognitive-behavioral
Supportive solutions-focused methods
Supportive-mindfulness-based
Supportive Eclectic Psychotherapy
Supportive/Client-Centered Approach
Supportive/Educative Counseling

If the concept of support can be attached to this variety of approaches to therapy, what is the meaning of the concept? In what specific ways may the concept of support or supportive therapy be appropriately attached to all of these approaches and maintained as a viable clinical concept? As this discussion proceeds, the randomness of a virtually limitless variety of such attachments will become obvious and disturbing.

To Sing or Swim?

"I'm really into soccer. Can I use soccer in therapy?" This question came from an individual who sought postdegree clinical supervision. He had located a clinical position in a private practice that included several licensed therapists. Dialogue with the individual indicated that he had no clinically relevant training that incorporated soccer or other similar activities. Therefore, the response from the prospective clinical supervisor was "no." The prospective clinical supervisor also stated that he had no soccer training and lacked qualifications to oversee the appropriate integration of soccer into therapy. The clinical supervisor observed that the prospective clinical supervisee wished to practice soccer as therapy because, as he said, "I'm really into soccer." Apparently, the prospective supervisee assumed that his interest in soccer qualified him to practice "soccer arts" as therapy. Can this individual's assumption be generalized to other mental healthcare providers?

Martin (2020) observed that many therapists' preferred activities became clinical practices because the therapists had an interest in them, but often lacked clinical understanding of using them and indicated no training that would qualify them for such practices. The list below is merely a partial one, limited to activities that begin with the letter "S." The list illustrates how therapists convert their personal interests into clinical activities, often having no clinical or evidentiary basis for such a conversion.

This short list of 24 activities represents hundreds of activities that licensed mental healthcare providers advertise as their approach to treatment. If there are twenty-six (24) that begin with "S," how many more may there be? If the list of activities was complete—if it could ever be complete—it would include hundreds of others, such as fly fishing, piano, guitar, hiking, running, climbing, riding, pottery, baking, drawing, culinary arts, and painting therapies. The inevitable question is, "Are these activities really 'therapy' or 'therapeutic?'" Of course, other questions almost inevitably arise. How are these approaches to therapy selected? More than therapy, do these approaches to therapy express the personal interests of those who advertise them? Who or what endorses these therapies? Do these therapies have any specific clinical training or relevant evidence to support them? Would they be approved by insurance claims reviewers? Would they be endorsed by professionally accountable therapists who seek to fulfill the normative mandates of professional ethics with regard to selecting and implementing treatment approaches? If a client were injured while receiving, say, Sailing Therapy, Swimming Therapy, or Running Therapy, and the client sued for damages, would a jury or a judge endorse these therapies? Would licensing boards that issue licenses for mental healthcare providers endorse these therapies? By what criteria would an ethics panel approve of these approaches, if such approval could be given?

As Table 4.4: "S" Related Yoga Therapies indicates, therapists advertise numerous therapies that involve physical movement activities. Among the "S" related therapies, there are likely more yoga therapies than the ones listed

Table 4.3: List of Activity-Oriented Approaches to Counseling and Psychotherapy That Begin with the Letter "S."

Sewing Therapy	Sailing Therapy (Adventure Therapy)
SAX [Saxophone] Therapy	SCUBA Skills for Eco-Therapy
Sculpture Therapy	Seed Digging Therapy
Shakuhachi Flute playing	Shaolin Kung Fu QiGong Therapy
Shiatsu/Martial Arts	Shooting Therapy
Shutter Therapy [Photography]	Singing Therapy
Skateboarding Therapy	Ski Therapy
Soccer Therapy	Social Presencing Theater
Scrapbook Therapy	Scripture Reading
Songwriting and Lyric Analysis	SoulCycle Barre or Pilates
Spiritual Ecstatic Dance	Surf Therapy
Surfing Therapy	Swimming Therapy

Table 4.4: "S"-Related Yoga Therapies

Satori Yoga	Schoolhouse Yoga
Self-Esteem Yoga	Simple Yoga Asanas
Slow Vinyasa Flow Yoga	Somatic Yoga Therapy
Spiritual Healing and Yoga	Street Yoga
Street Yoga-Trauma Informed	Sundara Yoga
Svaroopa Yoga	Sivananda Yoga

below, because some of them do not specifically include the word "yoga," such as Siddha, Sivananda, and Strala. Quite apart from "S"-related yoga therapies, The Big List includes more than 100 additional yoga approaches to therapy.

Limited only to those that begin with the letter "S," what is the possible meaning of such a list of approaches to therapy? Is yoga, particularly in all of its forms, an approach to therapy that licensed mental health care providers should offer? How are such approaches screened into practice when they are appropriate, or how are they screened out of practice when they are inappropriate? More broadly, whether the focus of attention is a form of yoga or one of the other activities, such as Sax Therapy, SCUBA, Shooting Therapy, Skateboarding Therapy, or any of the other activity-based approaches to therapy, how do these "therapies" get screened into or out of therapy? Framed in at least one more way, recognizing that all activity-based therapies are not "created equal," in a legal contest such as a civil lawsuit, how may a therapist defend the practice of these activity-based therapies?

A Solution in Search

No doubt, Solution-focused Therapy (SFT), along with some of its clinical descendants, has grown beyond the early formulations of it by Steve de Shazer (1940-2005) and Insoo Kim Berg (1934-2007) and extended formulations of it by Bill O'Hanlon, Yvonne Dolan, and others. They nurtured SFT and, seeing it mature, would likely see its development and rising influence as a confirmation of their discipline, creativity, and commitment to clinical excellence. One of the virtually ubiquitous spin offs of SFT is Solution Focused Brief Therapy or SFBT, for example.

However, as surely as the developers of SFT would likely find satisfaction in its rising influence, they would also likely feel disappointment in the multiple ways that others have co-opted their work and invented approaches to therapy that they would not recognize and would not accept. Just as many widely adopted approaches to therapy have been paired with approaches that render the associated therapies self-contradictory, some of the approaches with which SFT has been paired contradict, if not violate, SFT. While many more could be listed, Table 4.5: Descendants of SFT from "S" Words in Their Titles, only thirty (30) have been included here. They are advertised by practicing and duly credentialed therapists.

All of the approaches listed Table 4.5 begin with "solution-focused." Another 40 or more titles could be listed that include the words "solution-focused." The need for another listing hardly justifies another 40 or more solution-focused related therapies. However, some of the unusual pairings of solution-focused therapy with other approaches should be listed, only to illustrate the extraordinary variety of them. Thus, Table 4.6: Additional Solution-Focused

Approaches to Therapy includes another twenty (10) titles of advertised and somewhat unusual approaches to therapy. Each one combines with at least one other approach. Of course, the discussion of would be incomplete without a reference to "SOULution-Focused Therapy" and "Soulutions Counseling."

At the end of the discussion about SFT, a necessary question is "So, what?" The given facts do not necessarily point to a specific conclusion. However, the facts raise questions, at least, if not prescribe conclusions. The most basic question is, "What is Solution-Focused Therapy, if it can be paired with virtually any and every other kind of psychotherapy, including activities and ideologies that are not clinical?" After all, among the pairings Tables 4.5 and 4.6, SFT has been paired with Cognitive Therapy, Cognitive Behavior Therapy, Psychodynamic Therapy, Psychoanalytic Therapy, Bible-based Therapy, and

Table 4.5: Descendants of Solution-focused Therapy from "S" Words in Their Titles

Solution-focused Approaches
Solution Focused and Relational Cultural Theory Perspective
Solution Focused Approach (DBT)
Solution Focused Biblical Marriage Coaching
Solution Focused Brief Cognitive Behavioral Therapy
Solution Focused Christian Based Therapy
Solution Focused Energy
Solution Focused Experiential Framework
Solution Focused Family Systems/ACT/DBT
Solution Focused Gestalt
Solution Focused Mentoring and Coaching
Solution Focused Narrative Therapy
Solution focused Orientation Infused with Expressive Art Therapies
Solution Focused Person Centered Therapy
Solution Focused Psychodynamic Therapy
Solution Focused Sex Therapy
Solution Focused Spirituality
Solution Focused-Behavioral-Holistic Therapy
Solution Focused-Client Centered-Relational-Feminist Approach

(Continued)

Table 4.5: (Continued)

Solution Focused-Existential-Play Therapy
Solution focused Multidimensional Integrative
Solution-focused and Task-centered Therapy
Solution-focused Hypnotherapy
Solution-Focused Mindset Therapy
Solution-focused No-Nonsense Strategies
Solution-Focused Philosophy
Solution-focused Sex Addiction Therapy
Solution-focused Therapy Systemic View
Solution-Focused Transpersonal Care
Solution-Focused Ground-Based/Team Approach
Solution-focused Wilderness/Nature Therapy

Table 4.6: Additional Solution Focused Approaches to Therapy

Directive and Solution-Focused
Eclectic Solution-Focused Brief Therapy
Egalitarian Solution Focused Therapy
Empowerment-based, Solution-focused Ecological Model
Energetic Solution-Focused Therapy
Ericksonian/Brief Solution Oriented Approaches
Future-oriented and solution-focused Therapy
Practical Biblical Solution Focused
Psychoanalytic/Solution-Focused Work
Scripturally Based Solution-Focused Therapy

Transpersonal Therapy, to name only six. If SFT may be paired with all of these approaches to therapy and others, is it still SFT? If it can no longer be reasonably regarded as SFT because of these awkward, if not contradictory pairings, what is it? Whatever it is, an individual therapist may attach it to anything that their impulses desire, including Evolutionary Spirituality or Prayer Therapy.

Expanding the scope of questioning, what may be the larger implications of pairing one approach to therapy with another approach to therapy, when the two approaches appear to have little to recommend such a pairing, and when each one appears to contradict the other one? Do these somewhat random and prolific pairings indicate that practicing therapists lack a sufficient professional awareness of the approaches that they advertise? Do these pairings indicate a lack of professional accountability? Do these pairings indicate a degree of highly individualized thinking about the practice of therapy that appropriate accountability to clients and to the profession to which they belong is not possible? And, in the end, do these pairings indicate an escape from ethics?

"S" Words That Bellow, "Extinction, Please!"

As proposed earlier, the rationale for developing an analysis of "S" aims for understanding and actions that lie beyond merely lamenting the condition of therapy. And, as noted earlier, the accrued list of "S" therapies contains 4,285 approaches to psychotherapy. No doubt, many of the "S" treatment approaches cause little concern. Even if some therapists do not adopt some of the approaches, they would likely acknowledge that the approaches are acceptable ones, such as SFT, Sand Tray Therapy, Satir Family Systems, Schema-Focused Therapy, Secular Humanistic Therapy, Self-Psychology, and Sensate Focus Therapy.

However, the list of "S" approaches to therapy contains others that betray the best interests of the clients for whom therapy exists and the profession to which therapists belong. Such a list may be a tedious one to study, but if taken seriously, likely raises consciousness of the considerable challenges and threats to clients and the profession of therapy. Table 4.7: Unusual Approaches to Therapy from "S" List of Approaches makes clear that the challenges and threats are real and pervasive. Excerpted from the list of 4,285, the list of unusual approaches below contains only 100 approaches to therapy. All of them were harvested from the websites of practicing therapists.

This list of 100 approaches to psychotherapy should not be taken as a judgment about the importance of any of them to the individuals who believe in them. Any of these individuals may select any of these approaches to endorse and to practice. However, insofar as they advertise and practice them as licensed mental healthcare professionals, their judgment, ethics, and understanding of therapy should be questioned. Specifically, for example, an individual may choose to believe in Star Astronumerology but should not be allowed to practice it as a licensed mental healthcare provider or one

Table 4.7: Unusual Approaches to Therapy from the "S" List of Approaches

Sacral Bars	Sacred Acoustics
Sacred Activations Practice	Sacred Card Readings
Sacred Dance	Sacred Geometry
Sacred Heart Alchemy	Sacred Plants and Nature
Sai Shakti Healing	Salt (or Halo) Therapy
Salve Regina Expressive Arts for Healing	Samadhi Therapy
Santosha Psychotherapy	Sat Nam Rasayan Healing
Satvic Living	Scale-walking
Scalp Therapy	Scent Free Coaching
Scientific Wisdom (Ancient and Modern)	Scientology
Screaming	Scripturally-Rooted Therapy
Secret Garden Reiki Distant Healing	Seeing Stars
Seemorg Matrix Work	Seichem Egyptian Energy Healing
Senescent Sandrift Counseling	Seon (Zen) Buddhism
Shadow Alchemy	Shake Your Soul
Shakti Rising Model	Shalem Spiritual Formation
Shamanic and Ancestral Journeying	Shamanic Astrology & Meditation
Shamanic Healing (Mesa Carrier, Peruvian Inkan)	Shambhala/Tibetan Vajrayana Buddhist
Shaolin Temple Energy Healing	Shifaa Soul Counseling
Shinrin-Yoku walks (a.k.a. "forest bathing")	Shiome Therapy
Shiva Samhita	Singing Bowls/Coconut/Milk/Honey/CBT
Singing of Icaros	Skydancing Tantra
Slate Therapy	Slender Stoic Behavioral Coaching
Smileology	Solar Return Reporting
Somatic Archaeology	Somatic Astro Cartography
Somatic Tuning Method/Using Tuning Forks	Somota Respiratory Integration (SRI)
Soul Biofield Tuning	Soul Card Creation

(*Continued*)

Table 4.7: (Continued)

Soul Collage (Split Eye Reading/Lineage Work)	Soul Entrainment Therapy
Soul Journeys for Akashic Studies	Soul Retrieval & Past Life Regression
Soul Surfing	Soul Work—Christ-centered
Soul Writing	Soul-focused Feng Shui
Soulshine Astrology	Seven Visions Tranformaton
Sound Foundation in the Word of God	Sound Mnemonics and Crystal Healing
South American Toltec Shamanic Traditions	Spartan SGX Coaching/Sports Contexted
Spinal Release Technique	Spirit 2 Spirit-CTT
Spirit Junkie Masterclass	Spirit Releasement and UFO/ET encounters
Spiritual Ascension Therapy (SAT)	Spiritual Golden Angel Healing Support
Spiritual Herbalism	Spiritual Medium/Clairvoyant
Spiritual Mentoring (Order of Melchizedek)	Spiritual Sex Therapy
Spiritual Stargates	Spiritual Treatment/Theophostic Prayer
Spiritual Warfare Preparation	Spiritual Warriorship Therapy
Spiritually Fluent Psychotherapy	Splankna: EMDR TFT NET ACT RRCMT
Sri Kaleshwar Follower/Approach	Star Astronumerology
Stardreaming	Stoic Philosophical Orientation Therapy
Stress-relieving Aquamassage	Sufi Mysticism
Sundara Yoga	Superhero Therapy
Surrender Method of Craniosacral Therapy	Swami Omkarananda Model
Sweatlodge Ceremonies	Swedish Massage
Sychronizes Soul	Synastry
Systemic Trance	Syzygy Therapy/Fandom Therapy

who poses as a mental healthcare provider, licensed or not. To permit such approaches to continue beckons a tragic reckoning and likely demise of therapy. And, sadly, inexcusably so.

Clinical Adventurism

Those who read every word of this chapter may need an apology. The lists of approaches to therapy likely became tedious for them. If this is the case, I apologize. Gathering them was extraordinarily tedious, too. Among readers for whom the lists are tedious, they are encouraged to look over the horizon of momentary tedium and try to foresee the future to which the items on the lists are taking you and your profession.

Based on the analysis of "S," what conclusions may be drawn? First, before reading the conclusions posted here, I encourage readers to consider their own personal conclusions. When you read that "Sufi Mysticism" is an approach to therapy, what do you think about this? When you read that "Soul Entrainment" is an approach to therapy, what do you think about this? When you read that "solution-focused" has been an adjective for numerous other, often incompatible, approaches to therapy, what do you think about this? And when you read that Sailing, Sewing, Shooting, Skateboarding, Surfing, Seed Digging, or Song Writing and Lyric Analysis are advertised as approaches to therapy, what do you think about this? Those who advertise these approaches are your colleagues.

Many "S" therapies include dubious, if not apparently incompatible, combinations of therapies. For example, The Big List includes 278 Buddhist-related approaches to therapy. Omitting many approaches that do not begin with "S," such as Carl Jung and Mahayana Buddhism, Buddha-Christ Healing, and Buddhist and Sufi Integrated, and limiting the list to only ten approaches that begin with "S," the following ones likely evoke questions about the clinical judgment of those who practice such approaches.

Samatha Samadhi (Buddhism)

Self Compassion-Buddhist Framework

Self-Healing and Buddhist

Seon (Zen) Buddhism

Shamanism and Buddhist Psychology

Soto Zen Buddhist

Spiritual Buddhist Meditations

Spiritual Counseling (Christian and Buddhist)

Spiritually Focused Traditions (Advaita and Buddhism)

Shambhala and Tibetan Vajrayana Buddhist Traditions,

However, whether the religious orientation is Buddhist, Christian, or something else, it has very likely been linked and blended with almost every conceivable approach to therapy. Among thousands of such approaches, the following ones illustrate this phenomenon. For example, "Christian" approaches to therapy may be Christian Freudian Psychoanalysis, Christian Brain Assessments, Christian Existential Therapy, Charismatic Christian Counseling, Christian Rogerian Therapy, Christian Behavioral Therapy, Christian Worship Therapy, Christian Cognitive Behavioral Therapy, or hundreds of others.

All of these and others have inherent connections with something "Christian" and usually a specific theological and religious point of view, including Baptist Counseling, Methodist Counseling, Mormon Therapy, Catholic Counseling, Bible-based Therapy, Prayer Therapy, and so on. More explicitly, theological views become therapies, based only on the individual therapist's wish to have such a therapy. However, more than their obvious linkages with something "Christian," the necessary question is whether these presumed approaches to therapy are relevant to a professionally accountable delivery of therapy.

Taken together and regardless of the sincerity of those who practice them, the "S" therapies appear to be mostly non-clinical and possibly harmful self-indulgences. Tens of thousands of individual therapists presume to advertise these approaches and enact them as therapy and, through their enactments, ensure that the future of therapy is a dystopian one. They confirm the view, "I want to do what I want to do and, because I want to do it, I am right to do it as therapy." Insofar as they view themselves and therapy this way, they put their clients at risk. They put their profession at risk. At least, the risk is that their profession will continue to lose its competence, credibility, integrity, and relevance. Collectively, they perpetuate the largest category of unethical behavior among therapists by practicing approaches to therapy that satisfy only their impulse to practice such approaches.

This is clinical adventurism.

In mental health care, clinical adventurism can be defined as the expression of highly individualized ways of thinking about and implementing therapy, regardless of the consequences for the therapist, the profession, or clients. It is an abrogation of normative and minimal professional standards. As such, it has little or no basis in clinical reasoning—or even adult reasoning—concern about client welfare, the good of the profession of which these therapists are members, and, generally, the consequences of their actions. This is a way to say that clinical adventurism becomes an expression of ways through which therapists demonstrate their readiness to put their profession and their clients at risk, by giving priority to their personal interests. Possibly, their positive interest in their clients feels right for them, but their identified approaches to therapy appear to fall seriously below minimal professional standards. Their approaches waste the time and money of their clients or other payors, as welll as promise far more than these therapists can deliver. By promising so much more than they deliver, they compromise their integrity, set up potential harm to their clients, erode the welfare of their profession, and inevitably increase skepticism about their profession and resistance to it.

Insofar as clinical adventurism widely displays itself in the large community of mental healthcare professionals, it has an impact. If its impact were negligible, it could be ignored and, maybe, forgotten. At this time, clinical adventurism is neither negligible nor forgettable. The precise number of those who exhibit it is not known or knowable. No doubt, though, it involves tens of thousands of participants. Some studies, such as those reported by Martin (2020, pp. 48–84), suggest that the percentage of them among all duly credentialed providers is likely between 20% and 30%, because of offering aberrant approaches to therapy. However, when evidence about the decline of competence among mental health care providers is reported (e.g., Goldberg et al., 2016; Spengler & Pilipis, 2015), it appears to be more than half are not competent. In addition, among other factors that may increase the percentage from a low of 20–30 percent, the evidence from reports (e.g.,Walfish et al., 2012; Cuijpers et al., 2010; Knapp et al., 2024; Nuttgens, 2023; Ronnestad & Skovholt, 2013) suggests that clinical adventurism may pose a threat to professionalism from a majority of practicing therapists, due to considerable over-estimation of their abilities and effectiveness.

No other profession permits adventurism. Structural engineers do not construct skyscrapers on a bed of flowers, no matter how much they love flowers. Urologists do not implant a layer of crunchy peanut butter around an inflamed prostate, no matter how much they love crunchy peanut butter. Accountants do not advise their tax-owing clients that they can submit one miniature pig figurine for every thousand dollars they owe in taxes, no matter how much they love miniature pig figurines. In contrast, analogous approaches to therapy are quite common, as the analysis of "S" approaches indicates.

The consequences of clinical adventurism may be summarized in the form of several conclusions.

Psychotherapy is largely out of control, permitting numerous, inappropriate, unethical practices, including the massive proliferation of aberrant approaches to counseling and therapy.

Therapists have no identifiable way of bringing widely approved clinical orientations into clinical practice and no way to dispose of inappropriate clinical orientations.

Standards of ethics lack the practical applicability that makes them relevant to the preponderant volume of clinical judgments and actions, depending almost entirely on selected disclosures made by therapists themselves or the attorneys who pursue them through legal actions.

The utilization of aberrant approaches to therapy probably constitutes—by far—the largest category of unethical behavior among therapists.

Visible, useful, and effective regulation of therapy is far too distant from clinical practice. Exaggerated individualism, closely accompanied by personal and institutional ideologies, has overcome professional accountability.

Numerous therapists make claims that cannot be supported by agreed-upon evidence, good clinical judgment, or professional ethics. With increasing clarity and certainty, therapists do not demonstrate that they may be uncertain about how and whether to implement evidence-based approaches in their professional services. They actively deny and/or oppose evidence. If therapists practice Seichem Egyptian Energy Healing, Syzygy Therapy/Fandom Therapy, or any of thousands of other approaches, they oppose evidence.

Development of professional accountability appears to have broken down at several critical stages, including professional preparation programs, clinical supervision, continuing education, and independent clinical practice.

Clinical adventurists compromise the work and reputation of conscientious, competent counselors and therapists.

Clinical adventurists have the impact of institutionalizing and perpetuating unethical conduct. For example, if those who prefer to practice Past Life Soul Retrieval and other past life therapies can do so with no apparent constraints, they will have institutionalized such practices.

Those who advertise and deliver aberrant and often harmful approaches to therapy should be monitored and, in the absence of changing their approaches, excluded from clinical practice. However, given the astonishing volume of aberrant approaches that currently occupy considerable space and visibility in the professional community, those who pay no attention to them may be tacitly approving of the harm to clients and to their profession

> that practitioners of these approaches perpetrate. Such tacit approval comes from leaders of professional associations at every level of leadership, legislators, peers whose work is conspicuously compromised, credentialing agencies, licensing boards, and others.

Exacerbating the impact of these observations, psychotherapy mostly lacks a professional community and identity, neutralizing its potential for self-monitoring and correction. The lack of minimal cohesion comes from pronounced disorganization, individual self-interestedness, and the ongoing rise in unethical behavior. The codes of ethics of the American Counseling Association, American Psychological Association, and the National Association of Social Workers, and at least forty-two other codes of ethics (Martin & Turner, 2020, pp. 15–16) have virtually no monitoring or enforcement mechanisms, given the fact that the preponderant majority of therapists do not belong to professional associations. For example, apparently relying on large numbers of new members each year to sustain its numbers, the American Psychological Association (2023) reports that its "renewal rate for 2023 is 80%," similar to most years. The Bureau of Labor Statistics (2025) says that there are more than 750,000 social workers, but only 120,000 are members of the National Association of Social Workers (Wikipedia, 2024). In this context, including the data from the analysis of treatment orientations that begin with "S," does psychotherapy have viability over the long term without major reforms?

This chapter has been an analysis of treatment orientations that begin with the letter "S." If a similar analysis came from an examination of any other letter from "A" to "Z," it would encompass numerous treatment orientations, such as Acutonics and Zapoteca Healing Practices. In other words, the inclusion of a much larger body of evidence would not change the conclusions presented here. More than a worried, hand-wringing exercise, this analysis is a loud shout that carries a message: mental health care and the clients who receive services from caregivers deserve and should expect clinically relevant and professionally accountable services that they are not now receiving. With evidence, determination, organization, and active and persistent advocacy, mental health care can be and must be better than it is now.

This discussion confirms that those who make up stuff and those who blend therapy with approaches that are inherently hostile to therapy are blunting, if not bludgeoning, the profession of which they are members. Their presumed clinical approaches to therapy include more titles and practices than imagination alone could possibly create. The number and inappropriateness of thousands of approaches to therapy appear to be almost totally ignored by the peers of those whose licenses they share and the leaders of professional associations and preparation programs. However, much like physicians who ignored infection control initiatives for decades [Refer to the Introduction.], all of these individuals should consider interventions that may save their profession or, alternatively, consider that the profession of which they are members may not continue to exist as a viable profession.

Toward offering encouragement for others to consider their level of commitment to allowing their/our profession to become further imperiled, the following questions may be useful. At least, the questions may solicit and facilitate discussions.

> If I am an active member of a healthcare profession in which I cannot recognize thousands of the treatments and treatment approaches that my peers advertise, am I really a member of the profession?
>
> If I confidently and reasonably conclude that a very large number of these treatments are unethical, should I be a member of the profession?
>
> Is my profession really a profession?
>
> If, for good professional reasons, I reject virtually countless approaches to therapy, what can I do to protect myself and my profession?

These are truly formidable questions. Regardless of the angst that these questions may evoke, they acknowledge serious concerns about the welfare of the profession and the clients who are served by it.

Mental health care holds an unspeakably large potential for healing and hope. This book is an attempt to advance the cause of this potential. To achieve the immense potential of mental health care, therapists must energetically address the problems that currently beset it.

Clinical Adventurism and the Humanity of Therapists

A general statement about the humanity of clinical adventurists should be made because their adventurism, like many awkward or deficient behaviors, bespeaks the realities of being human. Such a statement should reflect the features of humanity that were introduced in Chapter 1. It offers a comment on clinical adventurism, as it may be viewed through an understanding of these features. In the context of the analysis of treatment orientations that begin with "S," the question of what these treatment orientations may say about the humanity of those who practice them should be answered, at least partially.

Common assets and vulnerabilities of being human. Those who practice many of the aberrant approaches to therapy appear to mask their assets and vulnerabilities insofar as they assert certainty about their respective therapies that have neither evidentiary support, clinical rationales, nor experiential validity. Such approaches include Standard Chakra Patterning, Soul Work—Christ-Centered, and Soul-focused Feng Shui. If their treatment approaches are not credible for their professional community, how credible are these therapists to themselves? A reasonable speculation is that their strong commitments to their respective approaches to therapy immunize their thinking from relevant facts, clinical efficacy, professional accountability, and their felt vulnerabilities.

Humanity is a community. Therapists who practice approaches to therapy that pose the probability of harm to the professional community appear to reject community as a feature of their humanity and their profession. Worse, they pose significant risks to their clients. Is the selection of approaches to therapy a means by which those who choose them have determined that they will alienate the professionally accountable community of mental health care providers? What may they expect from the larger community when they select approaches such as Stardreaming, Sound Biblical Theological Principles, Sufi Healing Circle, or Spiritual Treatment/Theophostic Prayer?

Inherent in the community is communication. If only, say, two or three therapists practice Scripture-based-Christian Healing, South American Toltec Shamanic Principles, Spirit-oriented Paganism, or another bizarre approach to therapy, is this a de facto statement about their interest in and capacity for healthy communication with others? Clearly, the answer to this question is at best "Maybe" and more accurately "No." Moreover, adding to the bizarre nature of their therapies, their presumed clinical practice has no clinically credible basis for its implementation. As such, their failure to engage with the professional community around questions about their approaches to therapy signals another dimension of their incapacity to communicate. More specifically, if therapists practice, for example, South American Toltec Shamanic Principles, they bear the burden of explaining the meanings of "South American," "Toltec," "Shamanic," and "Principles" to individuals whose cultural orientation and normative language very likely depart from the cultural orientation and normative language from which these terms emerge. In other words, why would minimally competent therapists practice such an approach and expect their clients to understand it?

Self-awareness characterizes humanity. The best of therapists struggle with self-awareness, because it is never complete, let alone perfectly integrated into personal and/or professional functioning. Although the professional obligation to pursue self-awareness has been a long-standing and historic necessity among practicing therapists, those who offer aberrant therapies appear to be shouting about their profound lack of self-awareness. To frame this idea in a specific way, would a minimally self-aware, professionally accountable therapist offer Synastry Forecasting, Sufi Mysticism, or Starseeds Astrology as an approach to therapy? Probably, they would not. Likewise, the fact that these approaches join numerous other aberrant approaches to therapy challenges the self-awareness and integrity of all other practicing therapists, insofar as such approaches encroach on their profession and call its viability and integrity into serious question.

Humanity is multiple forms of differences. Delivered appropriately, therapy affirms numerous differences among clients, therapists, and the larger society of which they are members. Such an affirmation stands solidly on values that not only inhere in competent clinical work but also those that hold potential for contributing to a positive, life-enhancing society. Do some treatment models unnecessarily direct clients and others away from living in such a society, including Star Astronumerology, Salvation Divine Therapy, and the Soteria Treatment Model?

Humanity is possessed by needs. Obviously, needs energize behavior. When individuals feel hunger, their need for food energizes food-getting behaviors. When certain approaches to therapy, such as Sacred Path Cards, Sai Shakti Healing, or Sailing Therapy, are selected, do they reflect the needs of those who select them? Apart from their need to be unique, somehow especially important, and defiant of normative clinical standards, what could their possible needs be?

Humanity embodies the reality of change and the necessity of adaptability. Many aberrant approaches to therapy appear to epitomize rigidity, not adaptability. Approaches such as Spiritual Biblical Counseling, Sacred Heart Alchemy, Spiritual Guidance/Biblical World View, Spiritual Biblical Framework, or Soulshine Astrology appear to have much more in common with firmly and rigidly held ideologies than professional accountability. As such, they likely inhibit change toward health.

Humanity enacts the rise and fall of the urgency of maintaining life. Sobbing, but notably unrepentant, the man confesses that he has had more sexual partners than he can count. He reports that he discovered the excitement and pleasure of sexual partnering when he was a pubescent child and that he has not been able to stop his aggressive pursuit of partners. As an above-average man, he acknowledges his confusion from his relentless sexual urges. He is a high achiever whose intelligence, skills, and efforts have made him a very wealthy individual. After numerous therapy sessions, including group and individual therapy, he begins to speak of his desperate need to connect with others while also speaking of his compulsive sexual pursuits as ways to "guarantee that it's not going to happen." He is correct. He desperately needs to connect with someone. His desperation erupts in urgently enacted behaviors. What a paradox. "I need what I will work hard to avoid getting. My chronic sense of urgency will perpetually betray my ability to have a life worth living." This is the paradox of selecting approaches to therapy that are not likely to effectuate clinically relevant and needed changes for clients. If these approaches do not deny the potential of maintaining life—healthy life—they muffle or neutralize such potential.

Human individuals need a reason to want to live. When therapists enact Sacred Geometry Practice, Sacred Gongs, Sacred Dance, Sacred Acoustics, Sacred Activations Practice, Sacred Card Readings, Sacred Circle of Healing, an observer of their enactments may reasonably conclude that they have good reasons to live. Likewise, a professionally accountable mental healthcare provider may also conclude that their reasons for living are not clinically relevant.

Recognizing the humanity in one another necessitates ethics and law. The professional community of therapists must define what is ethical and legal for clinical practice. The community is not a police force, though. Thus, the burden for living within the appropriate boundaries of professional ethics and law should be borne by those who function as therapists. If anyone in the community intends to enact an approach to therapy, with emphasis on those approaches that are unusual, they have the burden of clarifying and being public about the ethical and legal propriety of their respective therapies. They should be able to make clear that Shamanic Astrology & Meditation, Spring Forest Qigong, Splankna (Christian) Methods, Soul-centered Psychoshamanic Approach, or Soul Entrainment Therapy comports with ethical and legal standards. They should be able to provide evidentiary support for their approach(es) so that everyone else, particularly clients who will receive their services, can present their clinically relevant needs and that their needs will receive clinically relevant responses. In the absence of normative professional standards, those who offer these approaches are likely engaging in unethical practices.

Any characterization of the humanity of the therapists who practice aberrant, clinically unworthy approaches should be carefully scrutinized. Allowing for the limitations that inhere in any such characterization, conclusions may, nevertheless, be stated. As a general characterization of the humanity of these therapists, they appear to carry the awkwardly naïve, needy, and excessive individualism that permits them to ignore and reject normative standards of professional accountability. Insofar as this characterization is correct, it reveals as much about the profession of which these individuals are members as it reveals about these individuals. The picture is one in which these individuals and the clients whom they serve have been betrayed by preparation programs, professional associations, licensing boards, and other related groups.

As a general statement, regardless of their particular title or type of license, mental healthcare providers continue to hold immense potential for equipping their clients to live improved lives. Regardless of their personal preferences and values that guide their lives outside or inside of providing therapy, client welfare—what the profession deems to be plausibly professional and good for clients' health and well-being—therapists maintain their focus on achieving this potential. At this time, this immense potential has been grossly compromised, and such compromise will likely be sustained without vigorous intervention by the mental healthcare community. The profession must orient itself toward achieving the good that has long motivated it. More personally, those who practice aberrant approaches to therapy that are named in this chapter betray their clients. They ensure that their clients' needs will not be met. Still, much more than a lament about the condition of therapy, this book is a call to action, based largely on the profession's individual and collective obligation to fulfill its promise to clients and its society. The welfare of clients and the immense potential of our profession mandate the necessity of action.

References

American Psychological Association. (2023). *APA state of membership.* https://connectguide.apa.org/apa-state-of-membership

Barlow, I., & Brown, R. J. (2020). A systematic review of measures of therapist competence in psychodynamic, interpersonal, and/or relational models. *Psychology and psychotherapy: Theory, Research, and Practice*, *93*, 408–427.

Bilgrave, D. P., & Deluty, R. H. (2002). Religious beliefs and political ideologies as predictors of psychotherapeutic orientations of clinical and counseling psychologists. *Psychotherapy: Theory/Research/Practice/Training, 39*(3), 245–260.

Bowes, S. M., Ammirati, R. J., Lilienfeld, S. O., Costello, T. H., & Basterfield, C. (2020). Cognitive biases, heuristics, and logical fallacies in clinical practice: A brief field guide for practicing clinicians and supervisors. *Professional Psychology: Research and Practice, 51*(5), 435–445. http://dx.doi.org/10.1037/pro0000309

Bureau of Labor Statistics. (2025). *Social workers.* https://www.google.com/url?client=internal-element-cse&cx=013738036195919377644:6ih0hfrgl50&q=https://www.bls.gov/ooh/community-and-social-service/social-workers.htm&sa=U&ved=2ahUKEwiwqq2i5_CKAxX8LlkFHfBHH3gQFnoECAoQAQ&usg=AOvVaw2iro8q8M4brjn_pW4Vg459

Campbell, T. H., & Kay, A. C. (2014). Solution aversion: On the relation between ideology and motivated disbelief. *Journal of Personality and Social Psychology, 107*, 809–824.

Cuijpers, P., van Straten, A., Bohlmeijer, E., Hollon, S. D., & Andersson, G. (2010). The effects of psychotherapy for adult depression are over-estimated: A meta-analysis of study quality and effect size. *Psychological Medicine, 40,* 211–223.

Cummings, N. A., & O'Donohue, W. T. (Eds.) (2011). *Understanding the behavioral healthcare crisis: The promise of integrated care and diagnostic reform.* Routledge.

Goldberg, S. B., Miller, S. D., Nielsen, S. L., Rousmaniere, T., Whipple, J., Hoyt, W. T., & Wampold, B. E. (2016). Do psychotherapists improve with time and experience? A longitudinal analysis of outcomes in a clinical setting. *Journal of Counseling Psychology, 63*(1), 1–11.

Hodson, G. (2014). Ideology matters (Too much): Does super-sizing ideology make ideology a risk to society? *Psychology Today*. https://www.psychologytoday.com/us/blog/without- prejudice/201511/ideology-matters-too-much

Holden, G., & Barker, K. (2018). Should social workers be engaged in these practices? *Journal of Evidence-Informed Social Work, 15*(1), 1–13.

Knapp, S. J., Gottlieb, M. C., & Handelsman, M. M. (2024). Avoiding failures when applying principle-based ethics to difficult ethical situations in psychotherapy. *Practice Innovations, 9*(3), 205–214.

Lilienfeld, S. (2014). *Evidence-based practice: The misunderstandings continue.* https://www.psychologytoday.com/us/blog/the-skeptical-psychologist/201401/evidence-based-practice-the-misunderstandings-continue

Lilienfeld, S. O., Ritschel, L. A., Lynn, S. J., Cautin, R. L., & Latzman, R. D. (2014). Why ineffective psychotherapies appear to work: A taxonomy of causes of spurious therapeutic effectiveness. *Perspectives on Psychological Science, 9,* 355–387.

Martin, F. A. (2020). *Therapy thieves: How to save mental health care from its providers.* Oxford University Press.

Martin, F. A. (2024). *The challenges of integrating religion and spirituality into psychotherapy: Integrity, competence, and cultural pluralism in clinical practice.* Routledge Publishing. (In press).

Martin, F. A., & Cannon, W. C. (2010, May). A profession in peril. *Counseling Today, 52*, 50–53.

Martin, F. A., & Turner, J. P. (2020). *Clinical supervision in the real world: A practical guide to ethics, legal Issues, and personal development.* Routledge.

Martin, F. A., Turner, J. P., & Fugate, J. (2023). Post-degree clinical supervision in Tennessee: A report about the advertising by supervision dyads. *Tennessee Counseling Association Journal* (in process.)

Michaels, T. M., & Datta, V. (2016). Evidence, not ideology, should guide the use of psychotherapy. *The British Journal of Psychiatry: The Journal of Mental Science, 209*(2), 171.

Noble, A., & Rizq, R. (2019). "It's led me astray": How cognitive behavioral therapists experience personal therapy in clinical practice. *Counseling and Psychotherapy Research, 20*, 29–38.

Nuttgens, S. (2023). Of interventive doppelgangers and other barriers to evidence-based practice in psychotherapy. *Journal of Psychotherapy Integration, 33*(1), 20–33. https://doi.org/10.1037/int0000279

Plante, T. G. (2022). Religion has a public relations problem: Integrating evidence-based thinking into clinical practice. *Spirituality in Clinical Practice*. Advance online publication. http://dx.doi.org/10.1037/scp0000292

Ronnestad, M. H., & Skovholt. (2013). *The developing practitioner: Growth and stagnation of therapists and counselors*. Routledge.

Singer, M., & Lalich, J. (1996). *"Crazy" therapies: What are they? Do they work?* Jossey-Bass.

Spengler, P. M., & Pilipis, L. A. (2015). A comprehensive meta-reanalysis of the robustness of the experience-accuracy effect in clinical judgment. *Journal of Counseling Psychology, 62*(3), 360–378. http://dx.doi.org/10.1037/cou0000065

Thyer, B. A., & Pignotti, M. G. (2015). *Science and pseudoscience in social work practice.* Springer.

Walfish, S., McAlister, B., O'Donnell, P., & Lambert, M. J. (2012). An investigation of self-assessment bias in mental health providers. *Psychological Reports, 110*(2), 639–644. https://doi.org/10.2466/02.07.17.PR0.110.2.639-644

Whitney, B. M. (2021). Ethical considerations for the study of potentially harmful or ineffective treatments. *Professional Psychology: Research and Practice, 52*(1), 12–20. https://doi.org/10.1037/pro0000341

Wikipedia. (2025). National association of social workers. https://en.wikipedia.org/wiki/National_Association_of_Social_Workers

Chapter 5
I Am Therapist
The Humanity of Encounter

This chapter is an attempt to answer a simple question. How does the humanity of a therapist appear in and influence clinical work? As simple as the question may appear, it may be the most difficult question to which therapists should have an answer. In this discussion, the answer is given in the form of an allegory. Specifically, it is given as a dialogue between two individuals, "Counselor" and "Curious Public." The term "Counselor" or "Therapist" is intended to be inclusive of all mental healthcare providers.

The Encounter

Counselor (Co): Hi, I'm Counselor. I'm glad you're here. What's your name?

Curious Public (CP): I'm Curious Public. It's so nice to meet you. Your name is Counselor? Odd. What does that mean? I mean, it's okay; it's just that I've never met someone with that name before.

Co: No problem. Thanks for asking. Well, it means that I am a Counselor. Just like you and your name, I come from a family. I come from a family of Counselors. That's who we are. That's who I am.

CP: I'm not sure who the Counselors are. I'd like to hear a little more about your family and who you are. So, who are you? After all, I represent a lot of people. My name is Curious Public. So, I come from a family, too—a very large family. And all of us would like to hear about you.

Co: Good Question. I hope I can give you enough that you can make sense of who I am as a Counselor. Maybe a little family history would help.

CP: Sure, go for it. I'm kind of into genealogy. As I said, I come from a family, too.

A Counselor's Family History

My story is simple, but complicated, like climbing Mount Everest. The idea is simple, but getting to the top is not so simple.

My parents started with strong commitments. One was Caring, Compassionate, and Committed, with a lot of spontaneity and probably too much emoting. The other was Disciplined, Data-based, and Detached, with a lot of analysis and probably too much intellectualizing. One was driven by passion, and the other was driven by science. So, then, I came along. And, I've carried the delicate integration of my parents' genes.

A part of me is fueled by passion for helping others, and the other side is coolly objective about what I see in my clients. Somewhere, I picked up the phrase "disciplined improvisation" to describe what I do. I think that this describes my work really well, but it also describes me pretty well. For me, the idea of disciplined improvisation is that I try to meet my clients with a huge reservoir of training and commitment. I try to bring research and reasoned analysis of a variety of human problems, and then do my best to combine this with a lot of human relations skills, such as respect, curiosity, compassion, empathy, support, and things like this. It just depends on what a client might need.

I wonder how well this communicates. You might catch most of it, but you may wonder about the idea that suggests, "this is who I am." May I elaborate on this, just a little? I will try to be brief.

Well, even as a child, I really felt for those who suffered. Back then, of course, I was concerned about the kids who were left out or the ones who got hurt somehow, like breaking an arm on the playground. Then, as I aged, even as a teenager, I wanted to include the outsiders so they wouldn't feel so bad—like the gay kids or especially the shy and introverted ones—and pay attention to the kids who got hurt. I got involved in helping to start a food bank in our neighborhood. I didn't do nearly as much as other people did, because I was a teenager and they were adults. So, they led the way. But, still, even back then, I wanted to help other people.

When I started to college, I began with a plan to become a lawyer. I completed an undergraduate major in pre-law. When I thought about being a lawyer, I almost always thought about taking on causes that helped people, maybe even a career in politics. I wanted to provide free legal help for those who could never afford to hire an attorney. Back then, one of my causes was single mothers and their children because I saw how extremely deprived they were, especially when the men who fathered the children provided nothing to help them. I think that got started because I went to school with kids who really didn't have much. I always wondered what went wrong. How come they didn't have much, like nice clothes, and looked sad most of the time?

Also, back then, as a teenager, I was more angry about how deprived many other kids were. It was easy to look at adults and wonder why they were not doing more to help those kids. Now, I am an adult. Being an angry adolescent doesn't work anymore. I have to be involved in finding ways to help those who are deprived—of wages, of health care, of opportunity, and so on.

At my high school, we had a counselor and a school psychologist. Just because they were there and did so much good for kids in my school, I kept thinking that maybe I should consider becoming a counselor or therapist. As I continued to move toward becoming an adult, I met people who were counselors and other mental health professionals. They did not tell me to consider counseling as a career. Just because they were there, though, I began to see that there were opportunities for helping others and advancing causes important to me. So, I took a careful look at counseling and decided to get on board. I remember what I was like back then, and I almost burst out laughing. I thought that I wanted so much to help other people that the strength of my desire was more than enough to make me a superior therapist. I can't believe how naïve I was.

Now, here I am. To get here, though, I started to ask about how to become a counselor. I knew I had to find a solid training program. So, I did that. I found a graduate program, applied, got admitted, and went to work.

The Question of Growing

I figured that I could take all the courses and pick up what I needed to become a counselor—a therapist who could change people's lives because I would be armed with the best information available. Back then, my motivation to help others was pretty strong, but now I see how magical my thinking was. It was more of a journey of change than I had expected. I started with a serious commitment to becoming a counselor because I wanted to help others. I figured that if I could just help others, I would be a counselor—and probably a superb one. And I figured that if I gathered all of the information I needed, I would just put it to work and change those who needed to be different. I imagined that I would meet a suicidal teenager like some of them I went to school with, and change them into optimistic kids who would immediately be back into life and never think about suicide again. I really was naïve.

And, of course, I met some older therapists back then who seemed to have all of the answers to all of the problems that people could bring to them. I really was in awe of them. Not so much, now, because as I have matured as a therapist, I'm not so sure what I think about them. Some of them were and still are pretty good therapists. The ones I worry about, though, seemed to promise much more than they could possibly deliver, especially the religious ones. We can talk about that later, if you want to.

My big misjudgment back then was that I didn't need to change myself so that I could help others. It only slowly occurred to me that I needed to change myself. Maybe, when others hear this, they wonder what it is that I had to change. If someone had asked me about this before I started my graduate program, I would not have thought that I needed to change, and if I did think that, I still didn't know what exactly I needed to change. This probably sounds kind of mysterious. I had to change? Oh, yeah. I had to make a lot of changes.

One of my aunts is a cardiologist. Of course, I don't know precisely what all of her experiences were as she worked toward becoming a cardiologist. From what I could observe, though, she migrated from a passionate, concerned, empathic, relational, and really energetic beginner to someone who integrated all of this into an objective, scientific, analytic, and professional woman who has been an apparently effective cardiology caregiver. This isn't the same thing as becoming a counselor, but it says something about having to change one's self so that professional caregiving can be what it should be.

When I started, I believed that I needed to have the right information. Of course, this meant that I would know how people got mentally sick and how I could heal them. And, of course, it also meant that I could enter a room with a set of proven techniques and use them on clients—quickly healing them, of course, no matter what kind of problem they brought to me. After a while, I saw how very hollow this was. It was necessary, but it failed to account for the fact that, in deeply personal ways, I needed to be real and full of meaning—for me first and then for them. That was a big change.

When I started, I knew that I should comply with expectations. I needed to show up on time, armed with a lot of counseling techniques. Along the way, I discovered that I needed to find a way to live well—sort of like having "to practice what I preached." When I started, I understood that "living well" meant that I would show up for work, earn an income, heal others, go home to my family, and have all of the nice times that a family should have, and so on. But then the reality of being a good therapist got heavier and heavier—not so much as a burden, but as a demand for growth.

As I look back on my thinking around the time I began to try to help clients, I squirm with what I must have done to my clients. I could not recognize how incompetent I was. Of course, I didn't understand how normal this was. I convinced myself that I was competent until I had to admit that I was just like every other beginning therapist—inadequate. I suppose I wanted to skip the "beginner" part of being a therapist and immediately get to the part where I was a superior therapist. Now, I know that it just doesn't work that way.

Probably, other counselors look at their growth in ways that are different from mine. For me, though, I had to confront myself. One of the things was that I had to confront my tendency to escape from mismanagement of my anger. Don't misunderstand me here. I have never had a problem with letting my rage go and harming or assaulting others. It was nothing like that. Instead, I hid my anger from myself. So, as I met my first few clients, some of them were angry people. And, sure enough, just as I hid from my anger, I subtly maneuvered them to avoid their anger, too.

This really wasn't a HUGE deal. I don't think I really harmed anyone. But, I surely kept my clients from the growth that they should have had under my care.

Joseph P. Corbin or "Joey" came to see me when he was seventeen. Looking back, I now see that Joey did not want to be there. His dad insisted that Joey get some counseling. Joey and I met several times before he angrily told me "You can just go to hell." The trigger for his anger, if I remember

> correctly, was that I referred to his dad's expectations from therapy. Probably, I assumed that, if Joey's dad wanted him to get help, especially from me—a truly "wonderful therapist"—his fatherly interest and support was loving and positive. I did not see that Joey's dad, Everett, was an angry guy who was full of rage, apparently demanding that Joey accept and comply with occasional and quite unreasonable expectations.. Slowly, as Joey and I met for several months and trust built up in our relationship, he told stories of his dad's explosions of rage. After we had been meeting for a long time—I'm not sure exactly how long—I had an epiphany. And, it came with awkward self-doubt. How could I not have seen how angry and hurt Joey was? Was there something about me and my responses to Joey that turned me away from his anger and hurt? Did my experience with Joey tell me something about my anger and hurt that I should see and understand more clearly? Somewhere along the way, I had to tell myself that I had subtly interacted with this angry kid in ways that were kind, thoughtful, supportive and a lot more, but also in ways that kept me from seeing and respecting him as an angry and hurt young man. I struggled to make sense of this. In the end, I had to acknowledge that I had not treated Joey very well because I did not know how to manage my anger and hurt very well. At least, on one occasion, I said this to Joey and apologized for my mistakes in trying to help him. I remember well how he laughed—a kind of forgiving laugh—as if to tell me it was okay to be human and to make stupid mistakes. So, the relationship gained positive momentum from this. And, I was able to help Joey. In fact, for several years after our sessions ended, Joey would call to say hello. In a way, I was a safe place for him. I have to say, too, that a couple of my peers made a big difference in how I came to think about my anger. They are still good peers. But back then I remember one of them saying something like "Why can't you just let yourself be pissed? You are, you know?" A lot changed for me because of them.

And, then, there was the business of loss. When I started to train as a counselor, I had never considered that some of my early losses made any difference in my abilities to help others. I really did not think about my losses. I suppose that they were just wrinkles in the fabric of my life. The further I went, though, the more this thing about losses kept coming up. My dad suffered a stroke when I was in middle school, about ten years old. My grandfather died about a year later. My grandmother died about three or four years after that. We lived with my grandparents during this time. So, these were people I saw every day. There were other losses, but those are the big ones. I think that's all of the big ones.

Anyway, as I pursued my training, even without thinking about losses, something about losses kept coming up. Then, it began to occur to me, "I'm working very hard against losing." So, even when it made no sense, I tried to hang on to friends who were no longer friends. Worse, I tried to hang on to clients, even when we were finished. These things were so subtle that I easily missed them. I never really kept clients coming too much beyond the time they were finished, but I was really slow to let them go. In my most careful scrutiny of myself, it never occurred to me that my early losses defined some of how I related with others, including clients, thirty years later.

"Duffy," a pleasant 48-year-old woman, requested help with her stress about living through major changes. Specifically, she reported that she had given her adult life to her husband and her five sons, emphasizing that she would not have had it any other way. Repeatedly and with conviction, she stated that she loved her husband and her sons. She indicated that her husband seemed to be pleased with her and his career. With regard to her sons she indicated that she had done all that she could for them, but that they needed to move into their adult lives with independence. According to Duffy, her sons had stayed in her home much too long. As a doting mother, she had sensitive, supportive and loving conversations with her sons about her need for them to move out of her home and make lives for themselves. She stated that all of this proceeded very well, with her husband's full involvement and agreement. Now, however, after initiating changes, she began to feel the stress of seeing what she may want to do with her life, without having to care so intensively for her sons and her husband. "I just need to get a life of my own. And, I don't know what to do." Duffy indicated that she must be slow to recognize what was happening to her. Openly and with apparent genuineness, she cried about the fact that the changes that she had sought had happened and that as a result she had lost her security in knowing what to do with herself. She mourned, feeling that all that she had been committed to was disappearing.

On my side of this, I was inwardly cheering for Duffy. Given her age and interests, I wanted her to make the changes that she had made and wanted to make. I understood her stress from having to make changes. However, I clumsily minimized her grief. As I discussed my awkwardness with a colleague, she stated, "You don't handle loss well, do you?" The moment was one of recognition. My colleague was right. As if to make her case, she observed several somewhat inconsequential behaviors that illustrated her point. She reminded me of the a scene that she believed was ordinary for me. She observed that I was usually the last to leave one of our group luncheons, suggesting that I may not have been tolerating the small loss of

> leaving my colleagues. She was right. Actually, although I recognized the truth of what she said, I felt really bad about it. It exposed me to myself. As I tried to find ways to improve myself, based on my strange way of mismanaging losses, I felt surprised by how obvious this was to others and not so obvious to me.

Obviously, as you probably know from your own experience, our personal histories shape the way we think and act toward many different things. That's certainly true of me. That's why I mentioned my experience with loss. I remember losing my dog when I was seven years old. I felt this ache in my stomach, but no one would have known it was there. And, I associate losing my dog with some other losses. I remember a kid who came to our school. He had no hair. He looked really odd. I had never heard of leukemia, but I learned about it from him. Apparently, he was receiving chemotherapy at the time. And, one of the results was hair loss. Anyway, he was a good teacher for a lot of third-graders like me. But when he died, I assumed that everyone else would just move on and not give it much attention. I was wrong. The kid who died was publicly celebrated and remembered for quite a while in public ways. Looking at it now, I realize that I had somehow determined that I would not show how much I hurt when I lost something or someone important to me. I wanted to escape from the loss, instead of feeling it.

So, again, I had to learn that I had to be an authentic human being or at least try. Now, I realize that I started with the naïve and corrupt idea that I could help others, without having to be truly honest with myself.

More important, though, I learned that really good counseling is not an achievement. It requires growth—from me, the counselor. And, it goes on. It's growth that is a lifelong process. When it stops, good counseling stops, from my view of things.

Now that I have been in my professional role for several years, I'm still working on this. As one of my professional heroes said, "Counseling is a way of being, not an achievement." For now, though, I can tell you that life is better, now that I can be genuinely pissed, although I'm still pretty cautious about this. Life is better now that I can see myself losing and grieving in honest and real ways. And, one of the enormous discoveries is that, for me, the good life is not really about being pissed or grieving. It is about being genuine, honest, authentic, real, and living with the understandable ambivalence of being human and being more than human. This empowers me to be accessible to meaningful love, affection, friendship, sharing, pleasure, and so much more. Way back then, I did not realize how much I was missing in my relationships. The strange thing is that I was working hard to help others get what they needed from their relationships. I guess it's sort of like a plumber whose house has a lot of leaky pipes, while he's out there working hard to repair others' pipes. I suppose that another way to say the same thing is that I can be very imperfect and love being human.

With regard to counseling, it means that clients are no longer problems to be solved, but human beings who invite me into their lives, even when they are the least loveable, the least valued—suffering with the worst pain that they can possibly carry. And, it's there that I can be very much at home. At least, I can provide a safe and understanding place for them. Of course, some of them need help but are not suffering from extreme problems. No matter how severe their problems are, I have found a place to feel extraordinary gratitude for all of the clients I see, instead of looking around my internal space and trying to find a door through which to escape their pain. Now, I welcome their pain, just as I would want someone else to welcome mine. This sounds so simple, but getting here has not been simple.

In ways that were not really very clear to me, my changes began before I finished my degree, but from the time I entered my graduate program, I have been changing—sometimes because I recognized the need for change and other times not so much. And, ever since I completed my graduate degree, I have been on this journey.

The journey is not like being born again. For me, it has never been a one-day thing. It's more like being adopted—entering a family where I can discover and grow in my true identity, making a lot of discoveries along the way. Maybe I should try to tell you what this is. When I try to grow as a therapist, and every time I tell someone else about who I am, I discover that I have to tell the story a little bit differently. I take this to be a sign of growth.

Who Are You, Now?

CP: I'm not tired of hearing what you have to say, but I imagine that living through all of that makes you tired. Maybe you're tired, just telling me about it?

Co: Yes. I feel a little tired. When I immerse myself in who I am now, I feel less tired. I feel more alive now than I have ever felt before.

CP: So, maybe, picking up on what you just said, you can tell me about who you are now.

Co: Okay. Let's go there. So, as I see myself now, here is my view of me as a therapist:

I am a counselor. I became a counselor through a lot of growth. Without significant growth, I would not be a counselor.

I have joined a great family of counselors. This may seem to be a peculiar way to say how I belong to "my people," but it's just a way to say how seriously and importantly belonging to my profession is. If I describe this only in terms of the memberships I hold in professional associations, I leave out too much that is important. I guess that it might be like reading from the menu, instead of actually eating and enjoying the food on the menu. Reciting my credentials is not a bad thing to do, but it is a lot like reading a menu—it gives me a lot to think about, but doesn't really feed me or help me to grow. Still, maintaining my memberships is important because they are indicators of who I am and with whom I belong. They are my professional "homes." I should say, though, that my memberships are important, but they do not guarantee that I am good at what I do. When it comes to being effective in my work, I carry the responsibility for it, whether I am a member of a professional organization or not. Still, if you know a counselor/psychotherapist who is not a member of a recognized professional organization, you should probably be wary of them.

Also, I should say that, just like a family helps a member to know how to be a member of the family, my family helps me to know how to be a counselor. One of the big signs of this is our ethics, but it's not the only one by any stretch. Still, all of us who do what I do should be clear about being faithful to professional ethics, even when compliance may be inconvenient. If you were a member of my family and looking for a therapist, I would encourage you to take a look at the ethical standards that a prospective therapist should be following. It could be one of the most common codes of ethics, including codes from the American Counseling Association, American Psychological Association, National Association of Social Workers, and the American Association for Marriage and Family Therapists Code of Ethics.

The importance of professional ethics cannot be exaggerated. The codes of ethics I mentioned are not all of them by any means. For example, if you need a play therapist to help your child, you should make sure that the therapist is certified in play therapy. And play therapists have their own code of ethics. Or, if you or someone in your family needs a sex therapist, the same thing is true. Look for a certified sex therapist. They have their code of ethics, too.

Beyond saying, "I am a counselor" or "I am a therapist," my simple affirmation of my professional work is that "I belong to my profession." This is a personal and a professional statement. It's both. And, it's a way of saying that, no matter what I do in my work, I represent and in some ways speak for my profession. That's just the way it is. I think that this is important because, as I represent my profession, I must try to meet the highest standards that I know about, instead of doing only what I want to do. Maybe another way to say this is that the personal dimensions of this cannot be separated from the professional dimensions. I figure that, if I honor my profession, I try both to be as independent and professionally accountable as I can, while also complying with the expectations that my profession has of its members.

Sometimes, I grow weary of reading about professional identity. Some of the materials seek to differentiate one kind of therapist from another. In a way, this may be necessary because some of us really are very different from some of the others. For example, a therapist who specializes in helping senior adults in an assisted care facility will be very different from a therapist whose focus is on young adults who need career counseling. For me, those who want to separate counselors and therapists into small, unrelated groups are thinking vacuously about counseling and therapy. To define myself by making clear what I am not may be helpful, but it is empty and incomplete. I might put it this way: "I'm not a Russian, but this does not make me an American or tell me who I am as an American. Or, I may not be a Martian, but this does not tell me that I am an Earthling."

So, what am I as a counselor and therapist? Well, maybe I can give you some details about this. Trying to be brief, I am

Personal and professional.

Individually accountable, but also accountable to my profession.

Compliant with external authority (i.e., professional ethics, accreditation standards, licensing regulations, and more) for guidance and direction, but also committed to autonomous decisions about professional behavior, including clinical judgment.

Compassionate and sometimes anguished, but also detached and objective.

Confident in making clinical judgments, but also open to experiencing the professionalism of others, particularly with regard to work that I do not understand.

Defined by my training, ethics, licensing, certifications, and other markers of what I do. However, more than these markers, I am defined even more as a therapist because of other counselors and therapists with whom I associate and with whom I join in common causes through my professional associations.

Committed to a focused and professional relationship, when I meet with clients, as a distillation of my identity as a therapist and counselor and as an expression of personal and professional values. This is the fundamentally important reason for my existence as a therapist. This is the reason my profession exists—to deliver competent professional services. This is what I try to do as a counselor.

In other words, in response to clinically relevant needs that clients bring to me, I try to provide clinically relevant services.

Advantaged with opportunities to represent counselors.

In short, my purpose for my existence as a therapist is fairly simple. First and always, I am a therapist when I meet with clients. This is who I am as a professional person. And others who share this outlook with me are my professional family.

What Do Therapists Do?

CP: Good. I think I catch on. I'm wondering, though, about what exactly you do. Your ideas sound good to me, but can you tell me about what you do, in specific terms? If I were to follow you through your work day, what would I see? I think that this would help all of us.

Co: This is great. I love to talk about what counselors and therapists do. When I think about it, though, I feel some frustration, not because of your need to know but because of the many different things I do. Is it okay with you if I list some things in a fairly random way, without having to try to list everything?

CP: Sure. Any specific information would be helpful.

Co: All right. Here goes. If you have any questions, just let me know. Here is the list that comes to mind just now. Probably, after some thought, I would add many more items to this list, but this is what comes to mind right now.

Probably, before listing items, I should give you some idea about how extremely varied some of my days are. On any given day, I am celebrating with a client who has made huge advances toward gaining stability after a prolonged period of personal disasters and also giving attention to the most stressed and traumatized individual in the world—well, maybe not in the entire world, but surely an individual who would be universally recognized as having been seriously traumatized.

I remember how blown away I was when a man came for his first appointment. When he sat down, he said something like, "I really don't know what to say. I've never done anything like this before. I never thought I would need somebody like you, but here I am." Then, almost like he was in a trance, he began to tell me his story.

"My wife and I have been married for thirty-six years. She is in the end stages of cancer. Breast cancer. We caught it too late. It had metastasized. It's all over her body, now. She's in pain. All day. Every day. I know it's crazy, but I feel like I failed her. Somehow I should not have let this happen. She's dying and there's not a damn thing I can do about it. And, then, my daughter showed up at our house. She's pregnant. She looked awful. So, I thought that something had gone wrong with the baby. But that wasn't it. I hugged her and she started to cry. She couldn't stop crying. We just stood there, with her crying and me just holding her. After what seemed like hours—and maybe it was. I don't know. I lost track of time. Anyway, when she could finally speak, she told me that she had cancer, too. She said they would need to take the baby because the baby could not live through the treatments that she needed. That was about two months ago. Anyway, now she's not going to make it, either. But the worst was yet to come. I know I need to talk about it, but I don't know how. But I've got to. We have two sons. The older guy—Sonny—is just fine. God, I hope so. I really need for him to be okay. Our younger son. He's the one I've got to talk about. On Sunday, Chris and his buddies went to the lake. As a really good athlete, I feel like he would be the one to outlive all of us. On Sunday, he suffered a ruptured aneurysm—an aortal aneurysm—and died. I'm lost. Just lost. What the hell am I supposed to do! My son is gone. My wife . . . And my daughter. . . . . I'm so wiped out—tired—so tired I can't think straight."

The point of this story is to contrast it with the meeting that I had immediately after this one, just to give you an idea about how varied my work can be. The session I described was followed by one that was extremely different.

Julie had been coming to therapy for approximately eight months. Initially, she complained about feeling helpless and depressed. She accounted for this by reporting that she had been away from her work for nearly three years so that she could take care of her twin sons from the time they were born. She suggested that they were truly difficult babies, with one of them having chronic health problems. This led to financial and emotional strain for her family. Julie looked really tired. The thing that brought her to therapy was that she was anticipating going back to work, but believed that she had fallen so far behind in her profession that she may not be able to hold a job if she got one. Anyway, without trying to account for everything that

> transpired in therapy, Julie made steady progress and, then, the meeting I'm talking about, now, seemed to be light years away from where we began. On this day, Julie came happily into the office. She smiled broadly. She moved with a lot of energy. And, she brought a cake. As she entered my office she said something like this: "Okay. I hope you like the cake. I tried to get you to tell me what your favorite cake is and lucky for me, you gave me several options. Now, today I'm in charge. We're going to have cake. You can have your usual coffee. And if there is anyone else out there, let's give them some cake, too." [We usually had another two or three therapists and our administrative assistant at the office.] "This is my way of saying thank you. Thank you! Thank you! Today, my life is worthwhile because of you."

Well, you get the idea. In the space of only minutes, I went from attending to an individual whose story was overwhelmingly painful to an individual whose story was celebratory, very happy, and extremely positive. It's almost like attending a funeral and a birthday party at the same time. And, for me, it's really important to value therapy as therapy as well as I can deliver it and not take my clients' pain or joy as a sign of my work, just because one feels bad and the other feels good.

> Anyway, I need to answer your question about what I do and tell you what I do.
>
> Mostly, more than anything else, I sit with clients. I try to interact with them in ways that empower them to change. When I refer to "empower them to change," it may communicate, but I really cannot empower anyone. I can help them to discover their own power. If I had the power, enough influence, to empower others, my work would be a lot easier. As it is, helping a client to discover her own power may be harder, but it works much better this way.
>
> I spend a lot of time trying to improve my understanding of the problems my clients tell me about. This is never-ending. When I began to help people, we had very little useful information about how to help people based on brain studies. Now, we have a lot of this information. So, the demand to keep up with changes is ongoing. And, it's almost inevitable that we will have changes in the manual of diagnoses. So, if I take my work seriously, I have a lot of new learning to do. Even when I am most confident about what I know, I also recognize that I have so much more to learn.
>
> I attend professional meetings. Workshops and conferences help me to stay current on issues—an ongoing challenge. Also, I get to have time with professional friends. I never assume that my professional competencies are as good as they will ever be.

I help clients find the best help for their particular needs. If I can help someone who comes to me, I will do all I can to help. If not, I make referrals. I don't assume that I can help everyone with all possible problems.

I keep secrets. More than just keeping secrets, though, I protect the trust that clients have in me. We call it "confidentiality." Or, in legal terms, clients are entitled to "privileged communication." There are exceptions to protecting information, but even the exceptions are handled with great discretion. For example, if a client's situation involves the possibility of child victimization, I will report the situation to civil authorities. I will also protect the client's information as best as I can.

When I think about what some of my clients say about what I do, I remember some of their comments:

He listens like no one else ever has.
He encourages me to try different ways of doing things.
He helps me to find real answers for my problems.
He is kind and offers support.
He really reads me well—like hearing what I mean to say.
He helps me to gain insight into my problems.
He offers information that is new and useful for me.
He lets me be myself.
He invests time and effort in helping me.
He gives me great freedom to grow, even if growing is painful to see.
Of course, there's a lot more to it.

On my side of this, I think about the same things as my clients, but express them in a different way. When I do the things that my clients tell me are helpful, I am genuinely expressing care for them, but I'm also maintaining my professional role. I hope to be genuine with clients, but I am not their friend. I think it should be said that clients sometimes express their doubts about therapy and me. "I need more clarity from you." Or, "You are slow to give advice." Or, "You think too hard about things; I need someone who is more spontaneous." All of my clients' feedback should be taken seriously.

I focus on specific behaviors and their consequences, implications, and contingencies, and help my clients find new ways of thinking about them. The other side of this is that I refuse to get caught up in moralistic thinking about my clients' situations. Whether we're talking about drug abuse or infidelity or theft or whatever, my job is not to be moralistic, but to provide clinically relevant responses to their clinically relevant needs.

I listen for the discrepancies, incongruent meanings, and inconsistent information, and try to help my clients to "see" these things so that they can more likely make good decisions about them. Sometimes, clients wrestle with these things. For example, a woman tells me, "I love my husband, but I wish I didn't. I just don't like him much."

I try to help my clients maintain focus on their personal goals—goals that are desirable and that we have agreed to. If we have no goals, we usually don't achieve good results. You know that quip, "If you don't know where you're going, any road will take you there." Something like this applies to what we do in therapy.

I work hard to base my decisions on clinically sound foundations and a coherent, consistent rationale for my clients' behaviors. Of course, there's a lot more to it here, too. My purpose is not to be right by having the right theory or the right philosophy; it is to deliver a competent clinical service. To do this, I try to gather the best evidence I can. And, I try to utilize the best evidence I can get.

I try to stay informed about legal and ethical matters. Sometimes, I have to investigate to know how to handle a sensitive situation. Sometimes, I help colleagues with their legal and ethical questions. This sometimes involves getting involved in things that I did not know I needed to get involved with, such as social media. The explosion in the use of social media has had huge consequences for children and adolescents. So, I have needed to study social media and integrate some of my understanding of it into therapy. Generally, it's a sad situation, in that children suffer more than they gain from social media. They have become targets of profiteering individuals and corporations.

I spend a lot of time at my computer. This isn't what I enjoy most in my work, but it is necessary. It's necessary because I write reports about many of my clients. Some of these reports go to schools or attorneys, or other professionals, all in service to my clients, although most of what I write doesn't go anywhere, except in my clients' files. I exchange e-mail messages with other professionals, including my work associates around my office. I conduct searches about numerous aspects of my work—ranging from child abuse reporting to reading articles to getting information about a professional meeting and a whole lot more. Also, a lot of my computer work is completing intake information about my clients and writing case notes. Much of this is "hidden" work. It never really shows up anywhere.

During meetings with clients, I have an obligation to monitor them as carefully as I can. But I also have to monitor myself. Sometimes, when it's useful for my client, I share my feelings about what I see in them and the ways I am experiencing them. Sometimes, they need to know what I feel. It's not at all a matter of needing to share myself with my clients; it's more a matter of judging what may be clinically useful and productive for my clients. I should never make clients' sessions about me. My needs during my meetings with clients are irrelevant.

I keep appointments with clients. And, I show up on time. It's a matter of respect.

I try to help my clients understand the implications and dynamics—the risks and benefits—of the counseling approaches and techniques I use. This is often a real challenge for me, mainly because the process of counseling is something like an adventure and sometimes involves a lot of subtlety. So, often, we don't know where it's going. So, how do I prepare my clients for this? Allowing for this, I try to maintain a focus on what a client needs and on the goals that we are trying to reach.

When I evaluate my clients, I try to explain the evaluation as clearly as I can and in terms that leave little doubt about how I may have reached conclusions about them. I find that, when I am most honest about this, clients almost always accept what I have to say or report to them. On the other hand, when I obfuscate or try to soften the impact—and sometimes fail to be appropriately candid—clients understandably resist or reject what I have to say.

A common struggle for me is to see and accept cultural variations in my clients, especially when they appear to be similar to me. When the differences are obvious, we generally deal with them openly and in a productive manner. This may not appear to be much of a struggle. After all, what's so hard about relating to clients who are similar to me? I won't try to describe what this may be like for other therapists, but, for me, when a client is very similar to me, I may easily miss—just not see—important features in the client just because they are so familiar. It's like the old adage about the elephant in the room. If this means that you can't see what's obvious, just because it is so obvious, that's what I mean.

I try to accept my clients as they are and try to envision each one as changing in positive ways through the services they receive from me, but more importantly, through increasing their ability to claim health for themselves. This is usually easy, but sometimes it is very hard. Just like everywhere else in life, some individuals are more easily accepted than others. Sometimes, I find that I have succumbed to thinking in stereotypical terms. For example, I remember a client who was a huge man—much taller than I am and weighing, maybe, three hundred fifty pounds. He looked more like a brawler than a poet. And, I assumed that he was a lot like the way he looked. He wasn't like that at all. I misjudged him. To my surprise, he turned out to be really alert to others, a sensitive and flexible thinker, a truly complex guy, and, yes, a real poet.

Sometimes, my clients just do not have enough information about their problems or the situations they encounter. So, where it's feasible and clinically sensible, I try to educate them about these things, such issues as self-care, dealing with anger, managing parent–child conflicts, understanding loss, and so on.

I provide counseling services for individuals, families, and groups. In one session, I may meet with four members of a family and then meet with only one individual.

When we come to the end of our work together, I try to make this a smooth transition and to equip my clients with useful plans that they can use on their own.

I commonly check with my clients, just to be sure that I am accurately identifying their concerns and issues. This is just a simple matter of asking about whether they are getting from therapy what they need. Or, I sometimes ask whether I am interacting with them in ways that they believe are useful or whether there are things that they expect me to do that I am not doing.

Frequently, I try to take a step back from my work and evaluate what I do. I'll review my clients' records, just to try to ensure that I'm remembering details as I should. I have surveys that I will ask my clients to complete. And, sometimes, I will share cases with my colleagues. This may be where I get the most help. For me, it's good to get feedback from professional peers whose judgments about my work I can trust.

For my clients, I try to be clear about my counseling approach in ways that are consistent with my personal values and professional beliefs, so long as I can also have confidence that I am compliant with high standards of clinical care. Of course, I have doubts about this sometimes. This is where my peers and research literature prove to be helpful.

I look for covert messages when I listen to my clients, and try to interpret them skillfully for my clients. I also try to be alert to any of my own covert messages. I think most of us, whether we are therapists or not, try to do this. Or, as someone else told me, "I listen for what they have to say, but I have learned to listen for what they mean."

I try to give useful feedback when my clients do something well, mainly because when they're discouraged, they are not likely to see the things they do well.

I pay attention to relational skills and practice them as well as I can. I have forms that have scales in them so that I can judge whether I am utilizing the skills that are needed and how well I am utilizing them. However, knowing that I can easily assign halos to myself and miss things that are important, I also ask my clients to complete these forms sometimes, or ask some of my professional peers.

I help my clients to define and achieve specific, concrete goals for themselves.

When it's feasible and my clients give me permission, I will record a session and play it for my peers to evaluate. I'm always amazed at how helpful this is. The feedback and support help me to help my clients. Nothing is as valuable as getting feedback from my peers.

I try to give useful feedback, especially when a client asks for it and when things look like they're going very wrong for a client.

I have learned that I should never assume that I am doing things perfectly well. I don't. But, before we turn away from what I do as a therapist, I strongly believe that what I do outside of therapy is critically important for what I do during therapy. This is a way to say that I must, as a matter of personal commitment to myself and others, take care of my health. So, except for a few indulgences, I try to eat well. I try to exercise. But, maybe, most important, I try to stay close to the people I love. They keep me grounded. They care for me. Of course, I care for them, too. It's just that I never want to be in the position of taking unmet relational needs to my clients.

Well, this may be enough for now.

CP: That's quite a list. I get the idea that there must be a lot more that you could put on your list.

Co: No doubt about that. The list could go on for a long time.

CP: How about another question. Are there things in your counseling that you struggle with? How about this: Of all of the things you do, what do you like the most and what do you like the least?

Co: Good question. To start with what I like least, it's probably times when I am providing professional care for a child who really needs help, but has parents or others who actively undermine the child and the work that we are trying to do. Sadly, I have seen children who were destroyed by their parents. Many times, parents who declare their love for their children also do things that hurt their children.

About the things I like the most about my work as a therapist, I would have to say that there are many of them. If I have to choose one, though, I would say that I am most gratified when I see a client claim or reclaim health. One of the ways I've seen this is when an individual has lived in a cage of denial of her or his sometimes very visible thoughts and feelings. I remember a man who led a large corporation. The short story is that his board of directors told him to get help or he would be terminated from his employment. Apparently, the members of the board liked some of his decision-making and the productivity that came with it, but they also knew that he was costing the company a lot of money and a lot of employee dissatisfaction. My impression right away was that he was an extremely over-controlling individual who frustrated almost everyone who worked with him. He caused a lot of employee turnover. Anyway, he denied any accountability for the complaints that were made about him. He said many times, "I do my job. I do what I'm paid to do and I do it damn well." After about six months of therapy that seemed like a kind of warfare for both of us, I remember really well when he came into the office and I saw something different. Instead of beginning the conversation with his usual sarcasm, he was mostly silent. After what seemed like an hour had passed, but it was only maybe five minutes, he said, "You're right." He said it with great emotion. Of course, I asked him to explain. I had never really argued with him. So, I was not expecting to be proved right. However, I made observations that probably scared him. Like, "How do you account for employee turnover?" Or, "When you say to an employee what you told me you said, what message do you want to get to the employee?" Or, "What's it like for you to be here with me, knowing that if you don't come here, you could be fired?" Anyway, once this client began to be honest with himself, he also began to move toward claiming his mental-emotional health. That's a very good thing for me to see.

CP: Have you ever been scared of a client?

Co: Yes. But the threats have been somewhat distant. Distant, but real. A couple of situations come to mind. One was a slightly paranoid client who apparently concluded that I may have been trying to harm him. I saw him driving around our office building several times when he did not have an appointment scheduled. He was scary, but he never directly threatened me. Another individual, also an adult male, was a huge man and one who was full of rage that sometimes got away from him. He was a fighter who talked about how he enjoyed fighting and beating other men. He was a very scary character. Unfortunately, some of my fear of him rose up when I was in an office with only the two of us there.

Eventually, everything worked out well for him. He learned to direct his frustration and rage toward socially acceptable expressions.

CP: What does it do to you to fail to help a client when you think you should be able to help?

Co: Oh, wow. I wish that failing a client had never happened, but it did. And, if I continue in this work for a while, it will happen again. For me, at the heart of what I do—or try to do—is to take to my clients the best of intentions. At least, this gives me an opportunity to convey to the client that I am genuinely concerned and that I am quite ready to work for them on their behalf. Still, no matter how good my intention may be, they sometimes do not prepare me to be as effective as I want to be and should be. Anyway, there are a few things I should say about this.

One, some clients are, by definition, very difficult clients. For example, a client whose diagnosis is Antisocial Personality Disorder or Narcissistic Personality, or almost any personality disorder, is going to be a client with whom normative success is unlikely.

Another thing is that clients sometimes keep secrets and, because they hide important information from me, their secrets keep them from receiving the best help, no matter who is trying to provide it. It's like the guy who goes to see his physician, but never says anything about seeing blood in his urine. When I think about this, several clients come to mind. One individual's case was fairly simple. She successfully hid her drug addiction from me, although I suspected it. In the end, she overdosed and needed hospitalization. Later, she went to a drug treatment facility in another state, and I never saw her again.

Then, there is the category of my failures. I remember a family I tried to help. The family included a mother and two sons. For too long, I missed the fact that the mother hated her sons. She was a pleasant person with whom I related fairly well. For reasons I could not account for, I did not seem to be successful in helping her or her sons. My work with them ended when the boys—both teenagers—were arrested for breaking into a neighbor's home and stealing a lot of valuables. They faced charges for assault with a deadly weapon. Anyway, I should have seen how vulnerable the boys were and how hostile the mother was toward them. At the end, I learned that she had been violently violated by men several times. There have been other failures, but for now, this one rises to the top of my thinking.

I suppose that, just like any other kind of health care, the providers sometimes fail. For me, the challenge is to welcome my experiences with clients, no matter what the experiences are. Some of them make me squirm. When I fail, I usually don't pay enough attention to what makes me uncomfortable.

When I tune into this, though, I become curious. If I'm curious, I will not fail. And if I'm not curious, I will almost inevitably fail. I remember hearing, "When we're curious, we discover unexpected things." I have taken this to heart.

When I first started to do this kind of work, every sign of possible failure or even a hint of possible failure bothered me deeply. With a lot of mulling and support from my peers, I came to see that I needed to think in terms of what I should learn from my failures and not so much what I should fear from them.

CP: If I started to look for a therapist today, what should I look for?

Co: What a great question. I'm glad you asked it. It's one of those issues that I have thought a lot about. I hope I can help with this. Here are some things that you may want to ask a prospective therapist. Please, stop me if I give you too much here. This is one of the most important things we may talk about.

Are you licensed to practice in my state? Do you have a state-issued license?

I'm here for help with "my problem." Do you have experience in helping people with this kind of problem?

Do you have any special training to help people with my kind of problem? What are your special areas of practice?

Based on my problem, how much therapy do you recommend? How long will it take?

Would you describe your treatment style? What should I expect to happen when we meet?

Do you involve me in planning my treatment? How do you do this?

How do you make treatment decisions? Do you use measurable criteria to make treatment decisions?

Do you use treatment standards from published clinical practice guidelines to guide your treatment?

How do you work with other healthcare providers, including physicians? This question may be important if you need both therapy and medication. In this case, your counselor and your physician should know what the other is doing.

If you are overseeing the treatment of your child, you may want to know how your child's mental health care may need to be coordinated with school-related personnel. You may need to ask, "How will you work with my child's school and teachers?"

I hope that we do not have any emergencies, but if we do, how do you handle emergencies?

Do you charge a fee for phone calls? Or, are there fees for email messages? Does insurance cover this kind of thing?

Who has access to information about me?

Do you file insurance, or do I need to do it? What types of insurance do you accept?

Just in case you haven't already done it, check the therapist's website, if there is one. Look carefully at what kind of presentation the therapist makes.

And, do you really like your work as a therapist?

The main thing that you or anyone else needs to keep in mind when you're looking for a therapist is that your needs are what matter most. If a therapist meets your needs, therapy is a success. And, if you maintain your focus on getting your needs met, you will likely be a part of a therapeutic process that works for you as well as for your therapist.

The Future

CP: Are you okay with one more question?

Co: Sure. If I can, I would love to be helpful.

CP: Well, you've been in the profession for a while. I'm wondering what advice you would give to a therapist who is just beginning to function as a therapist. What advice would you give?

Co: Thank you. I had hoped that you would ask this kind of question. Probably, most of us who have been in the role of therapist for a while reflect on how awkward we were in the beginning. There is so very much to say about how to help a beginner. I feel like I could go on with this answer for a long time, if not forever. I'll try to be brief. Here are some things I would tell a beginning therapist.

Never believe simply that you're being effective. Never. Unless you have good evidence for being effective, do not get comfortable with the idea that you are effective because you enjoy what you're doing. You might enjoy playing tennis, but your enjoyment of playing tennis doesn't mean that you're ready for Wimbledon.

Recognize your goodwill and genuine interest in your clients, but don't conclude that these things alone are sufficient for conducting good therapy. They aren't. Your sincerity is critically important, but having solidly good clinical skills is important, too.

Welcome complexity. Clients are almost always ambiguous, just like the rest of us. Welcome their complexity as an immense resource from which you can gather clinically relevant information.

Let yourself see what clients need. Something motivates them to seek help from you. Their motivation may not be immediately apparent, despite what they say.

Take good care of yourself. This includes being patient with yourself. More importantly, it means that you have good friends and others—maybe, a dedicated partner—with whom you can meet your social and intimate needs. Don't take these unmet needs to your clients.

Think in terms of validating your questions. Be curious when you meet with clients. Let yourself wonder what lies behind and beneath what may be somewhat obvious.

Maintain connections with peers who can teach you. None of us is good enough to see all that we need to see in and about clinical work. It's the blind spots that inhibit our effectiveness. And, all of us have blind spots. If you can locate a mentor, someone who can oversee your work for, maybe, several years, your effectiveness will increase, but so will your enjoyment of doing therapy.

Look for what you do well and try to invent ways to improve what you do well, but also look for your weaknesses or failures. Your weaknesses and failures give you the most important lessons and guidance about how to be better than you are.

Be kind to yourself. Always seek to improve, even when you fail, but also always be kind to yourself. This is what you want to help your clients show themselves, but it's also what you want to model for them. And, by being kind to yourself, you will like yourself as a therapist.

Do your best to accommodate the standards of our profession, including compliance with professional ethics and best clinical practices, but also practice independence. Trust yourself, including your skills and understanding, to make good clinical judgments that you can respect and value positively.

This may be enough for now. I really appreciate this question. Thank you. And thank you for participating in this dialogue with me.

Chapter 6
Cold Feet and Masculinity
The Humanity of Discovering Self

This chapter presents word pictures of therapists who discover and claim their humanity. The pictures come from practicing therapists. The stories are modified to protect the identities of the therapists and clients to whom they refer. Their stories provide illustrations that confirm the importance of honoring one's humanity.

Cold Feet

The story of cold feet should begin when and where cold feet defined the core of my existence for several years. The years are the ones during which I emerged into the early childhood consciousness of the world. They somewhat mystically contextualized the rest of my life, so far, although I hardly recognized this for most of my life. The ways in which those years shaped me continue to rise into my awareness and cause me to consider their impact.

My mother and father married in 1966. At the time, they lived in a small town that nicely rested in the inside elbow of the Illinois River. Later, looking back at myself as a young and very literal thinker, I recall some confusion when I heard adults refer to the fact that we lived in Illinois, failing to understand why they would think that we lived in the Illinois River. This was similar to hearing music that made reference to "baby," as if the baby was an adult and doing things that babies do not do. Literal thinking hardly prepared me to understand what was happening back then or to anticipate what life may be like later.

Immediately, several major events defined the young relationship between my mother and father. For one thing, they had a child, my brother, Robert, later known either as Bob or Bobby. To me, he was almost always known as Bobby. Then, they had another child, my sister, Raquel, later known as "Rack," except for me. For me, she was, yes, Sis. Then, of course, they had me, a baby boy. And, as a male whose extended family included several manly men who were veterans of World War II, the Korean War, and the Vietnam War, I suffered the indignation of being referred to as "the baby of the family." I really hated that. I seemed to be the only one who felt the inappropriateness of this appellation. My mother and her sisters were the worst offenders, although I now realize that they intended to express affection for me in their matronly ways and not to offend me. Still, they could have been more sensitive to my maleness, just as the men could have supported me, too.

Hovering over this young and probably stressed family, the Vietnam War held us in an ominous shadow, apparently caged in the dread of military combat. Our dad was drafted. The family soon moved to a Quartermaster Corps facility in North Carolina. Because I was an infant at the time, I have pieced their story together, sort of like a fluid jigsaw puzzle. Sometimes, the pieces do not fit together very well.

The manly men, a slew of uncles, did many manly things. As military veterans, they loved to drink and hunt but not at the same time. In the year or two following their stint in military combat, they could not stop fighting. Sadly, brawls and arrests were fairly common. Thus, my early view of being an adult male was that drinking and fighting were just a part of it. Strangely, although they could not immediately stop fighting after Vietnam, they were pleasant and loving members of our extended family. Eventually, they settled down. I feel a lot of admiration for them.

Around mid-1970, the family relocated back to the small town in Illinois, but one of its members remained in North Carolina. Our dad did not return with us. Back then, I did not realize that he had been critically injured in some sort of military training accident. The Greyhound bus ride back to Illinois remains in my memory, but only in bits and pieces. The seats on the bus are a clear memory. Black. Stiff and rubbery. Cold. Our return to Illinois, more than any other fact, established the conditions under which cold feet became all too familiar.

The fact that our mother traveled back to Illinois in a Greyhound bus is something that sticks in my memory only because of the Greyhound on the side of the bus. Back then, I could not spell or read the word, greyhound. While I could not read or spell, I could sense that life was somehow not right. I have only the faintest memories of anything conversational that may have happened among my brother, sister, mother, and me. Surely, though, a young mother with three young children who traveled a thousand miles, knowing that her family had permanently changed, must have felt overwhelmed. Probably, she could not have anticipated that her life would get worse than she could have imagined while she traveled back to Illinois. Apparently, upon arrival in Illinois, my mother received news that her husband, our father, had died. To this day, it's still not clear to me whether they were still married.

Apparently lacking sufficient funding to secure a place for her family to live, my mother, as I later learned, sought help from her parents, my grandmother and grandfather. My grandfather refused to allow us to live with them. Apparently, his view was that my mother had made decisions that brought her to destitution and that she should have to live with it. Having only a few photographs with both my grandfather and me in them, I have no independent memory of him apart from the photos. I suspect that he declined opportunities to have a meaningful relationship with me or my siblings.

Lacking support from her family, my mother's options were limited, at best. Thus, as an unskilled young mother of three children and a woman with extremely limited means of supporting her family, my mother located a tiny tar-paper shack that would become our home for a few years. The shack had no plumbing. No electricity. Inside and outside, it was gray. The exterior walls lacked insulation and tight construction that could keep the wind out. Without plumbing in the shack, the family got its water from a natural spring about half a mile away from the shack. Among other things, this meant that simple cooking became a major source of often unwanted physical exercise, especially when the outside temperature was bitter cold or blazing hot. And, of course, without plumbing, the lack of ordinary conveniences of a bathroom for bathing and other basic human functions meant that we left the shack and walked approximately fifty yards to a creaky, stinking outhouse, although I took for granted that stinking outhouses were the norm. The kitchen floor was a worn-through linoleum covering that had a thin and disappearing color around the edges of the room. The rest of the color had worn away. The other two very small rooms lacked any kind of floor covering.

Among many other unwanted discoveries, I learned that hard, cold floors can be uncomfortable places to sleep, especially when they have cracks through which icy wind blows into the house and sneaks into spaces where we need to be protected from cold. And, when mom could not afford kerosene to heat the house, the cold bit even harder.

The resources that kept our little family afloat were thin and rare, as best as I can recall. Within the limits of trying to care for the three children, our mother held small jobs that provided funds for limited amounts of food. Food was donated through the only charity in town, but their supplies were erratic and quite inconsistent, at best. The outcome of the lack of food was that on any given day we would have enough, but that on other days—days that seem to come frequently—we had no food. I adapted toward recognizing hunger within me, but not honoring it. And holidays came to be events that I saw as celebrations for other people, not for my family and me. Anticipating my return to school after Christmas became an anxiety-filled time for me because my teachers would ask a question for which I had no good answer: What did you get for Christmas?

Now, fortunately, my experience of living in a shack has mostly faded into memory. More importantly, my memories of those times have been integrated into positive and productive memories and behaviors. Allowing for this, recently, I asked my sister what she remembered from the years our family lived in a shack. "Cold feet," was her reply. My thought was "Damn right! Cold feet." In an instant, I recognized that I had long ago adopted the belief that I should keep my feet warm, even in the absence of having cold feet. For me, like an approaching thunderstorm or hurricane, cold feet required me to protect them.

Today, as I review some of my personal habits from the last few decades, I see some that I had never seen before. For the purpose of reporting this story, one of the habits that I obviously knew about but gave very little thought to was doing things to ensure that my feet were warm. Mostly, during winter, I wore shoes and socks to keep my feet warm, just like everyone else, but walking around inside the house without shoes and socks was not something I did. And feeling comfortable about keeping my feet warm did not seem to require any thought. I just did it.

If we had no children, I may not have recognized that "cold feet" was a dread with which I had learned to cope. From the time he began to walk, our son seemed to feel alien in shoes and socks. When he was a preschool child, we could coax him to keep his feet warm because we believed that he should have warm feet. Probably, most parents would do what we did.

As our son grew, his disinterest in shoes and socks persisted. And, as he developed through middle childhood, neither of us—his parents—felt the need to require him to wear shoes and socks. We never scolded him for not wearing shoes and socks around the house. On his behalf, I should say that in social settings, such as a school classroom, he wore shoes and socks. Otherwise, he kept his feet bare. Just as I felt compelled to keep my feet covered and warm, our son felt compelled to keep his feet uncovered and cold.

As I saw our son's bare feet, I felt something about this. The sight elicited low-level discomfort, as if I should try to complete a chore that I could not recognize or a chore that I had already completed. Around pointless reflections on this discomfort, my conversations with my sister finally brought clarity and relief. "Cold feet." Finally, I recognized that from my early years when cold feet were painful and unavoidable, I had been feeling the persistent need to keep my feet warm, even when there was no need to make the effort.

Now, as I contemplate my work with clients, I see that many of them carry within them the learned experiences that may continue to guide their thoughts, feelings, and actions but without recognition of their experiences or their efforts to compensate for them. And, as I see this in them, I find renewed appreciation for my unusual predilection—a feature of my humanity that now evokes smiles. But I should also add that I have renewed appreciation for the heroic efforts of our mother as she determined that she would do anything necessary to ensure that her children could survive and possibly someday thrive. She showed us her humanity in life-saving, durable, gritty, dedicated ways.

On reflection, my experience with cold feet revealed how messy and alternately glorious human beings are, how twisted and alternately pure their thoughts can be, and how harmful to others and alternately magnificently altruistic toward others they can be. As much as my experience of cold feet shaped my perceptions of human beings, it also clarified and refined my perception of myself.

Manliness

Note: The circumstances depicted in this story are true. The names and some other facts have been altered so as to protect individuals but remain faithful to the character of the story.

Conversations can sometimes become extremely confusing if not contentious. Surely, numerous so-called "news programs" illustrate this phenomenon much too well. Often, they epitomize the challenge of believing that two individuals may agree about simple things, such as the time of day, the country in which they live, or the color of oranges. If an individual comes from the Democratic Party, Republicans are, by definition, wrong. Likewise, if an individual comes from the Republican Party, Democrats are, by definition, wrong. One is a "demon-crat" and the other is a "repugna-can." For the two of them, coming together for the common good takes a lower priority than self-righteously being right and close-mindedly winning.

In far more subtle ways, differences between individuals may be confusing, entrenched, deeply felt, and contentious. This brief essay in the form of a dialogue addresses a specific kind of difference that emerged in a conversation between two therapists. It became a difference that defined important aspects of their relationship and, moreover, of their clinical work.

Caleb: I've been working with this kid. He is one of the hardest cases I have ever had. He doesn't want to be in therapy.Dana: How old is this kid?

Caleb: Fifteen.

Dana: Man, that's not unusual—for a fifteen-year-old.

Caleb: That's right. There's more to it, though. His mom wants him there. She pretty much made him come. She claims that he has all kinds of problems. She says he's depressed. She says he hides at home, spending a lot of time in his room, ignoring her. She says that he is hostile toward everyone, especially her.

Dana: Sounds like a lot of fifteen-year-olds I know.

Caleb: No. Well, yeah, but he seems to be a pretty good kid. He does really well in school. He likes going to school. From what mom says, he has several good friends. It's mainly that he drives her crazy. Actually, if his mom talks about him, she glows with pride, as if he is the greatest kid in the world. The kid obviously does a lot of things right.

Dana: So, who else is in the house with this kid and his mom?

Caleb: Just mom and an older brother. From what mom says, the older brother is ID—intellectually disabled. I get the idea that almost everything about him makes her life difficult. He's constantly unruly. He's old enough to know a lot about sex, but seems to know almost nothing about sexual etiquette, but wants something from girls that he cannot comprehend. Mom says that she cannot take him anywhere if there are girls and women there. He might touch them in the wrong way or just ask them for something sexual. As a woman, she knows what it's like to be sexually manipulated or at least to get attempts at manipulation.

Dana: Where's dad? Or, husband?

Caleb: I wondered about this, too. Mom says he's dead. But when she talks about him, she seems strangely evasive. I really don't know what that's about, but I suspect that he may have killed himself. I just get that sense from her that something really bad happened. She won't go there.

Dana: Dad's dead, and mom is stuck with two boys. Damn. Sounds like she is stuck in a tough place. A woman raising two boys, with one of them disabled, is a tough slog. I really feel for women who have to do that.

Caleb: Yeah, man, you got that right. I guess my main concern is that this kid is so resistant, so shut down with his mother. I wonder whether he blames her for his dad's death. At least, I wonder whether she has kept a lot of secrets from him about all of that.

Dana: So, what is she wanting from him?

Caleb: She wants him to communicate with her. It's pretty simple, as far as she's concerned.

Dana: She wants him to communicate with her, but wants to force him to communicate? Your description of her approach to him looks like some kind of oppression.

Caleb: It may be. She's pretty determined to get help for him. And, for him, that probably feels like oppression.

Dana: So, where does this leave you?

Caleb: That's what I'm trying to figure out. On the one hand, I like this kid and would like to see him get along with his mother, but on the other hand, I want her to back off and give him some space for doing things his way.

Dana: That's going to be difficult. How do you respect mom's wishes while denying her wishes? Rock and a hard place?

Caleb: I don't know. On my side of it, I've got to think about how I can honestly and clinically think about this kid and/or his mom.

Dana: Any thoughts, so far?

Caleb: Yes. Of course. How about you, based on the information I've shared so far?

Dana: Well, I'd say that mom probably knows her son better than anyone else. She lives with him and raised him to be who he is. So, given that she is his mother, I begin to wonder how you best respect her rightful authority as mom and help him to share mom's concern about their relationship. So, I guess some good old CBT or DBT types of interventions would be the way to go, if I were working with them?

Caleb: Good thoughts. So, the way you see the situation, both mother and son have developed some skewed thoughts that interfere with their relationship and that if I help them to change these thoughts, they can engage with each other with fewer problems. Is that right?

Dana: Yes. That's about it, in a simplified form. No matter what you do, it will be more complicated than I just made it.

Caleb: I like this. My thinking about this kid is a little different, though. Let me try some ideas and see what you think. I begin with what I experienced with this kid. He doesn't want to be in therapy, but seems to like seeing me. He rejects his mother's ideas about him being depressed or distressed in other ways, but obviously has a good time talking with me. So, this difference seems to be important. Another thing is that the conflict between the two of them is not entirely new, but it seems to have gotten hotter over the last two years. So, I ask myself about what this could mean. Why was this boy a much easier child when he was seven, eight, or nine, than he is at fourteen and fifteen? The short answer I come up with is "puberty." But I don't believe that it's just about being pubescent. Whatever he expresses toward his mother is stronger than the most common adolescent indignation. So, again, what is it?

Dana: As you're talking, I'm wondering about this, too. My mom and dad were pretty evenly matched from what I can tell, but mom was the planner, organizer, leader, and dad was the playmate, dreamer, and follower, but also fiercely competitive. I'm exaggerating some of that, but they were and still are very different. I have always been close to both of them. And both of the provided great models for me to follow. They still do. And, as I think about your clients—this mother and son—I come back to my mother and father and wonder how you get this son to respect his mother as his model?

Caleb: This is a good conversation. But I don't want to get this kid to respect his mother as his model. As we talk, I am getting clearer about some of what his problem may be.

Dana: I think I like where you're going with this. Tell me more.

Caleb: He's male and his mother is female. In the absence of a man in his life, he knows, but really doesn't know, that he cannot let himself be too influenced by a female, as if he somehow accommodates becoming a female like her. So, how does he differentiate his maleness from her femaleness? Remember, he likes being around adult men but can't stand being around his mother. Is he trying somehow to figure out how to be a male?

Dana: That's not where I thought you were going. I was thinking that this fifteen-year-old had adapted to being a very special person after his dad died, and his mom could not think about her other child as giving her much satisfaction. The older son is really a pain to have around. So, she probably put a lot of hope in your client as a special kind of child who could give her a lot of satisfaction. Now, he is letting her know that he is truly special and that he can live his life of specialness without any guidance from her.

Caleb: You're right. We are going in different directions.

In this brief dialogue between Dana and Caleb, both of them may be right, or both of them may be mistaken in their conclusions about Caleb's client. Trying to answer the question of who is right could easily miss the importance of the differences between them. Clearly, the facts of the client's situation matter. And, equally clearly, both Dana and Caleb take these facts into account. As such, neither one is correct nor incorrect in their statements about the client. However, the significance of this dialogue, as Dana and Caleb later agreed, revolved around the assumptions they used to reach their conclusions about the client.

Following further dialogue, Caleb acknowledged that he had struggled with his masculinity during his adolescence and that, without giving it much thought, he often concluded that his adolescent male clients probably struggled with their masculinity, too. Further, he acknowledged that he, too, struggled with his mother, an unmarried woman who did not have a male partner in her life.

In contrast, Dana acknowledged that he and his dad had a positive relationship, along with having long and positive relationships with both of his grandfathers. He stated that he had never really questioned his masculinity, let alone struggled with questions about it. Dana also acknowledged that his experience of his masculinity probably caused him not to consider whether Caleb's client may have been struggling with his masculinity.

In the end, as simple as this dialogue and subsequent conclusions may be, they illustrate all too well the vulnerability to misjudgment about clients that can easily result from personal and longstanding assumptions, based on a therapist's personal history. Whether longstanding assumptions, beliefs, and other related commitments belong to a therapist or anyone else, they epitomize some of the essence of being human. More fundamentally, therapists carry the obligation to reflect on and attempt to minimize any undue, distorted clinical judgments that manifest their necessarily learned beliefs about countless aspects of the human experience.

Actualizing the Humanity of Therapy

All of the work of therapists surrounds a key, necessary fact: They exist as professional mental healthcare providers to provide professional services to clients. The client is the center of the therapists' concern and efforts. Client welfare—what is best for the client—transcends all other considerations. To actualize—to bring to life—this consideration, the following discussion presents the case of Bunting. It is presented as a means through which understanding of the humanity of the encounter between therapists and their clients may be enhanced, not to mention that Bunting's story alone is compelling.

The Case of Bunting. Bunting G. is a thirty-seven-year-old mother of two daughters. She has been struggling with depression, now having subsided, but still pressing her to get help, since the birth of her second child, who is now eleven years old. Before her second daughter was born, Bunting served as a counselor with a major mental health center. From the time her daughter was born, she had not been employed or otherwise involved in professional work.

Bunting—or "Bunny," as she prefers—has sought and received treatment. She has sought help through psychotherapy and psychopharmacology. These interventions seemed to moderate her depressive symptoms but did not eliminate them. Moreover, while functioning in an improved manner, Bunny reports that her depression "just kept breaking through." She avers that she is sometimes paralyzed by depression.

Now, seeking therapy again, her therapist Megan R. seeks to become acquainted with Bunny.

> I've looked at the material that you prepared for us, the intake forms. So, we can assume that I know what's there. Thank you for being so thorough in giving us information about you. The fact that you are a counselor comes through nicely in what you gave us. More than having information about you, I would like to get to know you. So long as you're comfortable with it, I would like to know more about your concerns and struggles, your obligations and circumstances, and, maybe, about the treatment that you have already had. There may be some things that have worked for you that we need to continue. Are you okay with this?
>
> Bunny: Yes. Sure. I will do all I can. I have to.
>
> Bunny softly cries. She seems to be overwhelmed by meeting her new therapist.

Therapist: Bunny, I see that this is difficult for you. Can you give me some insight about what's happening with you right now?

Bunny: I'm terrified. I've been here before. And, it hasn't helped. I'm scared to death that I will expose every raw nerve I've got, and I'll end up just hurting even more. I will find out again that no one can really help me.

Therapist: That makes sense to me. If you were not worried about this, I would be worried about you. Instead of being worried, I am comforted by the fact that you are worried about whether I can help you, whether you can get better. Maybe, as a place to begin, I want you to place as much of the burden on me as you can. After all, there are two of us here. If you don't make it, I don't make it, too. With all of that in mind, I take seriously that this is difficult for you. I can assure you that I will not overwhelm you. We will work at a pace that fits where you are. And if we get out of sync, I want you to let me know. Your well-being matters very much to me. For now, are you okay with me asking some questions just to get to know you?

Bunny: Sure. Anything. I will do my best to tell you all I can.

Therapist: If you're comfortable with telling me about it, what happened with the other therapist?

Bunny conveys a large volume of information in response to questions from Megan. It may be summarized as follows: Bunny was not clear why she sought therapy or how she located the therapist who treated her for approximately four and one-half years. She indicated that the therapist gave her a diagnosis of chronic depression and borderline personality disorder. "I knew that those diagnoses were not correct, but I have also learned not to argue with one's therapist. I have never been a borderline. That's just not me. I just don't know where the therapist got that." She reported that her previous therapist sought to treat her with cognitive behavioral/cognitive therapy. "I was just confused most of the time. I just didn't have the symptoms that chronically depressed individuals have or that borderlines have. Well, maybe, I had some of the depressive symptoms, but not the borderline stuff. I just do not like the idea that I am chronically depressed. It sounds like it's forever. I feel trapped, just by being called 'chronically depressed.'"

Therapist: Your previous therapist apparently took you seriously and tried to help, but may have missed seeing how you felt about what she was doing to help you. Is that it?

Bunny: Yes. Really, she understood a lot. But she seemed to have an agenda of her own. I'm not sure what it was.

Therapist: Again, if I do things that seem out of sync with you, please tell me. My job is not so much to be right about everything, but to be as helpful as I can be. So, please tell me, when I seem to be going astray. Would you do that for me—and for you?

Bunny: I'd be glad to. Thank you.

Therapist: Is there anything else about the other therapist that might be good for me to know? Or, maybe, anything that may be important to you?

Bunny: Maybe. I thought a little about this, but this has been fairly recent. When I went to get therapy, I was so depressed, so obsessed with what was happening to me that I think I just missed what was happening with the therapist. And, just recently, it hit me. I think she was scared or maybe intimidated. I'm not so sure that she knew how to deal with trying to help another therapist. I think I must have introjected her views so that I was the one who felt inadequate. That's really scary.

Bunny and Megan engaged in lengthy exchanges, mainly around inviting questions that the therapist posed to Bunny. Bunny's clinical picture slowly emerged.

Bunny concluded that her current, entrenched problems began after her second child was born. She reported that her daughter was born approximately six weeks prematurely. Apparently, her daughter's premature birth was less of a problem than several major health issues that beset her daughter. Bunny indicated that her daughter suffered from congenital heart and intestinal issues that required several hospitalizations and surgeries. She says that she withdrew from almost every other activity in her life so that she could care for her daughter. She took a leave of absence from her position with the mental health center. She moved from her home to a smaller home that provided easier access to and from the hospital and that cost less than the home she left. After sixteen months, she wanted and needed to return to work, but by this time had sunk into depression that kept her at home. Bunny says that she was thoroughly tired, defeated, and no longer competent to manage her health, her daughter's health, and her possible employment at the mental health center.

Bunny denies that she has seriously contemplated suicide or any other form of self-harm. "I know that that would not help anything. Besides, what would my daughters do without me? No, I knew that I had to go on, no matter how bad I felt."

After further reflection, Bunny cautiously but clearly recalled how helpless she felt as a child when impossible demands were put on her. She reported that her mother, Alyssa, was much too occupied with other people, including Bunny's troubled and demanding brother. She recalled that her "escape" from her mother and her brother involved time with her grandmother, Gramma

Katie. She provided extraordinarily detailed reports about satisfying times with her Gramma Katie, including times when they would shop for clothes for Bunny, bake jelly rolls together, feed the birds and squirrels around Gramma Katie's house. Notably, among the few times Bunny smiled in her early sessions, she remembered when one of the squirrels jumped on the table in front of Gramma Katie, causing her to jerk away from the squirrel while holding a glass of iced tea and splashing the full glass of tea all over herself.

Bunny reported that her brother suffered from developmental delays and probably autism. She said that he was not manageable, but that she increasingly carried the burden of managing him. She said that she always felt like a failure because she could not do anything effectively with her brother. Worse, she said that as she moved through her teen years, and wanted desperately to be involved in teenage activities with other teenagers, but that she was isolated and "unable to be normal." "I really resented that. And, I felt guilty for resenting it. I was 'damned if you do and damned if you don't.'" "I just carried around this feeling of despair, but I never thought of it as depression. And, I don't know that that's what it was." "I should have had therapy back then, I guess, but I didn't."

Bunny indicated that she has had no major medical issues. No thyroid issues. No family history of mental illness. "Just plain good health, until all of this postpartum stuff hit me." Megan was not quite settled with these reports.

Therapist: Bunny, it sounds like you lived with perpetual and unrelenting stress when you were a child, except for the times you shared with your grandmother. Is your grandmother still involved with you, and you with her?

Bunny: Well, no. Not really. I love her and she loves me. I have never questioned that. But I have to be kind to her. She is too old to entertain me. She still lives on her own, alone, but she just isn't as available as she used to be.

Therapist: Let's explore more about this later. For now, I'm also wondering about your father. In all that you have said about your family, you have not mentioned him. Can you tell me about him?

Bunny: Sure, but there isn't much to tell. When you're a kid, no one tells you anything. So, I don't really know what happened. I know that they married—my mom and dad. After that, the story gets kind of murky. However, having a lot of pieces of the puzzle, I believe that both of them got involved with others outside of the marriage. Both of them had affairs. They split, emotionally. They divorced when I was in my twenties. Dad remarried and had another family. He actually had more children. I think that his new wife was the one he had an affair with. They moved away, too. So, most of the time I was growing up, he visited her a lot in the Kansas City area or north of there, around Maryville, Missouri. So, I really didn't see him much, like a real father. And, even when I did see him, he was preoccupied with his other family. He has three kids with his wife. So, they really didn't have much time for me, and still don't.

Therapist: I wonder how your relationship with your father may have shaped your way of relating with me. But let's plan to immerse into that another time.

Bunny: I think that's a good idea. Right now, I'm just too emotionally raw to go there.

Therapist: Your mother did not remarry. Is that correct?

Bunny: Oh, no. The last thing she wants is a man in her life. I don't think she even liked my brother. Mom is just too busy with her own things. If she can walk—I mean, walk, like miles at a time—or bar hop with her friends, all female, she's doing fine. But, also, she will spend as much of her time as she can taking care of her flower garden. She loves flowers. She always spent more time with her flowers than she did with her children.

Therapist: You say that with some sarcasm, but I get the idea that your mother's lack of interest in you has caused you a lot of pain.

Bunny: Absolutely. She may have cared for me as her daughter, but she truly sucked at letting me know it. Maybe she was miserable and didn't want to dump her misery on me. I don't know.

Bunny described a relational history in which she appears to have developed the belief that she could not truly be important to anyone else. Adding to this, she developed the belief that she lacked the competence to develop a meaningful relationship. Megan acquired awareness of her extraordinary responsibility of engaging Bunny in ways that assured Megan of her importance in the therapeutic relationship.

Bunny described her older daughter as "close to ideal as a parent could want." "Meredith is outgoing, athletic, very caring—she dotes on her younger sister—sociable, very musical, and usually kind of nerdy." She indicated that Meredith has exceeded all developmental milestones, including her current achievements at age fourteen. She leads her school academically, with the highest scores in physics and chemistry. She holds the office of president in her high school as a freshman. Bunny wonders where Meredith gets her talent and determination. Somewhat cautiously, she expressed her dread that Meredith may need to make big impressions on others because she has failed to make such impressions with her mother and father—Bunny and Frank—at home.

Tearfully, Bunny talked about her relationship with Frank. She stated that the multiple health problems of their younger daughter have exhausted them. She said that she and Frank have not had a relationship since their younger daughter was born. She reported that because she needed to stay with her daughter "twenty-four/seven," she and Frank simply failed to keep in touch. She lamented the fact that they were in the same home but did not sleep together. "We hardly speak to each other." "He seems sad and pre-occupied with other things." She reported that Frank works as a human resources administrator with the local public school district. "We have just learned to be self-sufficient—lonely as hell, but self-sufficient. I think Frank is terribly lonely. I know I am." She said that she and Frank met while they were students at the state university near where she lived. She cannot recall where or when they first met but believes that it was probably at one of her girlfriend's home when several other friends were there watching football games. She remembered that they were in the kitchen of the home and met at the refrigerator when both of them were reaching for a beer. She remembered sitting with him on the porch swing and enjoying the evening with him. "As I look at him now, I think he was pretty lonely back then. I think he really needed me."

Usually, Bunny shared as much as she could tolerate. Maybe the sorest topic for her was her career.

"When I found counseling, I found an identity in which I could invest everything I had. I loved the idea that I could be a part of people's lives so that, as a result of what I did, they could live better lives. Happy lives. Fulfilled lives. When I had to quit work, I lost all of that. Now, I feel like I have nothing. Who am I, now? Nobody? Every day, I think about going back to work. That meant so much to me. But, right now, I would be scared to death to begin to see clients again. I need therapy so much, I can't imagine being helpful for them. Somehow, I have to get back there, though. I've just got to."

As Bunny revealed her story of involvement with her family, she provided a picture of herself as a mother who seriously, persistently, affectionately, and thoughtfully invested in her children. More than her career, protecting her children and advancing their welfare seemed to occupy her thoughts, plans, activities, and emotions. Paradoxically, while her children seemed to be securely attached to her, she gravely doubted her ability to be attached to them. "And, Frank, I just feel bad about what I have done to him. He deserves better than he gets."

Megan: Let's suppose that therapy works well for you. At some time in the future—and the sooner the better—your life is pretty much the way you want it to be. And, you no longer need therapy. What would this look like to you? What would you like to see, as the outcome of our work together?

Bunny: Oh, gosh. I've been stuck for a while. I guess that I would be back to work. My heart says that, if I accomplish nothing else, I will have a nice relationship with Frank. God knows, I need that, but I think he needs that, too. And, my kids. They will know that I'm okay—that I can take care of them, again.

Megan: Bunny, all of that looks like it's doable. I can't think of anything that would keep us from getting there.

Bunny's judgment about her previous therapist may be correct. The evidence that Megan, her new therapist, received from the previous therapist indicates that the previous therapist sought almost immediately in their therapist–client relationship to complete several assessments of Bunny, including intelligence testing, achievement testing, aptitude test, personality testing, and career test. Bunny's view of the previous therapist's initiatives is that her needs for understanding and support were avoided, adding that the therapist's interest in testing triggered the thought that the therapist could not relate with her and, worse, that the tests would reveal horrible surprises.

What may competent counselors and therapists think, feel, or do in response to Bunny? The answers to this question could, no doubt, take many different professionally accountable courses. Alternative theoretical orientations to case formulation make this inevitable, along with the extraordinary variety of personalities who deliver therapy. Surely, from Bunny's view, any courses of action should account for the fact that she was lonely, feeling isolated and worthless, and provide meaningful contact, such as a sensitive manner of hearing what she has to say and helping her to invent truly doable things that may improve her standing with herself. Relational purpose and meaningful contact, such as an improved relationship with her husband, would be curative for Bunny from her view of her situation.

Megan's views of her relationship with Bunting reveal several of her important professional assets but also her vulnerabilities. On reflection, Megan surprised herself when she said, "Mostly, I like what I did with Bunny, but I am uncomfortable with the thought that somehow I needed to be more like her—fresh, living on the edge, exploring parts of myself that I'm not well acquainted with, and that sort of thing. I need more of a depth of experiencing life, just like Bunny does. Frankly, I'm a little nervous about going there. What if I lay it all out there and engage with the depth of feelings that Bunny wants to take to Frank? I need to do some of that with my partner, and it scares me to death. Do I really practice what I teach my clients? I believe we made real progress in helping Bunny to see her pain as a real asset. Because of her experience of pain, she knows what it's like and how to overcome it. She has an understanding of suffering that she can take to her clients. Few of us have that kind of understanding. Bunny has risked so very much—much more than I have. I love working with Bunny, and I like that my work with her was pretty good, helping her to change. I'm just not a risk taker as much as she is. And, whether I'm comfortable with it or not, I must—simply must—explore some of this. I suppose this is Bunny's gift to me.

Thoughts about Humanity

Probably, most therapists have encountered distressed, discouraged, and depressed clients who have lost any expectation that their lives could be better than they are. With such clients, attention to their pain and other struggles is obviously needed. Possible courses of action, including specific clinical interventions, should be considered. Possibly, the most challenging and professionally accountable approach is to realize that the relationship with Bunny in and of itself is necessary. And, almost without exception, the therapist's discomfort with engaging in such a relationship with this client or with anyone else who is a client or not compels discomfort. No one passes by an open door in a hospital corridor, sees a suffering patient who is likely dying, and enjoys the scene. Instead, even if the response lasts for a few seconds, the scene of extreme suffering evokes discomfort. Within the space of a clinical consulting room, or wherever therapy is delivered, the pain of clients often evokes similar responses. Such responses are real. They are somewhat ordinary. Moreover, they are human. And, as such, they reveal therapists' humanity.

To be sure, clinicians can and do speak of clinical issues, empathy, transference, countertransference, therapeutic alliances, and so on, along with hundreds of other clinically related topics. More basically, the question is not whether they can speak of these things—they can—but how well they relate with suffering clients and, in the process of such relating, exhibit the best of humanity. Much more than easy assumptions and convenient beliefs about what is therapy, therapists who know who they are, including who they are when they meet their clients' suffering. When they meet with clients, they may justly embody the humanity and the paradox of healthy helping that feels both the pain that their clients bring and the hope that comes with their personal self-knowledge and its accompanying professional accountability. In doldrums of helping or the raging intensity of helping, their humanity lives within them. After all, they are undeniably human.

Scrutinizing these therapists in a quite limited manner, based on the characteristics of humanity that inhere in the practice of therapy [Refer to Chapter 1 for a discussion of these characteristics.] what observations, if any, may be shared?

The four therapists whose stories appear in this chapter demonstrate the important paradox of "owning" their vulnerabilities and, consequently, utilizing their assets.

These therapists appear to recognize the importance of having a professional community, although this is not quite as clear in the story of Bunting and Megan. Still, the therapist Megan appears to recognize the importance of community in the life of Bunting, largely from the adverse consequences of not having a community.

These therapists clearly possess a heightened interest in effective communication.

These therapists show that their level of self-awareness is high and that they can be curious about exploring what they don't know about themselves.

In quite different ways, each of these four therapists appears to engage with others in such a way that they respect multiple forms of differences among humans.

Each of these therapists appears to be guided by their understanding of their personal and professional needs and, in quite specific ways, demonstrates the outcomes of such guidance.

Quite remarkably, these therapists epitomize the significance of the reality of change and the necessity of adaptability.

The rising and falling urgency of maintaining life may be reasonably attached to an explanation of these therapists' actions, although "urgency" may be overstated as a description of their situations.

Assuming that meaningfulness equates with a need for a reason to want to live, this, too, would appear to expand the evidence beyond what is readily available in these stories, except for the story of Bunting and Megan. Surely, in the other two stories, the quest for meaning appears to be a salient but a somewhat quiet feature of their respective reports.

If recognizing humanity in one another necessitates ethics and law, the therapists in these three stories appear to have acquired an adequate, if not elevated, awareness of ethics.

These three stories express many of the characteristics of being human. They show the ambiguities that inhere in being human and embody the values and thoughts that result in positive, socially constructive actions. If utilized by others, these therapists' experiences can serve as invitations to careful self-examination and self-discovery.

Chapter 7
Healthy Helping
The Humanity of Being a Therapist

Achieving professional competency emerges from honestly honoring the humanity of therapists. Affirming this view, Knapp and his colleagues (2017) identified some of the qualities of humanity about which developing therapists ask themselves. They aver (p. 163) that developing therapists should wonder about whether they "are aware of their immediate reactions to patients, can evaluate their competencies accurately, effectively monitor potential biases, consider that they may use heuristics inappropriately in their decision-making, and think about how personal values may influence their professional decisions." Among others, these features of developing therapists epitomize the outcomes of serious self-examination of individual therapist's humanity and appropriate feedback from others.

To state what is obvious, therapists are neither exclusively therapists nor nontherapist humans. During every session with every client, the therapists are human. The specific indicators of this may be too many to report or imagine. In the clinical environment, while concentrating appropriately on the dynamic interaction between one's self as a therapist and a client(s), a therapist belches, becomes distracted by noises outside the consulting room, feels the pressure of flatulence, or suffers from the intrusive memory of his young daughter crying herself to sleep last night, among the numerous signs of being human. Allowing for a virtually limitless variety of such signs, the central question here is "What is healthy helping?"

Much too often, the space between healthy helping and unhelpful, socially sanctioned norms is small or blurred. A therapist's account of her meetings with a client illustrates this. The therapist whose words appear below is a young woman who is treating a young woman.

> I'm not sure what to do. My client stinks. I mean, she literally stinks. And we talk about it. She says that it's a good way to get people to avoid her. She's an attractive girl, but she says that if she never bathes, she can keep men at a distance. She's right. She stinks up my office, and I don't want to be there. I can't imagine that any man would want to get close to her. After she leaves the office, I'm afraid that the next client will think that the stink comes from me. I'd like to tell her that I will work with her if she takes a bath and comes to my office not stinking, but I'm not going to. At the moment, it just drives me crazy. Still, she comes to see me and wants to change her life. So, I try not to get caught up in judging her too harshly. As I listen to her, I really try to understand where she is. She's attractive, but does not like her body. From what I can tell, she has been shamed—extremely shamed—about her body. I do not want to do that to her. In the end, I have to think that her odor, her attitude, her history, and a lot of other things give me a lot to work with. So, I ask myself about any one of these things, "What is the clinical significance of it?" It's really hard sometimes—to smell her and to coach myself to think clinically.

The therapist's account of her interaction with her client illustrates the reality that therapy, including healthy helping, lies within the boundaries of being human, not outside of them. And, it is this bounded relational territory within which therapists demonstrate, enact, and embody healthy helping or not. No doubt, many others have documented the serious implications of human vulnerabilities as therapists present them. At least, these vulnerabilities should be taken into account when healthy helping is discussed but should not define healthy helping merely as their polar opposites, nor necessarily demand for attention and correction. The examples of these vulnerabilities or, possibly, failures, fall into several categories. Among others, Walfish et al. (2012) and others have reported about therapists' proclivity to exaggerate the positive outcomes of their professional services. Goldberg et al. (2016) have established that clinical competence continues to decline among practicing therapists, with the majority of them demonstrating incompetence. Martin (2020, 2024) joined several other researchers (e. g., Singer & Lalich, 1996; Holden & Barker, 2018; Thyer & Pignotti, 2015) to substantiate that therapists frequently promise much more than they can deliver by advancing nonclinical ideologies and other predictably failing approaches to their counseling and therapy. And, Rousmaniere et al. (2016) concluded that clinical supervision is not significantly related to client outcomes. Compatible with other major signs of failing clients, these important issues constitute and necessitate the conclusion that psychotherapy and psychotherapy education need "radical reform," in the words of O'Donnell (2011, p. 259). Also, these factors alone call for serious attention to the humanity of therapists.

As simple, stark, alarming, and real as it is to state that therapy may not be healthy, the observation has mostly been ignored by practicing therapists and their leaders. However, it should be noted that this chapter is not intended to dispute the findings of research that confirm this conclusion. Instead, along with many others, including hundreds whose research is represented in this discussion, it joins the expanding effort to move therapy toward clearer and universal professional accountability. Surely, multiple studies of highly effective therapists are signs of this effort (e.g., Silvia et al., 2024; Blatt et al., 1996; Delgadillo et al., 2022; Ablon & Jones, 1998; Eells, 1999; Fox, 2023; Goldfried et al., 1998; Huhra et al., 2008; Lafferty et al., 1989; Liszewski, 2022; Lilienfeld, 2014; Martin & Turner, 2020; Owen et al., 2019; Jennings & Skovholt, 1999; Skovholt & Jennings, 2004; Vaz & Sousa, 2021; Wampold & Owen, 2021). Also, allowing for caution about its practical implementation, building on relevant evidence for improving clinical effectiveness, those who teach in preparation programs should pay attention to evidence-based teaching (e.g., Feinstein et al., 2015; Allan, 2019; Mackrill & Iwakabe, 2013; Plakun et al., 2009; Malott et al., 2014; Osberg, 1997; Wheeler & Delaney, 2008; Valenstein-Mah et al., 2020).

Other efforts toward enhanced professional accountability have explored and developed innovative methods for improving clinical effectiveness. An example of this may be quantifying therapeutic language (Miller, 2023) as an indicator of competence or potential competence. Another example, provided by Montan et al. (2022), demonstrates a careful examination of how to improve training within a commonly known model of psychotherapy. In their study, the model was psychodynamic psychotherapy. Another contribution of an innovative method is Jewell et al. (2021), with their emphasis on "Utilizing Technology in Social Work Education: Development of the Technology Effectiveness and Social Connectedness Scale." Additional examples of innovative methods for improving clinical services may be found in Kühne et al., 2022; Hahn et al., 2023; Teichman et al., 2022; Kaslow et al., 2009; and, Westra and Di Bartolomeo (2024).

Healthy helping involves at least two major components. One is that therapists have a clear and useful understanding of what characterizes highly effective therapists. Therapists can elevate their competence by emulating and seeking to become effective therapists when they self-examine, consult with peers, gather evaluation resources, such as Feedback Informed Therapy (FIT) materials, and more. As this book and other sources establish, most therapists travel on roads that appear to go toward predictable ineffectiveness instead of intentionally traveling toward effectiveness. The other major component is the therapist's health. A healthy therapist is more likely to provide healthy and effective therapy than an unhealthy therapist. These two components are discussed below.

Humanity and the Highly Effective Therapist

As an apparent truism for practicing therapists, "If you don't know what characterizes good therapists, you are unlikely to become one." More than an intellectualized definition, the importance of the characteristics of a good therapist is that practicing therapists have committed to improving their clinical performance according to the best evidence for their aspirations, which they can achieve. Thus, the characteristics become personal.

As noted above, the information about highly effective therapists can be somewhat easily located. Adding to the sources already identified, the book by Miller and Moyers, *Effective Psychotherapists: Clinical Skills That Improve Client Outcomes*, can be located and ordered online. Or, if therapists subscribe to *The Journal of Mental Health Counseling*, they can find that the entire issue in January 2005 is dedicated to studies of "master therapists." Or, another book is Rousmaniere's *Deliberate Practice for Psychotherapists* (2016). With or without these resources or ones that have already been cited in this discussion, therapists can easily locate free presentations by virtually every prominent researcher on effective therapy if they have access to the Internet and look for YouTube videos. These videos include presentations by Bruce Wampold, Scott Miller, Tony Rousmaniere, Irvin Yalom, Lou Cozolino, and others. Or, useful and relevant materials, along with training possibilities, are available on the website of the International Center for Clinical Excellence. Instructive materials and other resources about highly effective therapists are readily available. Among them, an additional one is SAMHSA's Evidence-Based Practices Resource Center.

Improvement of therapy is an obligation of all therapists, including practicing therapists, instructors in preparation programs, officers and leaders in professional associations, among others. An essential question that all therapists should ask themselves is a simple but necessary one: "In what specific ways do I need to be better than I am?" The answer to this question transcends the somewhat mundane acquisition of information about what characterizes excellent therapists. Instead of merely gathering information, therapists should aspire to elevate their clinical competence so that their clients can achieve specific, measurable clinical outcomes. Still, the need to know what characterizes effective therapists is a good beginning toward improving clinical competence. The discussion of the following characteristics of effective therapists is a synthesis of the findings from the evidence that many researchers and others have reported, including those already cited in this chapter.

Before offering specific characteristics of effective, competent therapists, a description of the context for such a discussion is needed. For one thing, as Heinonen and Nissen-Lie (2020, p. 417) declare, "There is little understanding, and less consensus, on which characteristics explain the notable differences in treatment outcome between therapists." They confirm that therapists' evaluation of their own skills is important (p. 426) and that the "more effective therapists are characterized by interpersonal capacities" that emerge from their personal histories. While current research about effective therapists provides considerable guidance for those who aspire to improve clinical effectiveness, much more is required.

Another contextual feature is that self-care by therapists has been a consistent and persistent concern among those who discuss effective therapists. Those who maintain their personal health are more likely to be effective as therapists than those who do not.

A third contextual feature is that careful and evidence-based characteristics of effective therapists should provide guidance for preparation programs and other entities through which clinical training occurs. Currently, such guidance is quite inconsistently utilized. Sadly, the outcome of this deficiency prompted Lilienfeld (2014) to conclude, "There's plenty of legitimate debate in clinical psychology and allied fields, such as psychiatry, social work, and counseling, but at least one proposition should not be particularly controversial: The state of mental health care is in shambles." Concomitant to Lilienfeld's conclusion, professional education for therapists is "in shambles," too. The data that indicate this are overwhelming and longstanding. In short, among other related issues, many have described and attempted to explain the apparent, longstanding, and pervasive disconnection between preparation programs and clinical practice (e.g., Spengler & Pilipis, 2015; Cummings & O'Donohue, 2011; Daniel et al., 2019; Even & Robinson, 2013; Goldberg et al., 2016; Hill et al., 2015; Lane, 2023; Lilienfeld et al., 2014; Gonsalvez & Crowe, 2014; Lwin & Beltrano, 2022; O'Donnell, 2011; O'Donohue et al., 2008; Vannatta & Steen, 2019,

Society for the Advancement of Psychotherapy, no date; Wike et al., 2013). Stated tersely, O'Donnell (2011, p. 258) calls for "radical reform" of preparation programs.

A fourth contextual feature is that the characteristics of effective therapists provide guidance for clinical supervisors. Clinical supervisors who provide supervision to those whose professional development is critical for the clients for whom their supervisees provide therapy should know these characteristics and utilize them, at least, as desirable goals for their supervisees (Martin & Turner, 2020).

However, whether these things are taken into account by practicing therapists or not, they have an obligation to be vigilant about improving their clinical competence. When this obligation is taken seriously and integrated into clinical thinking and practice, therapists will likely elevate their effectiveness. Stated differently, they will also be able to review their clinical work and conclude that it is healthy and that, insofar as it is healthy, they have exhibited admirable features of their humanity, as the best of therapy defines it.

A good therapist demonstrates a readiness to help. A readiness to help may be assumed to be true of all therapists. No doubt, this assumption is largely correct. Seldom do therapists take indifference, hostility, or other negative attitudes to their work with clients. Some of the obvious signs of probable failure to deliver effective clinical services are detailed in Chapter 4. At least, the information in Chapter 4 strongly implies that large numbers of therapists succumb to the temptation to implement inappropriate ideologies as therapy, compromising the integrity of mental health care and the welfare of their clients, and tacitly rejecting their readiness to help. Generally, therapists' readiness to help manifests itself in normative availability for clients and in their commitment to optimize their professional assets on behalf of their clients.

Nevertheless, if a readiness to help may be important, how may it be demonstrated? The therapists who demonstrate their readiness to help recognize and provide professional care that gives priority to their clients' clinically relevant needs—and not their own needs. Significantly, from the point of view of clients who need help, they feel appropriately comfortable with the therapist. They believe that, even if their problems make them uncomfortable, they are comfortable with the therapist. They experience the therapist as one who genuinely likes to help others. They feel welcomed in the consulting room or wherever the therapy occurs. They conclude that the therapist has sufficient experience and knowledge and that the therapist invites the problem with which clients struggle instead of avoiding problems because they are unsure about how to react or feel fear of the problems. The therapists who demonstrate a readiness to help genuinely want to be therapists and enjoy themselves in this role, respecting their efforts to meet their clients' needs even when this is uncomfortable for them. The good will and positive attitude toward clients allows for common and easily forgivable errors in providing clinical services, without which common errors lead to therapy-threatening ruptures.

Effective therapists possess a proclivity for intellectual complexity. The relevance of this characteristic is that those who possess it will usually be able to engage with the real and common complexities that clients present. They understand that clients are almost always complex. Beyond the fact of such understanding, they welcome complexity because they know that to do otherwise involves rejecting clients and their needs. They feel respect toward their clients' sometimes desperate pursuit of simple answers to immensely complex problems and communicate appreciation for their clients' often painful need for answers. For example, when therapists encounter a client who suffers froman addiction to methamphetamines, they adapt their thinking to the complexities of the serious, long-term, inconsistent, and often painful process of recovery. Similarly, when they encounter a child victim of sexual assault, they feel the suffering of the child and reckon with not only the complexities of helping with the child's recovery but also the complicating factors of engaging the child's significant caregivers and those who are involved in legal proceedings.

Effective therapists want to know "more," usually demonstrating indefatigable curiosity. A common phenomenon in the delivery of therapy is that clients usually contain more clinically relevant information than clinicians seek from them. Effective therapists pursue clinically relevant questions with clients, seeing the value in helping clients to discover their potential for empowering themselves and solving their problems. They will ask about their client's internal events about which no one else knows or asks. Such therapists will hear from their clients: "I'm not sure how you did it. You never gave me advice, but somehow you helped me to find what I needed to do." While curiosity is not a stand-alone asset, it is one that facilitates clients' discovery of their personal power and useful solutions for their problems. Indeed, curiosity is in itself an important clinical intervention. Almost inevitably, it enables clients to discover information and insights that facilitate healing and recovery.

Effective therapists show a high tolerance for ambiguity. Tolerating ambiguity poses challenges for all humans. Quite apart from the matter of providing mental health care, clear and unambiguous information is often needed. After a biopsy that was needed to determine whether, say, an individual has lung cancer, no one is going to welcome the ambiguous statement, "Well, you may have cancer or you may not. We don't know, but we will let you know at some time in the future." Or, if a family is pursuing the purchase of a home and needs a mortgage, they need to know what the rate of interest on the loan may be and what their monthly payments may be instead of a vague promise by the lender to collect payments from the family.

Effective therapists recognize that humans are highly ambiguous and probably that their clients are often more ambiguous than others. Therapists' tolerance of ambiguity enables them to see ambiguity as an opportunity to help, insofar as it offers potential for discovery, whether a client is willing to be open or not. Thus, effective therapists expect and welcome ambiguity instead of attempting to pose solutions that defy ambiguity. Along with other critically important indicators of effective therapy, the importance of this one cannot be overstated. Very likely, the intolerance of ambiguity triggers therapists' defenses against the threat of their clients' ambiguous presentations, accounting for the rise of "narcissistic entitlement" (McWilliams, 2005, p. 139), "professional narcissism" (Knapp et al., 2024, p. 212), and "exaggerated individualism" (Martin, 2024, pp. 32–49). Professional narcissism manifests itself in many different ways. One of them prompted Martin to conclude, "Arguably, the most common violation of professional ethics is the intentional delivery of therapies that lack clinical credibility and that may cause harm" (2024, p. 231), as an unfortunate compensation for intolerance of ambiguity.

Most practicing therapists understand that they should develop and practice emotional attunement: Often, ttherapists assume that they should be emotionally attuned to their clients, a normative and necessary expectation. However, more than being emotionally attuned to their clients, therapists who demonstrate emotional attunement, with special emphasis on their internal coherence and authenticity, function more effectiveness than those who are out of sync with their emotions. They feel their feelings with an acuity that allows them to utilize these feelings on behalf of their clients and themselves. Based on such internal awareness, therapists increase the likelihood of being accurately attuned to their clients' emotions and of achieving clinically relevant outcomes with their clients. As experienced therapists often recognize, they "know" that something of significance is happening with a client, although the overt content of their dialogue does not necessarily account for it. While emotional attunement may not be singularly important, effective therapy cannot be delivered without it.

Effective therapists exhibit strong relational skills. The degree to which experienced clinicians demonstrate strong relational skills is the degree to which they are effective mental healthcare providers. Further, these skills protect the welfare of the clients whom they serve. Martin and Turner (2020, p. 151) describe relational skills.

> These skills encompass the ways a mental health clinician interacts with clients. Such interactions may be illustrated in multiple ways. For example, when clinicians model focus and reflective thinking for clients, they are exhibiting relational skills. Or when clinicians initiate conversations with clients about the quality of the relationship between themselves and their clients, especially in such ways that display openness to improving their relationship, they are exhibiting relational skills. Similarly, clinicians exhibit relational skills, when they choose to self-disclose or when they provide self-care for their clients or when they confront difficult client issues in ways that welcome troubling and often painful disclosures from their clients.

By definition and personal commitment, therapists provide professional care for their clients. As a necessary feature of such care, *effective therapists embody intentional and sustained self-care.* No one argues against self-care for therapists. However, a longstanding conclusion is that the failure to execute self-care plans has become normative among practicing therapists (e.g., Figley, 2002; Meadows, 2024; Molyneux, 2022; Posluns & Gall, 2020). Self-care for therapists not only needs careful monitoring among individual therapists but also needs to be emphasized in clinical training programs, professional associations, and relevant ethics panels.

A truism in relationships is that when an individual's relational needs are not met, the relationship lacks the potential for satisfaction and durability. Clearly, whether therapists' relational needs are met outside of therapy or not, their needs persist as important features of who they are as persons and as therapists. In the context of providing clinical services, *effective therapists meet their important relational needs and maintain social support outside of therapy*. And, apart from their role as therapists, they pursue ways to meet their relational needs. They find ways to care for others and meet their need for care from others. Generally, they like to be with others and, conversely, they are not usually loners or inclined to avoid others.

The importance of these qualities may be self-evident. When therapists possess them, they not only more carefully and precisely assess their own personal needs, along with ways to meet these needs but also engage with clients in such ways that they effectively respond to the clinically relevant needs of their clients. Collectively, these research-validated qualities equip therapists to understand and plan with their clients so that clinically relevant clients' goals are likely to be met.

Knowing that the characteristics of effective therapists are desirable and almost self-evidently admirable makes them tempting as measures of one's worth as a therapist. Therefore, those who aspire to develop these qualities should consider them as aspirations, not as signs of being an ideal therapist. After all, therapists have the potential to become ideal—whatever this may mean—as anyone else or any other category of humans. Aspirations for ongoing effectiveness and improvement should not become a means of self-punishment but should be utilized as markers of progress toward increased clinical competence.

Humanity and Clinical Judgment

Understanding the characteristics of effective therapists is important because such an understanding provides a solidly positive foundation upon which clinical skills may be built. Nevertheless, effective therapy often poses daunting challenges for those who try to provide it. They have learned that it is not a profession that is well suited for individuals who need constant reassurance from others. Effective therapists know this. They have largely reconciled themselves to the sometimes unwanted but inevitable thought that without disciplined self-awareness, they could harm clients. Thus, they know the importance of asking, "How do I protect my clients from me?" As terse as this question is, the necessity of asking it has been stated and implied several times in this book. It somewhat naturally follows from the research of Goldberg et al. (2016), Spengler and Pilipis (2015), Bowes et al. (2020), Martin, (2020, 2024), Cuijpers et al. (2010), Cummings and O'Donohue (2011), Lilienfeld et al. (2014), Martin and Turner (2020), Ronnestad and Skovholt (2013), and others. Chapter 4 offers additional strong evidence for the necessity of answering this question.

Briefly, to extend the need for therapists to ask about how they protect clients, those who presume to practice aberrant approaches to therapy pose the likelihood of harming clients and the profession of which they are members. At least, they prevent competent mental health care from being available for their clients when they presume to practice aberrant approaches, such as Smileology, Somatic Astro Cartography, Soul Biofield Tuning, Soul-focused Feng Shui, Soulshine Astrology, Spiritual Herbalism, Star Astronumerology, Swedish Massage, or Synastry, or thousands of other nonclinical approaches. Necessarily, observers of these approaches should ask whether those who practice them have also betrayed their own humanity, along with exhibiting a lack of professionally appropriate concern for their clients. Instead of exhibiting concern for their clients, they succumb to ideology-driven rigidity.

In contrast with the apparent abandonment of humanity, including their own, effective therapists recognize that when therapists meet with clients, something happens. A client gestures with her hands. A therapist asks a question. A client smiles broadly from a recognized, fresh insight. A therapist speaks words of encouragement. And so on. Therapists contemplate doing something or not. Therapists do something or not. At the core of functioning as a therapist, contemplating an action or enacting an intervention involves clinical judgment instead of enacting the therapist's ideology or reacting from personal needs. The term clinical judgment is used here to include similar and frequently used terms, including "clinical reasoning," "clinical interventions," and "clinical decision making." The core concept that inheres in these terms is that mental healthcare providers engage in a perpetual, second-to-second, "tick-tock" decision-making process when they provide clinical services to clients. In so doing, although therapists may hold appropriate clinical expectations for themselves and their clients, they welcome the challenge of not knowing what may come next. They see ambiguity as providing opportunities for inventing clinically relevant responses to clients in the moment.

In this perpetual decision-making process, the characteristics of effective therapists—or possibly ineffective therapists—manifest themselves. As these characteristics manifest themselves or not, the engagement with a client(s) establishes a living, relational process between two individuals. As in every other relationship, this process also expresses the humanity of these individuals. When the specific expressions of humanity include those that are described in Chapter 1 and are expressed by effective therapists in such ways that may be characterized as authentic, accountable, humane, and relevant, clients almost inevitably move toward meeting their goals. With allegiance to each client, effective therapists hold clinical ideologies in abeyance, pending their judgment about what each client may need. With this abeyance in place, they relate with clients in a manner that exudes understanding, warmth, respect, and more, forming a useful and positive foundation for conducting therapy. Allowing for the possibility that almost anyone can humanize their interactions with others, the added, essential characteristics of clinical judgment cover much more relational territory than this.

Another characteristic of professionally accountable clinical judgment is that it integrates as much clinically relevant evidence as may be available. Such judgment emerges from gathering clinically relevant information from and about a client. Broadly defined, gathering information is an important asset for effective therapists. They understand that their relational skills are important and that having clinically relevant information provides them with a necessary foundation for clinically relevant knowledge that contributes to their capacity to practice evidence-based, effective therapy. However, gathering information cannot stand alone. A therapist described her insights about information gathering in the following manner.

> Out of my frustrations of working with clients early, way back then, was that I could not determine what to do. Slowly, it occurred to me that I am never going to exhaust my ability and imagination to ask eliciting questions, if I look away from my client's emotional paralysis or my own and look, instead at my client's needs. I concluded that my client may be stuck, but that I cannot be stuck. If there are two stuck persons in room, my client cannot get the help needed. So, in the moment, I will find a way to allow my interest in my client to be expressed. Sometimes, this can look like most therapists believe it should look and at other times it simply looks odd. For example, I remember saying to a client, "You have a lot to say about a lot of things. I'm not sure what to think about everything you have said. So, if you're okay with it, I would like to narrow the conversation to a few things that come to mind. There's just so very much I don't know about you. How about this: If I were to visit your home, something I'm not going to do, what would I see? What would I see as I drive up to your home. If I were to go inside, what would I see? Maybe, you could give me a 'tour' of your home." The importance of something like this for me is not so much that I need to know what I would actually see at the client's home, but that, when the client tells me about her or his home, I will learn things about my client. Almost inevitably, the client will reveal important things about herself or himself.

Of course, the information gathered from clients and possibly other sources must be aggregated into a clinically relevant understanding of the client with an emphasis on understanding each moment of relating with the client. Further, the information from the client should somewhat naturally blend with the clinician's understanding of the client's clinically relevant needs. For example, if the client provides a useful body of information that the clinician correctly aggregates into a picture of an "excessively guarded, fearful, lonely, and avoidant person," the clinician may engage the client in useful and corrective reframing of their thinking about personal worth and their skewed valuing of external markers of personal importance.

Clinical judgment refers specifically to clinical decisions that therapists deem to be needed as they respond to clients. This is obvious. However, clinical judgment also means that the clinician decides to do something that other therapists—the professional community—would regard as appropriate "treatment." Far from being an assuring abstraction, clinical judgment translates into doing something, a compelling commitment of which good therapists are almost constantly and intentionally aware. As such, it may mean that the therapist says and does nothing. It may mean that the therapist directs the client to remain silent and reflect on their experience of the moment. It may mean that the therapist offers support (e.g., "Your readiness to smile and to show determination to balance your grieving with gratitude requires me to admire you. As I see you working through some really difficult circumstances, I conclude that you show real courage, even when you may not feel courageous."). The doing of something may be almost anything of which professionally accountable therapists can think and of which their similarly accountable peers would approve.

Haderlie (2011, p. 8) writes, "Although it seems intuitive that clinicians become more accurate in their decisions with experience, most results have not generally supported such a relationship . . ." Many others, including those cited by Haderlie, confirm this conclusion. However, as Haderlie adds, "Perhaps the most frequently-suggested means of improving clinical judgment is the provision of corrective feedback during training on judgment tasks" (p. 9). The explanations of this commonly reported phenomenon continue to elude researchers, except for the explanations that refer to therapists' exaggerated and extremely skewed self-confidence, an insular and inaccurate confidence in their clinical judgment, and their readiness to assign clinical efficacy to approaches that have no potential for effective therapy or, worse, that harm clients.

In contrast with the need for feedback-informed approaches to therapy, large numbers of therapists commit to their presumed clinical approaches, including numerous nonclinical ideologies. As Miller et al. (2015) conclude, "Contrary to prevailing assumptions our analysis of over 40 years of research on the appropriateness of confidence uncovered that clinicians' confidence has a small but statistically significant relation with psychological assessment judgment accuracy" (p. 561). Also, among others who pay attention to the discussion of clinical judgment, including Haderlie (2011) and Miller et al. (2015), already mentioned, the following sources provide useful information: Austin et al, (2023); Boswell and Constantino (2015); Boustani (2023); Dawes (1989); Faustino and Vasco, (2023); Garb (1998); Harding (2007); Isenberg and Venturo-Conerly (2024); Kraus et al. (2016); Lichtenberg,(2009); Rock et al. (1987); Spengler et al. (2009); and Walfish et al. (2012). Possibly, as the body of evidence that clarifies and establishes the qualities of effective clinical judgment and decision-making enlarges, the delivery of effective therapy will be enlarged, too. Through further investigations, understanding and developing highly effective therapists and specific measures of their clinical judgment may nudge the profession of therapy forward.

Health of the Therapist

Therapy is a relational process. The process involves at least two individuals, a therapist and a client, in a relationship that aims to increase the health and well-being of the client. Orlinski et al. (2005, p. 407) offer a cogent elaboration of this view.

> The fact that interpersonal relatedness is such a central aspect of the psychotherapies means that psychotherapists' *personal* qualities—their social perspectives, emotional resonance and responsiveness, motivation to help, self-understanding and self-discipline—are integral parts of their therapeutic work with patients, along with more generic *professional* qualities of technical competence, probity, and objectivity. [Italics appear in the original.]

Further, they appear to be quick to add that "those personal qualities need to be developed and maintained at a high level of sophistication and refinement—a higher level, in fact, than most people are expected or required to have in their close personal relationships" (p. 407), particularly when providing therapy for clients. Their view is that the sophisticated and refined personal qualities include mental, emotional, and relational health. As such, whether they demonstrate their health in clinical sessions, therapists should pursue and seek to maintain their personal health. Just as the good or bad qualities of being human appear in a wide variety of formulations, human health does so, too. Allowing for the wide variety of possible manifestations of human health, the necessary question is "What may characterize mental and relational health, with the emphasis on health?" And, in this discussion, the necessary companion question is "How may such a characterization manifest itself in therapists?"

In the history of the mental healthcare movement, several noteworthy efforts have defined healthy individuals. They include some widely recognized efforts, such as Maslow (1943, 1971), Erikson (1950, 1968), and others. In addition, many others have sought to define a healthy person (e.g., Shostrom, 1964; Goldstein, 1939, 1940; Barkham et al., 2001; Jensen & Bergin, 1988; Venter, 2017; Renger & Macaskill, 2021; Timulak & Creaner, 2012, Levitt et al., 2005; Balkis, 2024; Bleidorn et al., 2020). However, none of the attempts to define a healthy person has had as much influence and durability as Rogers' conceptualization of a fully functioning person.

As a clear and often reported and interpreted view of a mentally healthy person, Rogers' conceptualization of a fully functioning person continues to be an important reference for those who seek to understand human health.

In his various reports on what observers may see if they were to meet such a person, Rogers provided clear and convincing illustrations. A general encapsulation of Rogers's view (1963) of a fully functioning person includes the following three characteristics.

1. This person is open to his experience. This is a phrase has come to have an increasingly definite meaning for me. It is the polar opposite of defensiveness. In the past, defensiveness has been described as being the organism's response to experiences perceived or anticipated as incongruent with the structure of the self. To maintain the self-structure, such experiences are given a distorted symbolization in awareness, which reduces the incongruity. Thus, the individual defends himself against any threat of alteration in the concept of self.

   In the person who is open to his experience, however, every stimulus, whether originating within the organism or in the environment, would be freely relayed through the nervous system without being distorted by a defensive mechanism. (p. 18)
2. This person lives in an existential fashion. I believe it would be evident that for the person who was fully open to his experience, completely without defensiveness, each moment would be new. The complex configuration of inner and outer stimuli that exists in this moment has never existed before in just this fashion. Consequently, our hypothetical person would realize that "What I will be in the next moment, and what I will do, grows out of that moment, and cannot be predicted in advance either by me or by others" (p. 20).
3. This person would find his organism a trustworthy means of arriving at the most satisfying behavior in each existential situation. He would do what "felt right" in this immediate moment, and he would find this in general to be a competent and trustworthy guide to his behavior (p. 20).

However, whether the source is Rogers or one of the other luminaries in the history of therapy, the need for re-stating and maintaining currency is ongoing. Toward offering a contemporary picture of such a person, the characteristics discussed here may be adapted to defining healthy therapists. They express a synthesis of views, including those from publications already noted and professional experiences. The discussion of characteristics of mentally and relationally healthy individuals aims to encompass the essence of the insights that many others have carefully articulated, but to do so briefly.

One of the challenges in reporting about mentally healthy people is that they almost never get attention, particularly research attention. After all, they are not problems to be solved through research, and the funding that almost universally accompanies research projects is not available to investigate them. In addition, as a social and community issue, healthy individuals have attracted little attention for being healthy. Also, because they are usually fairly secure individuals, they do not crave attention and usually do not boldly present themselves so that others must give them attention. Mentally and relationally healthy individuals understandably occupy very little attention or effort from practicing therapists. Likewise, healthy therapists receive little attention from the professional community in which they are members. Instead, whether individuals are clients or therapists, those who receive necessary attention receive appellations such as disordered, pathological, bizarre, mentally ill, disturbed, harmful, delusional, and so on. Again, although these individuals require attention for the purpose of equipping them to move toward healthy living, this discussion is focused more on mentally and relationally healthy persons who are therapists.

The first characteristic is that *a mentally healthy person carries and tries to preserve an ever-present awareness of freedom to choose*. As many therapists readily recognize, the importance of this characteristic can be easily seen in those who deny their freedom to choose. For example, the widow whose husband died eight years ago continued to live as if he were alive, succumbing to the illusory comfort of denial. Or, the young man who "medicates" his failure—getting fired from his job—with alcohol has relinquished his freedom to choose and imposed harm on himself. Practicing therapists could immediately add countless reports of clients who reject their freedom to choose. Much too often, the temptation to avoid the freedom to choose may be irresistible when the temptation comes from "choosing a side" that protects individuals from choosing. This is commonly seen when individuals become members of a team, a religion, a political party, a corporation, or sometimes choose a clinical orientation. Clearly, among large numbers of therapists, the flight from freedom appears in the form of tightly and rigidly held ideologies (Martin, 2024), including clinical (e.g., Noble & Rizq, 2019; Martin, 2024) and religious ideologies. Instead of relinquishing the freedom to choose, the mentally and relationally healthy individual maintains a clear moral steadiness that rises above taking sides, such as these. Thus, such an individual places

as much value on cooperation as on competition,

as much importance on having a clear point of view as on accepting points of view that are different, as much demonstration on unity with others as on a readiness to create disunity on behalf of a morally defensible position,

as much focus on affirming life as on a readiness to sacrifice to defend life, and

as much energy toward gathering resources that make her/him secure as on generosity with resources.

Instead of mindlessly going in either direction, mentally healthy individuals maintain their freedom to choose. And, in maintaining this freedom, mentally healthy individuals show a balance in their lives. They often take a long view of difficult circumstances and work toward long-term solutions instead of giving in to immediate and often inadequate solutions. Their management of problems usually leads to outcomes that are somewhat more positive and durable than those of others. Within consulting sessions with clients, therapists frequently see "stuckness" but refuse to succumb to adopting stuck-ness as if it were their own. Instead, therapists maintain their freedom to choose.

Extending this idea, mentally healthy persons act with generosity, placing emphasis on ensuring that others have needed resources, particularly those resources that others cannot provide for themselves (i.e., Maslow's "Gemeinschaftsgefühl"). Typically, healthy persons maintain awareness of the pressure to take sides, to align with those who can bring benefits to them, but choose life-affirming actions as a way of being generous toward those who cannot meet their own needs. Drawing both admiration and enmity, they often stand in contrast with an American culture that is too often self-indulgent, self-promoting, and even greedy, a culture in which the "have-nots" have persistently increased in proportion to the population for almost four decades. Or, as Rogers asserts, "The direction that constitutes the good life is that which is selected by the total organism, when there is psychological freedom to move in any direction" (1961, pp. 186–187). Expressions of this freedom may or may not please others, but it is this recognition that confirms freedom. And, when therapists possess this quality, its positive value in their conduct of therapy is obvious.

Mentally healthy persons have a heightened and effective sense of proportionality. This simply means that a mentally healthy person keeps things relatively clear and free of distortions. This characteristic of a healthy person may be expressed in numerous ways, such as these.

They feel good about themselves, but not necessarily great. They take justifiable pride in good or excellent relationships, work, or other activities, but know that pride is much more about the future and the potential that the future holds than a record of self-satisfying accomplishments. They

> operate as if pride is good—based on real accomplishments—but that hope is better than pride.
>
> They are searching, curious persons who know that there are answers to many of life's pressing questions and that the answers are almost always tentative. They understand that life holds more adventure and change than fixed and certain things, encompassing the most satisfying, passionate, and romantic moments or the absorbing pain from a decaying and infected tooth.
>
> They understand that adversity comes with living and that this fact only partially describes human experiencing, insofar as companionship, good food, good sleep, and other "feel good" realities come with life, too. So, more likely than not, they understand that adversity or its opposite is momentary and that something significant happens after either one. It is this cognizance of "something" that permits the healthy person to maintain openness to possibilities.

To frame this idea another way, mentally healthy persons' sense of proportionality means that they welcome alternative ways of thinking about things. For example, healthy individuals may feel frustrated and angry when another driver cuts them off in traffic, but they are extremely unlikely to seek revenge. It means that they reasonably feel annoyed when their children challenge their authority but refuse to succumb to the thought or impulse to slap or hit their children. More than restraint or over-reacting to difficult circumstances, proportionality is usually joined with their freedom to choose. So, instead of beating their children when their parental authority is challenged, they may express not only their disappointment about the manner of being challenged but also appreciation for their children's independence. Indeed, the work of therapy often involves assisting clients with their need to reclaim their ability to think and act with proportionality, free of exaggeration, either-or thinking, or other unhealthy distortions. Among many familiar therapeutic attempts to assist clients with their need to overcome their disproportionality, Rational Emotive Behavior Therapy and various forms of Cognitive Behavior Therapy have demonstrated their effectiveness.

Implicit in proportionality, healthy individuals, including healthy therapists, demonstrate their inclination to adapt to circumstances. They adapt to the fact that their fifteen-year-old daughter experimented with consuming alcoholic beverages while visiting a friend. They adapt to the changing character of their intimate relationships, knowing that the ecstasy of newness and adventure that saturated the beginning of their partnering relationship cannot be indefinitely sustained. With conspicuous relevance, therapists adapt to the clinically relevant needs of their clients and provide clinically relevant services in response to these needs.

Mentally healthy persons demonstrate cognitive complexity. In other words, mentally healthy persons accept the fact that life is complex and adapt to this fact. For example, the human body is extraordinarily complex. This leads to the acceptance of believing in the expertise of physicians. More than this, though, mentally healthy persons are not concrete, either-or thinkers. This feature of a healthy person may be confusing. In application, this kind of thinking means that a mentally healthy person shows high tolerance for uncertainty, likes puzzles in many forms, and invites new experiences, including discovering new acquaintances.

As an asset for therapists, the importance of demonstrating cognitive complexity should be recognized. Frequently, this is confirmed when therapists encounter clients whose ability for cognitive complexity has been abandoned. For example, seeing a distressed client, therapists may observe that the client has long believed that she must be approved by everyone in her life. Or, another client irrationally concludes that he cannot leave his employment because he long ago decided that when he made a commitment to an employer, he should not renege on his commitment. This is to say that the opposite of cognitive complexity may be seen in individuals who seem permanently to think and believe the same thing under all circumstances. Often feeling overanxious, they cannot tolerate complexity. In contrast, complex thinkers may express their abilities in many different ways. They may enact their passions in ways that appear incongruous. For example, she may be a skilled quilter, but also take on the adventure of running marathons. Or, for example, he may not only be a devoted hunter but also develop his talent as a singer. Or, he may be an empathic, somewhat quiet therapist, as well as an aggressive, competitive athlete, maybe, as a basketball player. Or, she may be a devotee of solution-focused therapy, also comfortably practice cognitive behavior therapy or psychodynamic approaches because her clients' needs require it.

In practice, therapists who demonstrate complex thinking believe that their clients are much more complex than judgments that may be made about them. They recognize that mental-emotional problems are complex and difficult to understand. Healthy therapists appreciate this fact. They understand that the complex nature of most clinically relevant presentations from clients requires them to explore clients' problems and to avoid merely accepting them. The illustration below helps clarify this.

Jim seemed timid, almost afraid. However, when speaking with the therapist, Jim seemed to be comfortable. Later, as therapy began, Jim's

> fear came and went. When Jim revealed or spoke about his fear, his voice dropped to a barely audible whisper, as if he were trying not to be noticed. When he spoke about almost anything else, he showed energy and insight, as if he may not have any problems at all.
>
> Jim's story involves many facts that evoke thoughts and feelings in most others. As a thirty-four-year old man, he reports that his wife died after a long struggle with lung cancer. He reports that his adoptive father retired and relocated to another part of the country. Jim says that his adoptive father is his "real father," adding that "he has always been my rock." He reports that his biological father—whom he had never met—appeared without notice only a few months ago. Jim says that he faces daily challenges in trying to ensure that his three children get what they need. Jim indicates that his loneliness "bites hard." He suggests that his health has declined over the past couple of years, referring to nightmares, overwhelming fatigue, and moments "when my brain just turns off." He emphasizes that this is his problem.
>
> Jim says that he is not depressed. Somewhat persuasively, Jim says that he really is hopeful about his life, especially about his children. "It's just that I have these moments when "my brain just turns off," he says. He shrugs, "It really confuses me" and wonders, "What's wrong with me?"
>
> On hearing Jim's story, his therapist began to wonder about several possibilities among the many ways that he could understand Jim's mental-emotional problems. For example, when Jim said that his brain "just turns off," the therapist began to wonder whether Jim was describing a common result of prolonged fatigue. With enough fatigue, individuals lose focus. They can get so tired that, except for thinking about sleep and rest, they can think about almost nothing else. Similarly, the therapist began to wonder whether Jim was describing "dissociation," an event in which the individual slips into an altered state of consciousness, sort of like a prolonged and deeper than usual daydream. Also, in response to Jim, the therapist considered whether Jim may be carrying a long and hugely significant list of pressing problems "in his head" and while he is, say, preparing lunch for his children, slips into thinking about his hurtful loneliness because of his wife's death. And, of course, Jim's therapist, considers whether Jim may be showing the signs of grief. After all, grief, sometimes takes Jim from the present moment of enjoying his children into memories of attending to his dying wife.

Healthy therapists who respect the reality of life's complexities may see themselves in "Jim's" story. They can see Jim's complexity, as well as their own. They welcome the challenges and opportunities that inhere in recognizing that there are almost never easy or simple answers to complex human problems.

Whether they are more or less expressive of their feelings than others, *mentally healthy persons are considerably more tuned in to their feelings*, commonly demonstrating a capacity for expressing a wider range of feelings than others. In their relations with others, they show a readiness to be receptive to a wide variety of expressions of emotions, too. Generally, this equips them to be attuned to their own feelings and, therefore, to effective self-care and other care.

This characteristic may be confusing, mainly because there is no easy and reliable way to know who is attuned to their feelings and who is not. Being attuned to feelings is not the same as expressing feelings. And, much of what may be expressed often comes from family and social training and, not necessarily, an individual's ability to know what they feel. For example, a mentally healthy attorney may passionately present a criminal defense for a client whom she seriously dislikes. As an attorney, she is practicing her profession as effectively as she can, including expressing important feelings in her practice. As expressive as she is, she may not be attuned to her feelings or be able to authenticate them for herself.

More than anything else, individuals who are attuned to their own feelings have been taught by others that this is a good thing and that expressing feelings appropriately requires personal discipline. Healthy therapists accept their adult accountability for managing their own feelings. This is healthy, but it also provides a model of accountability for their clients and others. A sign of such modeling and accountability involves acceptance of difficult and positive feelings, but also the manifest ability to talk about their feelings in a straightforward, credible manner, relatively free of unhealthy contaminants, such as meta-emotions that too often become embedded in and distort honest and real emotions. Further, while recognizing the authority of their feelings as indicators of the way things truly are, they also recognize the normative subjectivity of such authority and the importance of alternative feelings that may be reactions to and associations with the same events. As such, they can openly address sensitive topics, such as their relational needs, sex, disappointments with themselves and others, albeit uncomfortable at times. Observations of these therapists indicate that they can attend to other's feelings. Whether they are providing therapy or relating with others elsewhere, these therapists are ready to support others when someone is having a difficult time, but they are equally ready receive such support. For example, to a friend, they may say, "You don't look so good. Are you feeling okay? Tell me about it." Or, "I know this is not a good time for you. Are you okay, if we just do something together?"

In short, healthy therapists maintain attunement to their own feelings. However, if therapists are healthy, they understand that this is not necessarily an attribute that they can or should claim or welcome in all clinical circumstances in view of discomfort with the feelings to which they are often attuned when they engage with clients. In practice, this means that, instead of cool, professional distance that disallows feelings, therapists see and hear from clients in such ways that they react with understandable feelings. For example, a therapist provides professional services for a five-year-old female whose parents relocated to another state without telling her, leaving her alone with no other family nearby. Or, a therapist hears from an adult male client who reports that his only sibling, an adult female, killed herself just days ago. Or, a therapist hears from a woman whose recent heart attack closely resembles his mother's recent heart attack. In response to these clients, neutrality is unlikely. Whatever feelings may emerge, such as disappointment, anger, sadness, mystification, fear, or others, they may be entirely appropriate. Therapists' management of these feelings is critically important. And, effective management of these feelings in ways that serve the needs of clients depends on how well therapists are accurately attuned to them.

Mentally healthy persons possess strong and positive relational skills. The importance of relational skills for therapists cannot be overstated. Many relational skills have been included in lists of those needed by therapists and formulations of these skills have taken many different shapes. As self-evidently important as relational skills are, they have not been clearly and consistently defined for therapists and those who train them. Nevertheless, several authors have attempted to overcome this apparent deficit.

During the last few decades, the attention given to investigating, understanding, refining and prescribing how to practice relational skills has been ongoing. Ivey and his colleagues have been leaders in this effort. Their book (2014), *Intentional Interviewing and Counseling: Facilitating Client Development in Multicultural Society* is a good example of their contributions. A common theme in the discussion of relational skills is that listening to clients is an essential skill. More than merely receiving information, such listening usually refers to the content of what clients say, the meaning of what they say, and the affect that may be embedded it. In addition, with appropriate grounding in their professional identity, therapists also establish that they are trustworthy, dependable, genuine, empathic, honest, and independent participants in the clinical process in which they maintain necessary and appropriate interpersonal and professional boundaries. Alternate presentations of necessary clinical skills have been published by Hill and Norcross (2023), Miller and Moyers (2021), Martin and Turner (2020), and others.

Recapitulated, the basic characteristics of a mentally healthy person, with reference to those who practice therapy, include these:

Holds the freedom to choose.
Keeps things in reality-based perspective through maintaining proportionality.
Thinks in complex ways.
Accurately attunes to one's own feelings.
Expresses strong relationship skills.

The characteristics of a healthy individual discussed here represent a sample of such characteristics. Additional ones include practicing self-acceptance but not self-indulgence, maintaining a clear conscience, accepting responsibility for one's thoughts, feelings and actions, laughing and enjoying humor, enjoying time alone and time with others, along with others. Just as the list of clinical skills has been presented in an extraordinarily large variety of ways, the characteristics of healthy individuals have been similarly presented.

Problems in life are inevitable. No one is safe from problems. Every mature adult knows this. Mentally healthy therapists know this, too. Instead of idealizing their mental health as a protection from all problems, they see their ongoing demonstrated commitment to sustaining their personal health as equipping them to manage their problems as effectively as may be possible. And, from this view of their own problems, they also see that they aspire to equip their clients to manage their problems effectively, too. In other words, "My humanity affects the humanity of others." This is both the limitation of humanity and the gifts of opportunity to improve the therapist's own life, as well as the lives of their clients.

Hope for Therapy and the Humanity of Therapists

As emphasized at the beginning of this book, therapy embodies and defines a view of humanity. Therapists embody this view when they seek and maintain their own health and healthy ways of practicing their craft. As such, they embody hope when they affirm this view. This affirmation says,

> Therapists raise potential for sharing common **assets and vulnerabilities** of being human whatever these assets and liabilities may be.

Therapists recognize that **humanity is community** that promotes the virtues and advantages of identifying with others. This is the opposite of isolation, loneliness and wanton aggression.

Therapists understand that **communication** inheres in community and that effective communication inheres in good therapy.

Therapists embody a relatively high level of **self-awareness** and operate well when it is present and active.

Therapists accept as real and necessary that humanity is **multiple forms of differences.**

Therapists see that humanity is **possessed by needs** that energize and activate behaviors that affirm and encourage living well.

Therapists confirm and affirm the **reality of change and the necessity of adaptability**, as a feature of being human and as commonly expressed as their belief in positive outcomes from their efforts.

Therapists respect the rising and falling **urgency of maintaining life,** as characterizing human thoughts and actions, including in and through therapy.

Including themselves, therapists know that human individuals **need a reason to want to live**. By definition, they help clients to move toward having health-promoting and health-sustaining reasons to live.

Therapists recognize that the humanity in one another necessitates **ethics and law** and defines how to engage with others in life-affirming ways.

A discussion and analysis of therapy necessarily encompasses, nurtures, and sustains the question of what is right and wrong. Truly, answering the question about how best to relate with others and, more generally, how to live well, positions therapy in such a way that it cannot be both morally strong and morally weak. Lived in a healthy manner, an accounting of an individual's humanity must reckon with the potential for both moral strength and moral weakness, acknowledging that all of the good and bad things that heightened self-awareness and self-knowledge inform.

From the Introduction to these closing paragraphs, this discussion has focused on the humanity of therapists. Their/our humanity poses both the potential for moral weakness and moral strength. No doubt, the discussion recognizes the fact of numerous compromises of moral strength and its blatant contradictions. However, much more than a lament about weakness or failure, it affirms the unspeakably large potential for improving the lives of countless others and, because of this, calls for change toward healthy therapy. More than a mere description of unethical clinical decision-making, it expresses the hope and, maybe, the promise that therapy will, as McWilliams (2005) asserted, preserve the humanity of therapists.

Including all its constituent parts, therapy as a profession must decide that the right—or moral strength—is always better than the wrong. To opt for the right means that the reality of humanity is not only acknowledged but also respected and honored. When this option is clearly and genuinely chosen, certain features of professional practice become obvious. In brief, among therapists, receptivity to truth and moral strength will be visibly and consistently demonstrated. And, regardless of who occupies the profession or initiates the discussion, professional accountability can be acquired only by those who are ready to pursue it, acquire it, and sustain it.

Appropriately framed professional accountability includes more than just providing effective clinical services, while such services are indispensable features of professional accountability. In addition, professional accountability asks the broader question of whether therapists carry the proportionate and necessary burden of contributing to the welfare of the society of which they are members. How well have they championed the cause of mental health? How well have they advocated for those who have no advocates, including the poor and hungry? How well have they represented those whose voices are silenced by various kinds of oppression, including spousal oppression, governmental deficiencies, corporate opportunism, incompetent therapy, or unhealthy social norms, among others? Along with others, these questions become distilled in the microcosmic community of person-to-person interactions between a client and a therapist.

> Many people are alert to the idea that when a person is before us, something infinitely more precious and profound is before us than a mere animated pile of molecules. We are in the company of *a person*, someone who calls for our attention as one person to another. Anyone who can sense this, who can genuinely receive and act on it, is in possession of a connection to, or sense of, a good that is the source of all goodness.
> (Italics appear in the original.) (Steane, 2018, p. 253)

On any given day, anyone of us may fail to honor our humanity. When we fail, we suffer the consequences, along with others who are influenced by our failure. But when we succeed in honoring our humanity, as daunting as this pursuit may be, we gain benefits, knowing that some of these benefits are unspeakably valuable. After all, which words best describe the importance of saving a life or mending a severely broken life? And, what is the value that the best of imagination could place on the health of a client who says, "I am so profoundly grateful. You saved my life. I feel like I can breathe now, not tied in knots of needing something but not knowing what it is. Now, I feel like a real human being. Thank you. Thank you!" Authentic hope comes from honoring one's humanity.

To close, therapy is effective and adds to the well-being of its larger society when humanity—indeed, life—turns to itself as the source of meaning, personal fulfillment, and sharing the adventure of being human. As therapists incorporate the best available evidence for their professional services, therapy thrives. As such, when they self-consciously and deliberately embody their humanity, therapists commit to creating a story of human existence that can be told with a smile and inner peace, if not outrageous joy. And, accounting for the slips and falls in human behavior, they see the results of their efforts and realize that they have moved their clients and society toward reconciliation, felt and predictable security, and honestly hopeful expectations. Authentic hope comes from honoring one's humanity.

References

Ablon, J. S., & Jones, E. E. (1998). How expert clinicians' prototypes of an ideal treatment correlate with outcomes in psychodynamic and cognitive-behavioral therapy. Psychotherapy *Research, 8*, 71–83. http://dx.doi.org/10.1093/ptr/8.1.71

Allan, R. (2019). Teaching and learning evidence-based practices: Promoting dialogue for counsellors and psychotherapists. *Counselling and Psychotherapy Research, 19,* 206–213. https://doi.org/10.1002/capr.12223Citations:3

Austin, B. S., Lee, C., McCarthy, A., & Sprong, M. (2023). Educators' perceptions of clinical judgment skill competencies in rehabilitation counseling. *Journal of Applied Rehabilitation Counseling, 54*(2), 148–166.

Balkis, M. (2024, February 21). The role of rational beliefs in promoting mental well-being: A validation of the rebt's psychological health model. *Journal of Rational-Emotive & Cognitive-Behavior Therapy, 42*(3), 669–679.

Barkham, M., Margison, F., Leach, C., Lucock, M., Mellor-Clark, J., Evans, C., Benson, L., Connell, J., Audin, K., & McGrath, G. (2001). Service profiling and outcomes benchmarking using the CORE-OM: Toward practice-based evidence in the psychological therapies. *Journal of Consulting and Clinical Psychology, 69*(2), 184–196. https://doi. org/10.1037/0022-006X.69.2.184

Blatt, S. J., Sanislow, C. A., Zuroff, D. C., & Pilkonis, P. A. (1996). Characteristics of effective therapists: Further analyses of data from the national institute of mental health treatment of depression collaborative research program. *Journal of Consulting and Clinical Psychology, 64*(6), 1276–1284.

Bleidorn, W., Hopwood, C. J., Ackerman, R. A., Witt, E. A., Kandler, C., Riemann, R., Samuel, D. B., & Donnellan, M. B. (2020). The healthy personality from a basic trait perspective. *Journal of Personality and Social Psychology, 118*(6), 1207–1225. https://doi.org/10.1037/pspp0000231

Boswell, J. F., & Constantino, M. J. (2015). Clinicians self-judgement of effectiveness. *Psychotherapy Bulletin, 50*(4), 15–19.

Boustani, M. M. (2023). Decision-making in modular treatments: Avoiding another research-to-practice gap. *Clinical Psychology: Science and Practice, 30*(1), 63–65.

Bowes, S. M., Ammirati, R. J., Lilienfeld, S. O., Costello, T. H., & Basterfield, C. (2020). Cognitive biases, heuristics, and logical fallacies in clinical practice: A brief field guide for practicing clinicians and supervisors. *Professional Psychology: Research and Practice, 51*(5), 435–445. http://dx.doi.org/10.1037/pro0000309

Cuijpers, P., van Straten, A., Bohlmeijer, E., Hollon, S. D., & Andersson, G. (2010). The effects of psychotherapy for adult depression are over-estimated: A meta-analysis of study quality and effect size. *Psychological Medicine, 40,* 211–223.

Cummings, N. A., & O'Donohue, W. T. (Eds.) (2011). *Understanding the behavioral healthcare crisis: The promise of integrated care and diagnostic reform.* Routledge.

Daniel, K. E., Jensen-Doss, A., Muroff, J., White, B. A., Reilly, E. E., Hollon, S. D., Mennin, D. S., Schuler, T. A., & Teachman, B. (2019). Characterizing evidence-based practice and training resource barriers: A needs Assessment. *Training and Education in Professional Psychology, 14*(3), 200–208.

Dawes, R. M. (1989). Experience and validity of clinical judgment: The illusory correlation. *Behavioral Sciences & the Law, 7*, 457–467.

Delgadillo, J., Deisenhofer, A-K. Probst, T., Shimokawa, K., Lambert, M. J., & Kleinstäuber, M. (2022). Progress feedback narrows the gap between more and less effective therapists: A therapist effects meta-analysis of clinical trials. *Journal of Consulting and Clinical Psychology, 90*(7), 559–567. https://doi.org/10.1037/ccp0000747

Eells, T. D. (1999). What do we know about master therapists? *Journal of Psychotherapy Practice Research, 8*, 414–317.

Erikson, E. H. (1950). Growth and crises of the "healthy personality." In M. J. E. Senn (Ed.), *Symposium on the healthy personality* (pp. 91–146). Josiah Macy, Jr. Foundation.

Erikson, E. H. (1968). *Identity: Youth and crisis*. Norton.

Even, T. A., & Robinson, C. R. (2013). The impact of CACREP accreditation: A multiway frequency analysis of ethics violations and sanctions. *Journal of Counseling & Development, 91*(1), 26–34.

Faustino, B., & Vasco, A. B. (2023, October 30). Development and preliminary analysis of a scale to assess client characteristics that influence clinical decision-making. *Journal of Rational-Emotive & Cognitive-Behavior Therapy*. https://doi.org/10.1007/s10942-023-00529-8

Feinstein, R., Heiman, N., & Yager, J. (2015). Common factors affecting psychotherapy outcomes: Some implications for teaching psychotherapy. *Journal of Psychiatric Practice,* 21(3), 180–189.

Figley, C. R. (2002). Compassion fatigue: Psychotherapists' chronic lack of self care. *Journal of Clinical Psychology, 58*(11), 1433–1441.

Fox, S. (2023). *Therapist perceptions on factors differentiating the most from least effective therapists.* [Doctoral dissertation.] Indiana University of Pennsylvania. http://gateway.proquest.com/openurl?url_ver=Z39.882004&rft_val_fmt=info:ofi/fmt:kev:mtx:dissertation&res_dat=xri:pqm&rft_dat=xri:pqdiss:29255578

Garb, H. N. (1998). *Studying the clinician: Judgment research and psychological assessment*. American Psychological Association.

Goldberg, S. B., Miller, S. D., Nielsen, S. L., Rousmaniere, T., Whipple, J., Hoyt, W. T., & Wampold, B. E. (2016). Do psychotherapists improve with time and experience? A longitudinal analysis of outcomes in a clinical setting. *Journal of Counseling Psychology*, *63*(1), 1–11.

Goldfried, M. R., Raue, P. J., & Castonguay, L. G. (1998). The therapeutic focus in significant sessions of master therapists: A comparison of cognitive-behavioral and psychodynamic-interpersonal interventions. *Journal of Consulting and Clinical Psychology, 66,* 803–810.

Goldstein, K. (1939). *The organism*. American Books.

Goldstein, K. (1940). *Human nature.* Harvard University Press.

Gonsalvez, C. J., Crowe, T.P. (2014) Evaluation of psychology practitioner competence in clinical supervision. *American Journal of Psychotherapy*, 68(2):177-93. doi: 10.1176/appi.psychotherapy.2014.68.2.177. PMID: 25122984.

Haderlie, M. M. (2011). *Enhancing therapists' clinical judgments of client progress subsequent to objective feedback.* Unpublished dissertation. University of Nevada, Las Vegas. http://digitalscholarship.unlv.edu/cgi/viewcontent.cgi?article=2225&context=thesesdissertations

Hahn, D., Weck, F., Witthøft, M., & Kühne, F. (2023). What characterizes helpful personal practice in psychotherapy training? Results of an online survey. *Behavioural and Cognitive Psychotherapy, 51*(1), 74–86.

Harding, T. P. (2007). Clinical decision-making: How prepared are we? *Training and Education in Professional Psychology*, *1*, 95–104.

Heinonen, E., & Nissen-Lie, H. A. (2020). The professional and personal characteristics of effective psychotherapists: A systematic review. *Psychotherapy Research, 30*(4), 417–432. https://doi.org/10.1080/10503307.2019.1620366

Hill, C. E., & Norcross, J. C. (2023). Psychotherapy skills and methods: Introduction to the special issue. *Psychotherapy, 60*(3), 237–245. https://doi.org/10.1037/pst0000483

Hill, C. E., Bauman, E., Shafran, N., Morrison, A., Rojas, A. E., Gelso, C. J. (2015). Is training effective? A study of counseling psychology doctoral trainees in a psychodynamic/interpersonal training clinic. *Journal of Counseling Psychology, 62*(2), 184.

Holden, G., & Barker, K. (2018). Should social workers be engaged in these practices? *Journal of Evidence-Informed Social Work, 15*(1), 1–13.

Huhra, R. L., Yamokoski-Maynhart, C. A., & Prieto, L. R. (2008). Reviewing videotapes in supervision: A developmental approach. *Journal of Counseling and Development, 86*(4), 412–418.

Isenberg, B. M., & Venturo-Conerly K. (2024). Microlevel clinical decision making: Challenges and suggestions to support early-career clinicians across care contexts. *American Journal of Psychotherapy, 77*(1), 39–41.

Ivey, A., Ivey, M. B., & Zalaquett, C. P. (2014). *Intentional interviewing and counseling: Facilitating client development in multicultural society* (8th ed.). Brooks/Cole.

Jennings, L., & Skovholt, T. M. (1999). The cognitive, emotional, and relational characteristics of master therapists. *Journal of Counseling Psychology*, *46*, 3–11.

Jensen, J. P., & Bergin, A. E. (1988). Mental health values of professional therapists: A national interdisciplinary survey. *Professional Psychology: Research and Practice*, *19*(3), 290–297.

Jewell, J. R., Anthony, B, & Murphy, A. (2021). Utilizing technology in social work education: Development of the technology effectiveness and social connectedness scale. *Journal of Social Work Education*, *57*(2), 372–382.

Kaslow, N. J., Grus, C. L., Campbell, L. F., Fouad, N. A., Hatcher, R. L., & Rodolfa, E. R. (2009). Competency assessment toolkit for professional psychology. *Training and Education in Professional Psychology*, *3*(4, Supplement), S27–S45. https://doi.org/10.1037/a0015833

Knapp, S., Gottlieb, M. C., & Handelsman, M. M. (2017). Self-awareness questions for effectiveness psychotherapists: Helping good psychotherapists become even better. *Practice Innovations*, 2(4), 163–172.

Knapp, S. J., Gottlieb, M. C., & Handelsman, M. M. (2024). Avoiding failures when applying principle-based ethics to difficult ethical situations in psychotherapy. *Practice Innovations*, *9*(3), 205–214.

Kraus, D. R., Anderson, P., Bentley, J. H., Boswell, J. F., Constantino, M. J., Baxter, E. E., & Castonguay, L. G. (2016). Predicting therapist effectiveness from their own practice-based evidence. *Journal of Consulting and Clinical Psychology*, *84*(6), 473–483.

Kühne, F., Heinze, P. E., Maaß, U., & Weck, F. (2022). Modeling in psychotherapy training: A randomized controlled proof-of-concept trial. *Journal of Consulting and Clinical Psychology*, *90*(12), 950–956. https://doi.org/10.1037/ccp0000780

Lafferty, P., Beutler, L. E., & Crago, M. (1989). Differences between more and less effective psychotherapists: A study of select therapist variables. *Journal of Consulting and Clinical Psychology*, *57*(1), 76–80.

Lane, D. (2023). Social work education and practice learning at a crossroads: Challenges. *Practice: Social Work in Action*, *35*(1), 27–45.

Levitt, H. M., Frankel, Z., Stanley, C. M., & Raina, K. (2005). An evaluation of outcome measures used in humanistic psychotherapy research: Using thermometers to weigh oranges. *The Humanistic Psychologist*, *33*(2), 113–130. https://doi.org/10.1207/s15473333thp3302_3

Lichtenberg, J. W. (2009). Comment: Effects of experience on judgment accuracy. *The Counseling Psychologist*, *37*, 410–415.

Lilienfeld, S. (2014). Evidence-based practice: The misunderstandings continue. *Psychology Today*. https://www.psychologytoday.com/us/blog/the-skeptical-psychologist/201401/evidence-based-practice-the-misunderstandings-continue

Lilienfeld, S. O., Ritschel, L. A., Lynn, S. J., Cautin, R. L., & Latzman, R. D. (2014). Why ineffective psychotherapies appear to work: A taxonomy of causes of spurious therapeutic effectiveness. *Perspectives on Psychological Science*, *9*, 355–387.

Liszewski, K. (2022) *The qualities and characteristics that distinguish most effective therapists: A survey of clinical supervisors and directors*. [Doctoral dissertation, Indiana University of Pennsylvania]. http://gateway.proquest.com/openurl?url_ver=Z39.88-2004&rft_val_fmt=info:ofi/fmt:kev:mtx:dissertation&res_dat=xri:pqm&rft_dat=xri:pqdiss:28860875

Lwin, K., & Beltrano, N. (2022). Rethinking evidence-based and evidence-informed practice: A call for evidence-informed decision making in social work education and child welfare practice. *Social Work Education*, *41*(2), 166–174.

Mackrill, T., & Iwakabe, S. (2013). Making a case for case studies in psychotherapy training: A small step towards establishing an empirical basis for psychotherapy training. *Counselling Psychology Quarterly*, *26*(3–4), 250–266. https://doi.org/10.1080/09515070.2013.832148

Malott, K. M., Hall, K. H., Sheely-Moore, A., Krell, M. M., & Cardaciotto, L. (2014). Evidence-based teaching in higher education: Application to counselor education. *Counselor Education and Supervision, 53*(4), 294–305. https://doi.org/10.1002/j.1556-6978.2014.00064.x

Martin, F. (2020). *Therapy thieves: How to save mental health care from its providers*. Oxford University Press.

Martin, F. (2024). *The challenges of integrating religion and spirituality into psychotherapy: Integrity, competence and cultural pluralism in clinical practice*. Routledge Publishing.

Martin, F. A., & Turner, J. P. (2020). *Clinical supervision in the real world: A practical guide to ethics, legal Issues, and personal development.* Routledge.

Maslow, A. H. (1971). *The farther reaches of human behavior*. Viking Compass.

Maslow, A. H. (1943). A theory of human motivation. *Psychological Review, 50*(4), 370–396. https://doi.org/10.1037/h0054346

McWilliams, N. (2005). Preserving our humanity as therapists. *Psychotherapy: Theory, Research, Practice, Training, 42*(2), 139–151. https://doi.org/10.1037/0033-3204.42.2.139

Meadows, G. (2024). "Does self-care need a rebrand?" It's a vital part of our commitment under the Ethical Framework - yet how much do we really think about what true self-care means? *Therapy Today, 35*(3), 34–35.

Miller, D. J., Spengler, E. S., & Spengler, P. M. (2015). A meta-analysis of confidence and judgment accuracy in clinical decision making. *Journal of Counseling Psychology, 62*(4), 553–567.

Miller, K. (2023). *Can we improve psychotherapy by quantifying therapists' language?* https://hai.stanford.edu/news/can-we-improve-psychotherapy-quantifying-therapists-language

Miller, W. R., & Moyers, T. B. (2021). *Effective psychotherapists: Clinical skills that improve client outcomes.* The Guilford Press.

Molyneux, C. (2022). The lost art of self-care. *Wounds UK, 18*(2), 64–67.

Montan, I., Dinger, U., Dück, J., Ehrenthal, J. C., Storck, T., Taubner, S., Weintz, L. P. H., Thake, M., Friederich, H-C., Schauenburg, H., Schultz, J-H., & Nikendei, C. (2022). Psychotherapy trainees' perspective on a longitudinal curriculum for the training of psychodynamic intervention competencies. *Psychoanalytic Psychology, 39*(4), 321–329. https://doi.org/10.1037/pap0000418

Noble, A., & Rizq, R. (2019). "It's led me astray": How cognitive behavioral therapists experience personal therapy in clinical practice. *Counseling and Psychotherapy Research, 20*, 29–38.

O'Donnell, R. R. (2011). Reforms in professional education. In N. A. Cummings & W. T. O'Donohue (Eds.), *Understanding the behavioral healthcare crisis: The promise of integrated care and diagnostic reform* (pp. 257–278). Routledge.

O'Donohue, W. T., Cummings, N. A., & Cummings, J. L. (2008). The unmet educational agenda in integrated care. *Journal of Clinical Psychology in Medical Settings, 16*, 94–100.

Orlinski, D. E., Geller, J. D., & Norcross, J. C. (2005). The patient psychotherapist, the psychotherapists's psychotherapist, and the therapist as a person. In J. D. Geller, J. C. Norcross, & D. E. Orlinski (Eds.), *The psychotherapist's own psychotherapy: Patient and clinician perspectives.* Oxford University Press.

Osberg, T. M. (1997). Teaching psychotherapy outcome research methodology using a research-based checklist. *Teaching of Psychology*. *24*(4), 271–274. https://doi.org/10.1207/s15328023top2404_13

Owen, J., Kivlighan III, M., Kopta, M., Drinane, J. M., Miller, S., & Imel, Z. (2019). Are high- performing therapists both effective and consistent? A test of therapist expertise. *Journal of Consulting and Clinical Psychology*, *87*(12), 1149–1156. http://dx.doi.org/10.1037/ccp0000437

Plakun, E. M., Sudak, D. M., & Goldberg, D. (2009). The Y model: An integrated, evidence-based approach to teaching psychotherapy competencies. *Journal of Psychiatric Practice, 15*(1), 5–11. https://doi.org/10.1097/01.pra.0000344914.54082.eb

Posluns K., & Gall T. L. (2020). Dear mental health practitioners, take care of yourselves: A literature review on self-care. *International Journal for the Advancement of Counseling, 42*(1), 1–20. https://doi.org/10.1007/s10447-019-09382-w

Renger, S., & Macaskill, A. (2021). Simplifying the definition of the fully functioning person for client use. *Counseling and Psychotherapy Research, 21*(4), 970–982. https://doi.org/10.1002/capr.12386

Rock, D. L., Bransford, J. D., Maisto, S. A., & Morey, L. C. (1987). The study of clinical judgment: An ecological approach. *Clinical Psychology Review*, *7*, 645–661.

Rogers, C. R. (1961). *On becoming a person*. Houghton Mifflin Company.

Rogers, C. R. (1963). The concept of the fully functioning person. *Psychotherapy: Theory, Research & Practice, 1*(1), 17–26.

Ronnestad, M. H., & Skovholt. (2013). *The developing practitioner: Growth and stagnation of therapists and counselors*. Routledge.

Rousmaniere, T. (2016). *Deliberate practice for psychotherapists*. Routledge.

Rousmaniere T. G., Swift J. K., Babins-Wagner R., Whipple J. L., & Berzins S. (2016). Supervisor variance in psychotherapy outcome in routine practice. *Psychotherapy Research, 26*(2), 196–205. https://doi.org/10.1080/10503307.2014.963730

Shostrom, E. L. (1964). An inventory for the measurement of self-actualization. *Educational and Psychological Measurement, 24*(2), 207–218. https://doi.org/10.1177/001316446402400203

Silvia, C., Sousa, D., & Cooper, M. (2024). Inside the consulting room of a highly effective therapist: An analysis of first sessions. *Counselling & Psychotherapy Research, 24*(2), 681–691. https://doi.org/10.1002/capr.12705

Singer, M., & Lalich, J. (1996). *"Crazy" therapies: What are they? Do they work?* Jossey-Bass.

Skovholt, T. M., & Jennings, L. (2004). *Master therapists: Exploring expertise in therapy and counseling.* Merrill Publishing.

Spengler, P. M., White, M. J., Ægisdóttir, S., Maugherman, A. S., Anderson, L. A., Cook, R. S., . . . Rush, J. D. (2009). The meta-analysis of clinical judgment project: Effects of experience on judgment accuracy. *The Counseling Psychologist, 37*(3), 350–399.

Spengler, P. M., & Pilipis, L. A. (2015). A comprehensive meta-reanalysis of the robustness of the experience-accuracy effect in clinical judgment. *Journal of Counseling Psychology, 62*(3), 360–378. http://dx.doi.org/10.1037/cou0000065

Steane, A. (2018). *Science and humanity: A humane philosophy of science and religion.* Oxford University Press.

Teichman, Y., Berant, E., Shenkman G., & Ramot, G. (2022). Supervisees' perspectives on the contribution of supervision to psychotherapy outcomes. *Counseling and Psychotherapy Research.* https://onlinelibrary.wiley.com/doi/pdf/10.1002/capr.12540

Thyer, B. A., & Pignotti, M. G. (2015). Science and pseudoscience in social work practice. Springer.

Timulak, L., & Creaner, M. (2012). Qualitative meta-analysis of outcomes of person-centred/experiential psychotherapies. In M. Cooper, J. C. Watson, & D. Holledampf (Eds.), *Person-centred and experiential therapies work* (pp. 65–90). Monmouth, NP25 3SR: PCCS Books.

Valenstein-Mah, H., Greer, N., McKenzie, L., Hansen, L, Strom, T. Q., Stirman, S. W., Wilt, T. J., & Kehle-Forbes. (2020). Effectiveness of training methods for delivery of evidence-based psychotherapies: A systematic review. *Implementation Science, 15*(40), 1–17. https://doi.org/10.1186/s13012-020-00998-w

Vannatta, R., & Steen, S. (2019). Pedagogical practices in CACREP accredited group counseling courses: A content analysis. *The Journal for Specialists in Group Work, 44*(2), 138–150. https://doi.org/10.1080/01933922.2019.1599477

Vaz, A., & Sousa, D. (2021). Persuasiveness: An underappreciated characteristic of effective therapists. *Psychology of Consciousness: Theory, Research, and Practice,* 1–16. https://doi.org/10.1037/cns0000309

Venter, H. (2017). Self-transcendence: Maslow's answer to cultural closeness. *Journal of Innovation Management, 4*(4), 3–7.

Walfish, S., McAlister, B., O'Donnell, P., & Lambert, M. J. (2012). An investigation of self-assessment bias in mental health providers. *Psychological Reports, 110*(2), 639–644. https://doi.org/10.2466/02.07.17.PR0.110.2.639-644

Westra, H. A., & Di Bartolomeo, A. A. (2024). Developing expertise in psychotherapy: The case for process coding as clinical training. *American Psychologist, 79*(2), 163–174. https://doi.org/1-.1037//amp0001139

Wampold, B. E., & Owen, J. (2021). Therapist effects: History, methods, magnitude, and characteristics of effective therapists. In M. Barkham, W. Lutz, & L. G. Castonguay (Eds.), *Bergin and Garfield's handbook of psychotherapy and behavior change: 50th anniversary edition* (pp. 297–326). John Wiley & Sons.

Wheeler, K., & Delaney, K. (2008). Challenges and realities of teaching psychotherapy: A survey of psychiatric-mental health nursing graduate programs. *Perspectives in Psychiatric Care, 44*(2), 72–80.

Wike, T. L., Bledsoe, S. E., Bellamy, J. L., & Grady, M. D. (2013). Examining inclusion of evidence-based practice on social work training program websites. *Journal of Social Work Education, 49,* 439–450. https://doi.org/10.1080/10437797.2013.796791

Index

Note: Page numbers in *italics* refer to tables.